To Nanette Cochran

from William Humphrey

5/87

# OPEN
# SEASON

# OPEN SEASON

*Sporting Adventures by*

# William Humphrey

DELACORTE PRESS/SEYMOUR LAWRENCE

Published by
Delacorte Press/Seymour Lawrence
1 Dag Hammarskjold Plaza
New York, N.Y. 10017

These essays, sometimes under different titles and in somewhat different form, appeared originally in the following magazines:
   "My Moby Dick," "Cast and Cast Again," "Great Point," "Bill Breaks His Duck," "The Trick-shot Artist," "The Guns of Boyhood," "Birds of a Feather," "Royal Game," "Guardian Dragon": *Sports Illustrated*
"The Spawning Run,": *Esquire*
"The Rigors of Bonefishing,": *True*
"Ditches Are Quicker,": *Life*
"The Fishermen of the Seine,": *Town and Country*

MANUFACTURED IN THE UNITED STATES OF AMERICA
FIRST PRINTING

Library of Congress Cataloging in Publication Data
Humphrey, William.
      Open season: Sporting Adventures.
      1. Fishing.   2. Hunting.   I. Title.
SH441.H948   1986      799
ISBN 0-385-29513-8
Library of Congress Catalog Card Number: 86-8830

*To my friend Nick Lyons*

# Contents

# OPEN
# SEASON

Time is but the stream I go a-fishing in.
*Thoreau*

# My Moby Dick

**1**

Call me Bill. Some years ago—never mind how long precisely—I thought I would go fishing. It is a way I have of driving away the spleen, and after a winter spent in the Berkshire Mountains of Massachusetts, I had a whale of a swollen spleen. Whenever this happens—whenever I find myself snarling at little children; whenever I stop being grateful that my bottle is half full and start grumbling that it is half empty; whenever I get to thinking of committing myself to a mental institution like the handy one there in Stockbridge—then I account it high time to go fishing as soon as I can, as soon as the season opens, if it ever does. The poet who wrote, "If winter comes, can spring be far behind?" had never spent a winter waiting for spring to come to the Berkshires.

Now, when I say I am in the habit of going fishing whenever I begin to go stir crazy, I do not mean to have it inferred that I am tormented by an itch for places remote, that I feel the lure of wild and distant seas and mysterious monsters of the deep. Not for me marlin in the Gulf or swordfish off the Patagonian coast. Such fishing costs money, and if I have been saved from evil it is by never having had much of the root of it all. I leave such sport to adventurers who enjoy airplanes and superhighways, motels and roadside franchise food. I never like to journey more than about five miles from home to go fishing, although a reliable report of really good sport can tempt me as far away as ten. When I go fishing I too want to get away from it all, for it is silence and solitude even more than it is fish that I am seeking; but I do not want to have to go far to find it. As for big fish, all is relative. Not every tuna is a trophy. Compared to, say, pickerel, every whale is a whale, but not every whale is a big whale. There are small whales. Every species has its prodigies, and these are not always found where you might expect to find them. While men go in search of them in wild and distant places, it may well be that the monarch of them all lies at this very moment in the shallow waters of that unlikely looking little stream just over the hill behind the house. Tarpon of a hundred pounds are common, and earn their catchers no glory; but Mr. T. S. Hudson got his name in the record book, where it has stood for a generation, by catching a four-and-three-quarter-pound bluegill. To land it must have taken fully five minutes. Which is the panfishing equivalent of the three days battle between Moby Dick and the crew of the *Pequod.*

Now, when I go fishing, I do not hitch a boat to my bumper or clamp a canoe on top of the car and head for the nearest lake. A lake is all too apt to have in and on it other boats, bathers, water-skiers, and for me fishing is an act as private as prayer. Besides, when you've seen one lake you've seen them all, whereas old Heraclitus tells us you can never ascend the same river twice. No boats for me. I do not travel light when I go fishing; I go laden with gear, much of which I seldom use; but a boat is too big a piece of tackle for me. A boat demands so much attention itself, either rowing it or bailing it out, that it interferes with the fishing. The fisherman who fishes from a boat must needs be a boatman, too; me, I am a fisherman pure and simple. To sit in a boat requires patience I have not got. I am sedentary but not that sedentary. I combine hiking with my fishing; when I catch nothing, as is most often the case, I console myself with the thought that I have at least gotten my exercise.

But the principal reason for my dislike of boats is my dislike of impounded water, still water, flat water, silent water, which is to say, stagnant, murky, tepid, weedy, scummy water; nor do I admire the kinds of fish that favor such water. Give me fast-flowing water, cold water, live water, and the fish that thrive in its cold, against its currents. If, in wading it, I sometimes slip on a mossy rock and take a dip myself, I am only the wetter for the experience.

I am particular about my fishing, as you see, requiring that it be cheap, nearby yet uncrowded, in a mountain stream or a meadow brook; and, since it is fishing more than fish that I am out for, I want a fish that will test me— my brains, that is, not my brawn, of which latter I have got even less than of the former. I want a fish that is fastidious and finicky, wily and skitterish, hard to lure, game when hooked. I want one that is not merely edible but delicious, and, while I am at it, one that does not have to be scaled, if you please. "Is that all!" you may say. "Why, the fish you would have must be as rare as white whales—if not as big." I am hard to please; but there is, among all the many kinds of fish that swim, one, just one, that fulfills all my many requirements.

And, that winter in the Berkshires, just over the hill from my house, there was my kind of stream. Frozen hard, still and silent, it was waiting, as I was, for a thaw that was so slow in coming, it seemed the Ice Age had returned.

## 2

I am not alone in my monogamous—even monotheistic —devotion to the trout. There are many fishermen like me—far too many, as far as I am concerned—and I am sure the others all feel that way, too.

What is the appeal of this fish, felt by more men than that of any, perhaps all, other varieties? The trout grows nowhere near as big as the pike, but is there a Pike Unlimited? The trout is not, "pound for pound, and ounce for ounce," as game as the black bass, but who is the black bass's Theodore Gordon, the hermit saint of trout fishing? The catfish provides sport for a greater number of people, yet the best-selling book on fishing of all time, after *The Compleat Angler,* is entitled *Trout,* and rightly so; if you do not agree, whether you be a fisherman or not, try *Catfish.* Whether the trout is the tastiest of freshwater fish is not even to the point, for many fishermen return to the water every one they catch.

I used to think it was the beauty of its habitat that made the trout attractive to fishermen. I thought that until I saw the Beaverkill River in the Catskill Mountains of New York. The Beaverkill is to American trout fishermen what the Ganges is to Hindus. Upon its waters the aforementioned Theodore Gordon floated the first dry fly in the New World—perhaps not quite so momentous an event as its discovery by Columbus, but not far behind that in the estimation of millions of Americans. They said it couldn't be done; that the dry fly, an English invention, was suited only to the placid chalk streams of England; that upon America's swift, wild mountain streams a dry fly would not float, or would float for so short a time before drag set in (more—much more—on this later) and alerted the fish to the fraud, that it would never work. But, in 1890, Gordon did it. A pilgrimage, once in his lifetime, to the waters upon which this miracle was first wrought, is as obligatory for the American fly-fisherman as one to Mecca is for a Moslem.

Let us continue with that comparison. Suppose, reader, that you are a devout Moslem. And that you still have not made your pilgrimage to Mecca, your *hajj*. What though you have prayed facing east five times daily, observed Ramadan, eschewed alcohol, abominated pork, saddled yourself with the prescribed four wives and upon them bred, then brought up a small army of soldiers for the Prophet—all for nought unless you see Mecca before you die. Now suppose that you have scrimped and saved and even borrowed, and you have managed it—just in time, too, for you are not getting any younger. You leave your affairs in other hands and you join the caravan on its long, dusty march. Now suppose that you get there, and you enter the Kaaba, the holiest of holy places to you, and you find that it has been turned into a pigsty.

I did that. I longed and I planned and I saved, I joined a caravan—it was a traffic jam, actually—and I went to the Beaverkill. And I found that along its banks and spanning its storied pools now runs U.S. 17, a four-lane superhighway that speeds milk trucks and tractor-trailers and mobile homes and traveling salesmen to Binghamton from New York City, and vice versa.

But the point of my story is this: Beneath those overpasses, beside those traffic lanes, indifferent to the din and the rumble and the exhaust fumes, were fishermen—even one fisherwoman. They were not out for meat, but sport of the purest; whatever they caught they were going to have to put back, for there that is the law. It was then that I learned that it is not the beauty and tranquillity of its habitat that draws fishermen to the trout. It is the *ding an sich*. To some brothers, and sisters, of the angle, *where* trout live does not mean a thing, so long as they live there. When I cross over the last current of all, I confidently expect to see a certain breed of sinners, oblivious of their burns, casting Rat-face McDougalls upon the waters of the River Styx.

### 3

The Housatonic at Stockbridge inspired Charles Ives to compose a symphony, but to the fisherman I met there years ago on opening day of trout season, he on his way up the bank, I on my way down to the water, it was Shit Creek. "I've heard of it," he said, "and now I've seen it." He was a fly-fisherman, and the sight of me, with my spinning rod and worm box, was all he needed to fill his daily limit of disgust.

## My Moby Dick

I am sure the man thought I was too thick-skinned to feel his barbed look of contempt. If so, he was wrong; he could not have found another more sensitive to its sting than I. Wormer though I was, and looking up from the bottommost rung of the social ladder of angling, I knew its gradations as well as he, who was on top, did. I had once aspired to climb to the top myself; I had tried and failed. I do not mean to say that I was like the fellow I met while fishing just the other day. He was worming his way downstream, and seeing me ply my delicate art with the tiniest of dry flies (for in the years between the time of the adventures I am relating and the time I am relating them, I have made that climb; what started me climbing again is the subject of this report) said that he had tried fly-fishing once—couldn't get the knack of it. I had tried for a whole year. In search of pleasure, I had spent the most frustrating, humiliating, and unhappy season of my life, before converting my fly rod into a spinning rod and, thereupon, catching, with a worm, my first trout. But I always felt coarse and inferior, and in the company of my betters I knew my place. Had the man I met on the Housatonic looked more closely he might have seen that mine was as sporting as a spinning outfit could be: a split-bamboo rod weighing just an ounce and a half, a line testing just two pounds. But to him even the most refined worm fisherman was still a worm fisherman, and as Dr. Johnson said, "How does one choose between a louse and a flea?"

As I soon learned, the man was right about the Housatonic, and had the right name for it. The river sounded good and, at a composer's distance from it, looked good —but not at a fisherman's. The worm I dunked in its waters that day did not survive five minutes, and it was not killed by a trout. It was poisoned.

Back at home I found out what had killed the river just by tracing it on the map. Upstream from Stockbridge, the Housatonic flows through Dalton, home of the Crane, the Eaton, and other paper companies. The wastes generated by their mills are—or were then—discharged untreated into the river. For miles downstream nothing could live in it.

Herman Melville had another name for the Housatonic, one even more repellent than that fisherman's: Blood River. Melville struck through the mask, the pasteboard mask, and got to the heart of the matter: not the acids generated in the manufacture of the paper, but the lifeblood of the millhands—that was the source of the pollution. There can be no doubt that Melville had Dalton and the Housatonic in mind as the setting of his sketch "The Tartarus of Maids," for he himself had recently made the trip he describes in it to Carson's Old Red Mill in Dalton to get "a sleigh-load of paper." He was writing *Moby-Dick*.

Melville's strange preoccupation with and horror of whiteness makes yet another appearance in this sketch. On a cold snowy day in January, the narrator, a seed merchant, goes by sleigh to the paper mill to order the envelopes that his business requires by the thousands. His horse is named Black, yet once inside the icy gorge where the mill sits, the horse turns white with frozen sweat. So intense is the cold that the narrator arrives at the mill with frostbitten cheeks, the color all gone from them. His business transacted, he is given a guided tour of the mill. There white rags are shredded by girls as pale as the rags, their lungs ruined by the airborne lint. The rags go into vats where they are turned into a milky mass that reminds the narrator of the whites of soft-boiled eggs. At the end of the production line another spectral woman gathers and stacks the endlessly accumulating sheets of paper. By company rule, the women are all unmarried. This sterility Melville equates with their paleness, the whiteness of the paper they produce (the process takes exactly nine minutes: a gestation period in miniature, resulting in blank sheets), the colorlessness of the wintry scene, the barren setting of the mill. Blood River is like a huge hemorrhage draining away all life from the place, which he calls "The Devil's Dungeon," and leaving all the color of death.

The narrator of the tale—plainly Melville himself in thin disguise—speculates upon the future use of all that paper: "All sorts of writings would be writ upon these now vacant things—sermons, lawyers' briefs, physicians' prescriptions, love-letters, marriage certificates, bills of divorce, registers of births, death warrants, and so on, without end." It does not occur to him to include the foolscap he himself is writing his sketch on, or the newsprint of the magazine that will publish it. Not to mention the dollar bill he bought the paper with, and those others he was hoping would be spent for that issue of *Harper's Monthly.*

A writer—even one who is a freshwater fisherman—has got to be careful how he curses paper mills.

## 4

The only other stream in that vicinity was of literary-historical interest only. A tributary of the Housatonic, this little creek originated in Stockbridge Bowl, the big lake below Tanglewood, summer home of the Boston Symphony Orchestra, and meandered down to Stockbridge, where it joined the river. I rode alongside it, and at one spot, in the hamlet of Interlaken, four or five miles downstream, over it, on my way to and from the library in Lenox, where I went to get the volumes of Hawthorne and Melville that had been my reading through that grim, gray winter just past. "Shadow Brook," the Hawthornes called it, and the dell it runs through they called "Tanglewood." In the little red cottage just below today's Tanglewood concert grounds (or rather, in the original of it, which burned, and of which this one is a reproduction) the Hawthornes had lived during the year *The House of the Seven Gables* was written. To that cottage, mounted on his saddle horse and accompanied by his big Newfoundland dog, Melville, himself busy that same year of 1850 writing *Moby-Dick*, rode over from Pittsfield to visit, and to tell, in Julian Hawthorne's words, "tremendous tales about the South Sea Islands and the whale fishery," looking, "when the narrative inspiration was on him, like all the things he was describing—savages and sea-captains, the lovely Fayaway in her canoe, or even the terrible Moby Dick himself."

In Tanglewood the Hawthorne children had listened

to Eustace Bright—a.k.a. Nathaniel Hawthorne—relate the Greek myths that became *A Wonder Book*. In Stockbridge Bowl and in Shadow Brook, Julian Hawthorne learned to fish—an enduring pleasure for him notwithstanding the accident that befell him when, out with his father on the lake one day, their leaky old punt capsized —fortunately, close to shore. Such an ardent fisherman was the boy Julian that he even fished for chickens! Using grains of corn for bait, he fished for them out of the barnloft door. Remembering Shadow Brook more than half a century later, Julian Hawthorne had this to say: "Water, in another guise [other than the lake, he means] dashed and gurgled for us in the brook that penetrated like a happy dream the slumber of the forest that bordered the lake. The wooded declivity through which it went was just enough to keep it ever vocal and animated. Gazing down upon it, it was clear brown, with glancing gleams of interior green, and sparkles diamond white; tiny fishes switched themselves against the current with quivering tails; the shaggy margins were flecked with sunshine, and beautiful with columbines, violets, arbutus and houstonias. Fragments of rock and large pebbles interrupted its flow and deepened its mellow song; above it brooded the twilight of the tall pines and walnuts, responding to its merriment with solemn murmurings. What playfellow is more inexhaustible than such a brook, so full of life, of motion, of sound and color, of variety and constancy?" By my time, well over a century later, it was largely unchanged, and then, too, the fish that switched themselves against its current with quivering tails were still tiny. It was suited, for fishing, for boys only. Indeed, in the section of it that lay in the lower part of Interlaken, the fishing was restricted to children under fourteen.

Boys were fishing in the pool just below the bridge, in upper Interlaken, one day in July when I, on my way home from the library, had a flat there. I watched them from the roadbank as I rested after changing tires. They were catching panfish. But they were neither keeping them nor throwing them back. Whenever a boy landed one he stepped on it to keep from getting finned while he unhooked it. When he had baited his hook again he left the fish to flop on the bank. Very intent they all were, yet no boy bothered to string or even keep track of his catch. Maybe they meant to gather them all together when they had enough and have themselves a fish fry. They ought to kill them quickly, though, not leave them to flop on the ground until they died.

I was withdrawing my eyes from the scene when they snagged on something. It was something lying in shallow water near the bank downstream from the boys. A log, probably. Or a long, narrow rock. The dappling on it had to be sunlight and shadow. It could not be what it looked like. Not anywhere—least of all in this little roadside puddle. To nobody but a nut on the subject, like me, would any other possibility have occurred.

I got my binoculars from the car. What they showed me was a trout thirty feet long. It could not be included in the glasses' field of view; it had to be scanned, section by section. The spots on it were as big as those on a dappled horse, and gave to it the look of a submarine painted in camouflage.

My binoculars being eight power, the fish was actually between three and four feet long. I skipped a breath. I was being shown—I put it this way because I had a strong sense of having been chosen, privileged—one of nature's prodigies, and given a glimpse into her inscrutable ways. Not in the remote, still, unpeopled wildness of Labrador (where it would still have been prodigious) but here in this little roadside pool where cars whizzed at my back and from the houses clustered all around came the mood music of daytime TV serials, lived one of the world's biggest trout. Few men—I mean by that, say, half a dozen —men, even, whose monomania, whose profession was the pursuit of trophy trout, had ever seen one anywhere near as big. I was of many minds about having been singled out to receive this revelation. I was proud and I was humble. I knew I did not deserve this distinction. I was glad and I was scared. Him whom the gods would bring down, him they first exalt.

Seeing me with my binoculars trained on them, the boys all quit fishing as one and, leaving their fish behind, clambered up the bank and fled on their bicycles as though they had been apprehended poaching.

I went down to the water's edge, treading softly so as not to spook the big trout. Some of the bluegills abandoned on the bank were still giving an occasional feeble flounce, others were dead and dry, curled up like shavings; all had had their eyes gouged out. I could account for this barbarity no better after finding a tangle of line with a hook baited with a fish's eye. In addition to being atrocious, it seemed senseless. Catch a fish and pluck out its eyes to catch another fish with, and all only to throw the fish away? This—to say the least—unsporting behavior seemed all the more shocking and saddening in this setting: in the same pool where a truly noble fish lived.

One thing I understood: the boys' flight. They knew that what they were doing was wicked.

The big trout lay almost touching the bank. I crept up on him cautiously. I need not have. It was to protect himself where he was unguarded that he lay so close to the bank. His eye on that side, his right, was blind. It was opaque, white, pupil-less; it looked like the eye of a baked fish. That, too, was saddening. One hates to see a splendid creature impaired in any way.

An explanation for those boys' behavior now dawned on me. It was pretty farfetched, enough to make me wonder whether I was not a little touched, but I could think of none other to account for the presence together there of the blind fish and the blinded fish. The boys were not fishing for the bluegills, only for their eyes to use as bait. With these they were fishing for the trout. I theorized that they were performing an act of sympathetic magic—or unsympathetic magic, if you will. That they credited the trout with an appetite for, or a hatred of, fishes' eyes because of resentment over the loss of that one of his. I may have been overinfluenced by the literary associations with the place in my mind. I may just have been reading too much Melville. A one-eyed Ahab of trout?

Be that as it may, something that has given me much pleasure, and possibly has kept me out of some mischief, fly-fishing, I owe to the two things that came together there at that little pool of Shadow Brook in Interlaken: that big fish and those boys. I was going to fish for the fish, and without reproach to myself that I had trespassed upon the boys' prior claim to him. They had forfeited all right to fish for that trout. It was my revulsion at that ugly business of theirs of gouging out the eyes of living creatures that made me forswear all live—or once live—bait, and determined me to try again, hard as I knew it was, badly as I had been beaten at it before, to learn to fish with artificial flies. Nothing but the most sporting of methods was worthy of that once-in-a-lifetime fish. On paper it sounds pretentious, but I felt I had been chosen to atone for those boys and to show that noble trout that not all his human adversaries were ignoble in their ways.

## 5

Trout are fished for at three depths: upper, middle, and lower. It is not immaterial that society, as we know it, is divided into the same layers. Three families of artificial flies exist, one for fishing at each of these depths. They represent the natural insect in three successive, and ascending, stages of its life cycle. The complete fly-fisherman ought to be adept with all three, and to know when to use which. In practice it does not work out that way. A man is drawn to wet-fly fishing—why is as mysterious as why some men take up the viola instead of the violin. He becomes a good wet-fly fisherman, and his loyalty to the wet fly turns him to it at times when one of the other two kinds might work better. Another man becomes a good nymph fisherman; that is the depth at which he likes to catch fish: when they are feeding on insects after they have left the stream bed and before they have hatched on the surface. He would almost sooner not catch them than catch them in another way. Upon hatching, the insect spreads its wings to dry and rides downstream for a moment before either taking flight or being eaten by a trout. It is this winged stage that the dry fly imitates. The dry-fly fisherman is the most stubbornly loyal of all to his way, and he is the snob of snobs among fishermen. He believes that his way entitles him to the topmost rung of that social ladder of fishing mentioned earlier. The odd thing is, the other kinds of fishermen agree with him on this, and defer to him. They acknowledge him their superior in fishing finesse. On second thought, is that so odd? The assertion of social superiority is usually all that is needed to make others accord it to you. The reason that all other kinds of fishermen look up to the dry-fly purist is not that he catches more fish than they; on the contrary, it is because he catches fewer. His is the sport in its purest, most impractical, least material form.

The wonderful obstinacy of the dry-fly purist! The odds which he knows are against him, and despite this— or because of it—his pertinacity, his lofty indifference to mere gross success, his concentration upon means, not ends! Let him be on public water, water without restrictions as to tackle and baits. Along comes a worm fisherman, his creel heavy with fish. The dry-fly man not only does not envy him his catch, he despises the oaf. Along comes a spin fisherman, one whose outfit allows him to fish bushy places where the fly fisherman cannot penetrate, and who, with his metal lures, has taken his limit. "Hardware merchant" is the dry-fly man's contemptuous name for him. Along comes (we are ascending, rung by rung, that social ladder, reader) a man who fishes with flies, but with streamer flies, which imitate not insects but minnows. Bit fish feed on minnows, and so this fisherman also has filled his creel. Along comes a wet-fly fisherman; wet flies imitate insects but are fished underwater. This fisherman, too, has fish, for a statistical reason presently to be explained. With differing degrees of intolerance, the dry-fly man looks down upon them all. For him, in the words of an old song, it ain't what you do, it's the way what you do it. His creel may be empty (he may not even carry a creel; he may belong to that most select group of all: those who would never dream of killing a trout, who put back all they catch) yet he will not switch, though he knows as well as any of them, indeed, better than any of them, that big fish, the kind he too is after, seldom stir themselves for a morsel of food that would require a diamond merchant's scale to register its microscopic weight, and he knows that all trout, even little ones, take only about ten percent of their food on the surface of the water, where he is fishing. And the strange part is that, though they regard him as daft, and subject him to much joking, down deep those other varieties of fishermen have a sneaking admiration for his quixotry, and yield him without grudge his place at the top of the ladder.

## 6

Measuring your fish before you catch him is counting your chickens before they hatch; but as I did not much expect to catch that big one-eyed trout, I measured him first. It was possible to do this because he always lay at his feeding station with his blind side almost touching the bank. I went to the pool at break of day the morning after discovering him, carrying with me a carpenter's six-foot folding rule. I stretched it, and myself, upon the bank. In addition to the rule, I took with me my wife, and while I do not expect to be believed myself, I trust that no one is unchivalrous enough to doubt her word. She, too, was stretched upon the bank, and she is ready to affirm that the fish measured forty-two and a fraction inches. I did not attempt to tape-measure his girth, but I have measured that of my own thigh, to which it corresponded. When the length and the girth of a fish are known, its weight can be roughly estimated. I estimated old One-eye's to be thirty pounds, give or take five.

He could never have attained that prodigious size in that little pool. He must have come down, and not very long before, from Stockbridge Bowl, perhaps been washed down in a flood. Nor could he have attained that size half blind. The loss of that eye, too, had to be fairly recent. Nor could he have attained that size on a diet limited to the tiny insects that he was now daintily feeding on.

But this was a very old fish, and old fish, like old people, experience a decline of appetite, and old trout do not like to exert themselves. Tables have been worked out showing how many calories, or fractions thereof, there are in a mayfly and how many ergs of energy a trout of a certain weight must expend per foot of movement in water with a current of a certain force, and what it all adds up to is: The more a big fish eats the more it starves. Old One-eye had once been even bigger than he was.

Now, a fish that big cannot be caught. That he has not been is all the proof needed that he cannot be. He is too wise. He never got that big without being wise. The allotted life-span of a trout—which only the tiniest fraction of them attain—is seven years, by which age the average one is twenty-two inches long. Cyclops was just under double that—had he likewise doubled the normal life-span? Was he, in age, the equivalent of a human being of one hundred and forty? He must in his time have seen—and seen through—all the three thousand patterns of artificial flies that are said to exist. Considering the odds against it, his survival to that age made him a Hercules, a Solomon, a Tithonus of trout.

On the other hand, a fish that big is too big not to be fished for.

What happens is that the fish hooks the fisherman.

I struggled hard to get free of that one. I knew he could not be caught, even handicapped as he was by being half blind. That would only make him all the warier. He could not be caught—certainly not in the only way worthy of him, the way in which I was obliged to fish for him, with a floating fly. Certainly not by me. I knew I was no match for that fish, very possibly the record American trout.

I considered sending this letter:

*Mr. Lee Wulff*
*Dear Sir:*
*In return for a season's private tuition in fly-fishing from you, I will guide you to the biggest living brown trout.*

I enjoyed the thought of Lee Wulff's rushing out and chartering a pontoon plane for us.

That would have been the fitting thing to do: to have given that fish to the man who was his match. That would have been the sporting thing to do. It would, and I knew this at the time, have been the prudent thing to do.

I knew how dangerous a sport fly-fishing for trout can be. I have since come to know personally some of its casualties—and to shudder. I speak not of the physical dangers—though every sufficiently old fishing club has on its wall one or more coiled leaders with a fly attached and a label that reads, "Tom Smith's last cast," meaning the one he had on when they found him and fished him out, drowned while wading, or the victim of heart stoppage, possibly brought on by excitement over the biggest fish of his life. Such cases, however, are comparatively uncommon; the danger I refer to is more widespread, and more insidious. It is mental, emotional. Fly-fishing for trout has wrecked men's marriages, their careers; when begun early enough in life it has prevented them from ever getting around to either marriage or a career and turned them into lifelong celibates and ne'er-do-wells. I have known some. Two whom I know had the strength of will to cure themselves of chronic alcoholism, but not of their addiction to fly-fishing. Theodore Gordon threw up his job at an early age, sponged off his relatives, remained a lifelong bachelor, neglected his old, dying mother, and did nothing but two things with himself: fish for trout and, out of season, tie flies to fish through the coming one. There are, incidentally, a great many fishermen who think his was an exemplary life. The danger of becoming that kind of addict not only scared me, it appalled me. Before all excess the healthy, well-balanced mind draws back in distaste and fright; such zeal for a mere sport is particularly unbecoming. I both pity and despise any person who makes a passion out of a pastime. I know that, like everything else, moderation can be carried to excess; nonetheless, I am a firm believer in moderation.

That is my belief—in practice I am excessive in everything I do, and I had long suspected that my failure to master fly-fishing had been a blessing in disguise—like the man prevented from becoming a lush because he could never hold down the stuff. Now providence had placed in my path a fish that was enough to unbalance a stabler man than I, and had restricted my method of angling for him by putting those boys there, committing a crime against nature that nothing less than the purest and most high-minded method, one I had tried, failed at, and forsworn, could make up for. I wanted that fish and I wished I had never laid eyes on him. I had not lost a leg to him, but he had certainly taken a big bite of my brain.

## 7

I equipped myself with the finest tackle. The fish deserved no less. I deserved a great deal less, and that was why I bought the best: I needed all the help I could get. To obtain it I went to New York City, there being no tackle shops anywhere in my area for the very good reason that there was no fishing, the only sizable river being a sewer. My purchases made the shopowner friendly—inquisitive he was by nature. My accent betrayed me and I owned up to being from Texas. On my way to Canada to do some fishing. Little celebration for bringing in another gusher.

I needed instruction, but I had no one to instruct me. In those days there were none of the fly-fishing schools of which there is such a proliferation nowadays. If there had been, I would have gone and enrolled under an alias and given a false address, and in just three days—at least so they promise in their ads—even I would have graduated a bachelor in the art and the science, and come back and laid educated siege to old Cyclops.

I had never known a fly-fisherman. Since my ignominious failure to make one of myself and my retrogression to worms, I had not wanted to know one. I had avoided any closer contact with the few I saw at a distance on streams from time to time. But even if I had known one, known him well, I would not have trusted myself to seek his help now. Indeed, I would have shunned him altogether. He would surely have noticed my state of excitement. His curiosity would have been piqued. My eagerness, my impatience to learn, and to put my knowledge to work, would have given me away. A wild look, that of one who has gazed on wonders, haunted my eyes in those days. Fly-fishermen are a suspicious crew, and their suspicions run on one thing. My secret would have been guessed, and I would have been shadowed to its source in Shadow Brook.

I sought instruction in books—no other sport has spawned so many. The literature of angling falls into two genres: the instructional and the devotional. The former is written by fishermen who write, the latter by writers who fish. I had read extensively in piscatorial prose of the devotional sort, searching always for the works of literature that some critics said were to be found there. I found one—if, that is to say, *Moby-Dick* is a fish story. I turned now to the manuals.

From the furtiveness of my manner in asking for a book on the subject anybody would have thought it was on how to do *It*. The salesclerk—one of those unfortunates whose dreaminess declared better than a blood test that he too had been bitten by the tsetse fly of trout fishing and would never amount to anything—guided me to volumes that he said were "the latest thing." That drew me up. Innocent that I was, I supposed that one manual on fly-fishing, updated periodically to include new tackle, would suffice for all time, the same as one on sex. That the sport had had a long continuity, I knew; but I supposed it just flowed quietly in the same old channel down to the same old sea, that its tenets had been laid down in one bible a long time ago and gone unrevised ever since. I learned now that it had a history, and that history was rife with revolutions and upheavals, especially, as might be expected, in these turbulent and changeful modern times. Fishing had indeed had its Age of Faith, its long, slumbrous, unreformated Dark Ages; but the era of inquiry and technology had affected it as it had all else. The days of fishing as an inexact art and a thoughtless pastime belonged to—only so archaic a *mot* is *juste*—yesteryear. If you were to compete with the crowds now on the streams in quest of trout, you needed to be a physicist, an entomologist, a limnologist, a statistician, a biometrician. The angler had metamorphosed into the ichthyologist, and the prevailing prose reflected the change—if mud can be said to reflect. I found myself correcting it as I had done freshman themes in my years as a professor. You had to hack your way through it as through a thicket. Participles dangled, person and number got separated and lost, clichés were rank, thesaurusitis and sesquipedalianism ran rampant, and the rare unsplit infinitive seemed out of place, a rose among nettles. Yet, instead of weeding their gardens, these writers endeavored to grow exotics in them: orchids, passionflowers. Inside each of them was imprisoned a poet, like the prince inside the toad. What came out was a richness of embarrassments: shoddy prose patched with purple—beautifully written without first being well written.

To solve that most basic of problems, which artificial fly to offer the fish, one of my authorities, the one I called The Efficiency Expert, counseled approaching the stream with a net, a bottle of formaldehyde, and the highest-power microscope you could conveniently carry. Plant your net in the stream like a seine stretching from bank to bank, go upstream and turn over some rocks on the creek bed, go back to your net, pick off the little nymphs that have washed down against it, get out your microscope and identify them, then with your handy streamside fly-tying kit containing an assortment of hooks in twenty different sizes, tinsels, threads of all colors, feathers and furs from all the world's feather- and furbearers, tie artificials to match—or to match not those nymphs, if you were a dry-fly purist like me, but the winged adults of which those were the nymphs. The same expert had done field studies and had counted and worked out the number of casts made by the average angler in an average day on the water. It came to 8,500. As his own approach, with its extended foreplay, left him time to make far fewer than that, he was concerned that every one of his should count. His goal—unattainable—was that his every cast should be free of drag, that deadliest of all the fly-fisherman's many, many enemies, for when the fly drags on the water the fish not only smells a rat and refuses the fly, he refuses every fly for the next twenty-four hours, more or less, because it scares the living daylights out of him. Using this dodge and that, The Efficiency Expert had worked out ways to avoid drag that resulted in adding as much as a week to the fishing season, practically speaking. Ah, yes, I thought, we could all of us use a little more of that drag-free float, in every walk of life, in every endeavor. And I thought, "Oh, Cyclops! Into what deep and murky waters you have led me!"

From The Entomologist I learned that when fish are being finicky—"selective" is the word—about the fly they are feeding on, the angler must match it. When, for example, it is *Ephemerella subvaria* that they are all eating like peanuts, then you must show them the Hendrickson fly, not the Quill Gordon, which was all they would look at last week when *Iron fraudator* was in season. A glimmer of hope in a fog of confusion: every species of aquatic insect has its hatching time fixed as surely as it takes you nine months to ripen; ready or not, it can no longer stay in its protective pupa, snug in the silt of the creek bed, past a certain hour of a certain date: willy-nilly, it must emerge into this cruel world of waiting and voracious trout. So it would seem that the angler could get away with something like "If this is Tuesday, then it must be Blue-winged Olive." Alas, there are, for trout, more different kinds of plats du jour than there are days of your years. There are, in the streams of North America, as

many different kinds of aquatic insects as there are stars
in the Milky Way. To be sure, not all of these are staples
of trout diet, and thus essential for the angler to know—
only some 1,500, with a few thousand variations as to
size.

> *When I read the learned entomologist;*
> *When the proofs, the figures, were ranged in columns before me;*
> *When I was shown the charts and diagrams, to add, divide,*
>   *and measure them;*
> *When I, sitting, read the entomologist*
> *How soon, unaccountable, I became tired and sick;*

and this vision of myself came to me: I stood waist-deep
in my waders in a heavy current with a swarm around my
head of some 1,500 insects, each infinitesimally different, and *I was able to identify each and every one of them!*

"*Heptagenia elegantula,*" I intoned. "*Ephemerella infre-
quens. Cinygmula ramaleyi. Rhithrogena impersonata.
Siphlonurus quebecensis. Paraleptophlebia adoptiva. Epeorus
pleuralis . . .*"

It was the learned but mindless mumble of the idiot
savant. I closed that volume as though slamming down
the lid on Pandora's box. Demented I might be, but that
way lay madness maddened.

> *I, sitting, read the learned entomologist;*
> *Till rising and gliding out, I wandered off by myself,*
> *In the mystical moist night air, and from time to time,*
> *Swatted in perfect ignorance at the bugs.*

## 8

It was I, alone, unaided, who solved my problem. I hit upon a solution which, though I say so myself, was brilliant. Crafty. Sly. Stunningly original. It was elementary, of course; every brilliant stroke is—after somebody has had it! Like so many advances, mine consisted in going at things backward. The problem: I needed a mentor. The predicament: I knew no one, could trust no one. As long as I kept thinking of my preceptor as a fisherman, I got nowhere. Once I thought of him as a fish—eureka! Who knew more about the ways of trout than the world's greatest trout, one of the all-time greats? Here I had him in a fishbowl of a pool, and he was blind on one side; without his seeing me, I could study his every move, every mood.

I went to the pool. I set out in plainclothes, taking no tackle with me. For a long time to come I would have no need of any. Then, suddenly seeing myself as others might see me, a man out at odd, twilight hours, stealthy, furtive, up to something or other, I reconsidered and went disguised with gear. When I got there I found those wicked boys up to their tricks.

I had forgotten about them. In my mind that fish had grown even greater than he was, and I had grown a great deal greater than I was, and in my mental photograph of the two of us, me smiling modestly as I held him up by his tail, those boys with their despicable tactics had been crowded completely out of the picture. Now there they were, one of them yanking a bluegill onto the bank, another stepping on his fish, still another with his bloody little paws busy at their grisly task. A fit resembling in all its symptoms an apoplectic stroke seized me. A superstitious dread, which turned instantly into a dead certainty, gripped me. I was convinced on the spot that those little Yankees, natives of the place, unlike me, knew something I did not know: that for a resentful old one-eyed cannibal trout, fishes' eyes were a surefire bait, that generations of Berkshire Mountain boys had known this; and so real that I all but saw it transpiring before my eyes was this sickening vision: one of those cane poles bent double, a shout of "I got him!" raised in a boyish soprano, and my fish, my trophy fish, was ingloriously hauled ashore by that whole brood of little imps.

As soon as I showed up, of course, they skulked away. And they made themselves scarce for however long I stood guard, defending One-eye against them and against his own savage proclivities. But I could not be there around the clock, not without neglecting both work and wife. Just the mornings, the afternoons, and the evenings until boys' bedtimes.

It was a change of season, bringing with it an annual American rite, that delivered me from the threat they posed. One day as I came on my afternoon shift, one sunny, shirt-sleeve, get-out-of-doors day, I passed the Interlaken playground and there they all were. The cry of "Batter up!" piped in clear, sweet, childish tones, trilled like birdsong on the vernal air. Baseball season had come to the Berkshires—late, like all seasons, except winter. Blessings upon those Little Leaguers and might they one and all grow up to be a second Babe Ruth! A small and rather dingy but nonetheless inspiriting copy of Old Glory fluttered on its staff above this enactment of The National Pastime. Proceeding on my way to the pool, my pool, I dilated with devotion toward this sports-conscious country of ours. I not only blessed baseball, I was grateful for golf, thankful for tennis, ecstatic for aquatics —for all those many health-giving, body- and character-building warm-weather pursuits that keep our people in tone, and out of trout streams.

### 9

My time to learn from old One-eye was short—what was left of this season. Neither he nor I would be here next year. I would be gone from the country; he would surely be dead. He was too old to survive another Berkshire winter. He could not live long in this little pool. No scope for his bulk here. He was home from sea, passing his decline in this sailors' snug harbor.

Each day that I went there to learn from him how to kill him, I waited anxiously for his appearance and rejoiced to find that he was still alive. I was not fearful that some other of his natural enemies might have gotten in ahead of me and killed him overnight. None had up to now; he had outsmarted, outfought them all. I feared only that he might have cheated me by dying a natural death. He was now fighting his first losing battle, the one against the common enemy of fish and men.

I logged his comings and goings like an assassin establishing his victim's routine. He came always to the same feeding station, an eddy at the tail of the pool where a tiny feeder stream trickled in, like an old regular of a restaurant to the table reserved for him. If there were other trout in the pool, none dared appropriate his place. When I had fixed the hours at which he issued from his lair beneath the bridge, then I was there, prone on the bank beside his spot, waiting for him to come to breakfast at dawn, to dinner at dusk. He was unfailingly punctual in keeping the appointment with me that he never knew he had. Almost cheek to cheek with his sworn enemy he lay. And though he was a prodigy of his kind and I merely representative of mine, yet nature had given to me a dubious superiority which made me pity him: Unlike me, he did not know that he must die.

But though he might be ignorant of the end awaiting him, the fish acted as though he felt himself threatened every moment of his existence. Such a jittery creature he was, ever alert, ever fearful, as though he understood that he lived his life in a medium that exposed to hostile view his every movement. The fleeting shadow of a cloud passing over him was enough to send him darting for safety underneath the bridge. Old and big and wise in his way as he was, he could never for an instant relax his lifelong vigil; indeed, he must redouble it, for now he had but one eye with which to be twice as watchful.

That blind eye put between him and me the equivalent of a one-way mirror, and, lying motionless in shallow, still, clear water, he could be observed as though he were in a tank in a laboratory, or in a home aquarium. Yet, long as I studied him, and at such close range, I never got accustomed to him, never quite believed in his actuality. His difference from all others of his kind was too gross, too offensive to the established order of things. Surely for the latter part of his life his very size must, paradoxically, have been a protection against man, a conspicuous cover, if you will, a kind of flagrant camouflage. He was simply too big to be believed. Not looking for a trout his size, fishermen did not see him, or if one did, he disbelieved his own eyes, dismissed the apparition as a figment of his fevered imagination, a fisherman's fantasy, and, knowing well how fishermen's tales are received by the world, never told a living soul. Thus, unseen, or else rejected as an impossibility and cloaked in universal silence, a wonder unrenowned, the fish had grown bigger and bigger.

It might be expected that such a monster, such a freak, would be clumsy, muscle-bound, weak, short of wind, but the fish's great bulk was no impediment to his grace, his agility, his might. From dead still, he could, when alarmed, accelerate to his full power with a speed that amounted to vanishing on the spot—a magician's trick: Now you see it, now you don't. His mastery of his element was total. Without the movement of a muscle he could maintain himself as stationary as a stone. By inflating and deflating his air bladder, he surfaced and sounded like a submarine, and just as stealthily. He would sight his prey as it entered the pool. Then, light as a bubble he rose, his dorsal fin broke water like a periscope, his huge streamlined snout silently dimpled the surface, and into that great maw of his a grasshopper or a late-hatching mayfly drifted, borne helplessly on the current. Mission accomplished, he sank soundlessly from sight. When he wriggled to propel himself forward, the undulations of his muscles caused his spots to ripple like those on the side of a dappled horse when it quivers to the bite of a fly.

Meanwhile, my studies were not confined to the fish, his hours, his preferences in food—which were, in any case, whimsical and unpredictable in ways which the books scanted. It was equally important that I familiarize myself with his immediate surroundings, that small dining area of the pool in which, if at all, he was to be taken unawares. I had to chart the currents I would be fishing as carefully as a riverboat pilot. That my river—the little feeder stream that served up the fish's food to him—was no more than two feet wide and not much longer than that before it was dissolved into the pool itself, that it was slow and unruffled, and that my fly would float on its surface, above any obstructions, might seem to make my task easy. Not so. The very narrowness of the channel would demand a cast of pinpoint accuracy, the very shortness of it would mean that my time of drag-free float would be fractions of a second, and the very stillness of the surface meant that my fly must fall upon it so unnoticeably as to seem not to have fallen but to have hatched from under it.

And even then there was still another worry.

There were—there always are, even in the narrowest stretch of flowing water—though barely discernible, more currents than one. This is what, sooner or later, always causes drag, that oft-mentioned enemy of the dry-fly fisherman. The fisherman's fly must ride down the current that ensnares the live insects and carries them to the lurking fish. Meanwhile, the leader to which the fly is attached lies across the adjacent current, or currents. No two currents of a stream, however small, however slow, however close the two, flow at the same speed. One of them will carry the leader downstream at a rate faster than that of the fly. After a while—about as long as it takes to read this—the leader bellies in the current downstream of the fly and begins to drag the fly faster and faster as it lengthens. Nothing could be more unlike the free float of the natural insect, and trout are all born knowing this. Furthermore, they not only refuse that one unnatural fly—so unsettling is the sight, they quit feeding altogether and hide themselves in fright. The fisherman's time in which to deceive and hook the fish is that brief interval between the alighting of his fly upon the water and the commencement of drag. Drag a fly over a wise, wary old trout, and you had might as well move on.

I would have yet another problem. The limitation of the fish's vision, which had worked to my advantage while I studied him, would be a disadvantage when I came to fish for him. The field of view of a normal trout is just 97.6 degrees. Within that narrow compass the fisherman's fly must be presented; if the fish is to take it, he must see it. Only half that would I have in which to attract, entice, and deceive old One-eye. To put down a fly, from a distance of some forty feet, on that small a target would be about like asking a bombardier to hit a one-lane bridge from five miles altitude, and, if it was not to frighten the fish away, the fly must alight with the delicacy of a wisp of down.

It was not that familiarity had bred contempt for him in me—if anything, my awe of him and my awareness of my problems had mounted to the point that I was almost paralyzed by them—that made me decide the time had come for me to take him on. I had just wakened to the realization that it was August—late August, almost September. The year's first yellow leaf falling to the water before me was what wakened me. The fishing season was fast running out. That wizard of a fish had cast his spell over me. Another of his protective devices; by his very fascination he could beguile you into forgetting your intentions toward him.

There is a way to land a really big fish—maybe. It is the opposite of the way to land an ordinary one. Instead of fighting him, you put no pressure on him at all; indeed, you do not let him know that he is hooked. You give him his head. You just hold on quietly and let him have the freedom of the pool, until the moment when you scoop him up tail-first in your net. That was what the fish had done to me. Without my even knowing I was hooked, he had had me all but ready for the net. Now or never, I must get up off my belly and into the water with him.

I then learned that we were not alone, my fish and I. While I had been observing him on that day of decision, I was being observed myself.

10

"After that big old trout?"

I was crawling backward away from the bank. Looking over my shoulder, I saw a towheaded little boy, as freckled as a trout. I spent another minute on my hands and knees searching for the thing I was pretending to have lost.

"After that big old trout, eh?"

"Trout?" I inquired, giving up my search and getting to my feet. "What trout?"

The boy stepped around me and started down the path to have a look for himself. He knew where to look.

"Don't go too near!" I said. "You'll scare him."

"Scare him? What's he got to be scared of? Hell, he's bigger'n I am."

"Well then, keep back. If you should slip and fall in he might eat you."

"You a foreigner?"

"Texan."

"Thought you talked kind of funny. Well, let me tell you something, Tex. You're wasting your time fishing for that big old one-eyed trout."

"Done a good bit of fishing yourself, have you?"

"Enough to know that. I'm just telling you for your own good."

"Son, if I'd always done what was good for me I would never have had much fun."

The boy watched as I rigged my rod. From a pocket of my vest I took one of my many fly boxes and selected a fly.

"What's that?" the boy asked.

I showed him the Hairwing Coachman, size 10, that I had chosen.

"What is it?" he asked.

"An artificial fly. A hook with feathers tied around it to look like a live insect." Actually, the Hairwing Coachman imitates no known insect. It's the fly for entomological ignoramuses, like me.

"What's it for?"

"It's my bait."

"That? You think you're going to catch that fish with that thing?" The boy pitied me. To him my foolishness was monumental. "Mister," he said, "there's just one bait you might get that fish to bite. Know what it is?"

"I suspect I know what you think it is," I said.

"It's—"

"Never mind."

"It's—"

"Never mind! You do things your way, I'll do them mine."

"You want to catch that fish, don't you? Well—"

"I do, but that's not all I want. There's more to fishing than catching fish."

With a shrug and a shake of his head, the boy gave up on me. He had done his best.

I went up over the bridge and around to the other side of the pool. I waded into the water behind the fish. I dared approach him no nearer than thirty-five feet. I flicked my line back and forth in false casts, adding to its length. When I judged it to be the proper length, I straightened it forward and let it drop. It touched water just where I wanted it to, and, so it seemed to me, touched softly. Nevertheless, the fish bolted for the bridge, much to the enjoyment of the boy on the bank.

11

What I had done was disregard the first and most famous dictum of fly-fishing, that of the earliest writer on the subject, Walton's friend and companion Charles Cotton: "Fish fine and far off."

In fly-fishing, the lure—the artificial fly itself—being weightless, it is the weight of the line that the fisherman casts. This makes it far too heavy and conspicuous a thing to fool even the most foolish fish, and among trout of any size there are few foolish ones. To get "fine and far off" the fisherman is forced to interpose between the line and the fly an additional piece of tackle, one which, in the already unequal contest between him and the fish, gives the decisive advantage to the fish. It is, of course, the fish that dictates—one might say, designs—every piece of the fisherman's tackle, but with this one he practically assures an outcome favorable to himself. This is the leader, the translucent terminal addition to the fisherman's line to which is attached the fly.

Nowadays leaders are made of nylon monofilament, but traditionally they were made of something that perhaps gives a better idea of their gossamer nature: the drawn and finely stretched gut of silkworms.

A leader's diameter is measured with a micrometer, in thousandths of an inch. It tapers from butt to tippet, going from about the size of carpet thread down to something that looks as though it were spun by an anemic spider. In fishing for trout, a leader nine feet long is the shortest ever used; anything less than that puts the heavy and highly visible line—or its equally alarming shadow—too near the fish. The maximum length? There is none. It is whatever the fish demands and the fisherman can cast—for the longer the leader the harder it is to handle. In broken water, early-season, deep, fast, turbid water, and with small, unsophisticated fish, one can get away with a shorter and coarser leader; later in the season, with the water low, slow-moving, and clear, and always with big, wise, wary old fish, the leader grows ever longer, ever finer, with the fisherman further handicapping himself with each foot he adds to the tippet, hoping to stop at the point where the leader is fine enough to fool the fish but still strong enough to hold and land him.

Now, when I say "big, wise and wary trout," it should be understood that I am talking about those of three pounds and over. Even the skilled and dedicated fisherman catches very few that big; rare is the man who has taken a single fish of four pounds or over in a lifetime. In the eastern United States nowadays a two-pound trout is a big one. My Cyclops was fifteen times that big and surely to the fifteenth power wiser, warier. Thus, paradoxically, the biggest of fish was to push me to use the lightest of leaders. Our campaign against each other was fought over thousandths of an inch, with me yielding steadily to him.

With each concession I made to him I came nearer to enticing, deceiving, and hooking him and further from ever landing him if I should. I had begun with a nine-foot leader terminating in a tippet of .011-inch diameter with a dead-weight breaking strength of nine pounds. This the fish not only disdained, he let me know it was a gross insult to his intelligence and unworthy even of mine.

As, over the succeeding weeks, I grudgingly added length to, and subtracted strength from, my leader—and as I learned to cast the clumsy thing (which took a great deal longer to do than it does to tell)—I had the satisfaction, and the anxiety, of seeing a growing change in the response of my adversary.

12

The Boston Symphony Orchestra was in its summer home and the concert season on up at Tanglewood, drawing music lovers from all over the northeast. On Sundays a steady stream of cars passed over the bridge in Interlaken—over me—on their way there, then when the concert ended, came down in a stampede. On one rather somber Sunday, when the people of the settlement were all shut indoors and when the low cover of clouds put a lid on things and sounds carried far and wide, down from above came the distant thunder of Beethoven's "Ode to Joy." The music seemed to be coming from light-years off, and so vast was the number of voices in the choir that had been assembled, it sounded like the hosts of heaven: ethereal harmony, music of the spheres.

Conscious that my time was short, I applied myself closely, and under the fish's strict tutelage I was becoming a better fisherman. He demanded nothing less than perfection. A careless cast, one that missed its aim by an inch or that landed with the least disturbance, and he was gone. Such ineptness seemed not so much to frighten as to affront him. He then retired beneath the bridge as though to allow me to beat an unwatched retreat. How fatuous of me it seemed then ever to have thought I was going to catch that wonder of the world. In this feeling I was unfailingly seconded by my companion, the tow-headed, freckle-faced little boy on the bank.

Until, that is, he gave me up as a hopeless case, lost

interest, and no longer appeared at the pool. The appeal of fishing as a spectator sport is limited at best; with never a nibble, I provided no excitement whatever, only the laughable spectacle of a wrongheaded and stubborn fool, deaf not just to local wisdom but to plain common sense. I was relieved to be rid of him.

I was improving steadily, and all the time I remained as far short as ever of the mastery, the magic, needed to entice this phenomenon of a fish into taking my fly. The longer I fished for him and the better I got at it, the more elusive he seemed to grow, as though he were leading me —as he alone among trout could do—into the most rarefied realms of trout fishing. I got good enough, or so I felt, to be justified in wondering whether there was a man alive who could catch this fish.

Steadily forcing me to yield to him in the battle of the lengthening leader, he now had me down to one eighteen feet long, spidery thin. With that I could see I was beginning to interest him. So big was he that even at my distance from him I could detect that rippling of his spots which denoted that he was tensing, readying himself to pounce upon his approaching prey. He looked then like a jet plane throbbing as its engines are revved up for the takeoff. I too throbbed with tension at those times. He would raise himself, wait, watch. Then at the last moment he always had second thoughts, sank back and let my fly drift past. I had said it to myself before, I now became convinced that this fish had attained his extraordinary size, his uncommon age, thanks to some faculty that made him unique among his kind, perhaps in the history of his kind. I alternated between cursing him for his invulnerability and feeling that I had been uniquely privileged to have made the acquaintance of so remarkable, so rare a creature.

I grew increasingly conscious of my debt to him, yet I remained ungrateful. He was giving me incomparable training in how to catch trout—lesser trout than himself, that is, and that included them all. He was testing me against the highest possible standards. Few fishermen had ever had such coaching as his of me. I should have been content with that. I was not. He himself was the fish I wanted to catch, I hardly cared whether I ever caught another, and, forgetting now that I owed my betterment all to him, in my increasing pride and vainglory I grew more and more confident that I could, that I would. Right up to the season's closing day I continued to believe that.

## 13

"Closing day," my small companion met me with at poolside.

"Has come. Aye, Caesar. But not gone," I rejoined.

"Huh?" My talking in riddles was all that was needed to convince him that I was hopelessly addled.

"Still using them artificial flies, I see."

"Mmh."

"Ever get him to bite one of them yet?"

"Can't say I have."

"Then what makes you think he's going to now at the last minute?"

"Don't think he's going to—just hoping he might. You never know when your luck will change."

But the truth was, the boy had dashed my hopes. Closing day it was, and that alone would be the thing to make this one different from all the other days I had sunk in this folly of mine. At midnight tonight the Fish and Game Commission of the Commonwealth of Massachusetts would extend legal protection over its most venerable trout, and he would live out his pensionage in this little pool. It was only out of a sense of obligation and to round out the fitness of things that I waded into the water. A sense that, having challenged the fish, I owed him his total triumph over me. It was I who had made today's appointment with him, and there he was.

As often happens, now that I had lost confidence, and, with it, the compulsion to perform, I excelled myself in my casting that day. Four times running I placed my fly—a number 12 Black Gnat it was, to match the ones that were biting me—over the fish without rousing his suspicions, putting him off his feed and sending him to sulk under the bridge. Those repeatedly ignored casts made my young companion smirk; I, though rather ruefully, admired my unproductive accomplishment.

My fifth cast would have alighted in the same spot, some four feet in front of the fish, as the others had. However, it never did. Exploding from the water, the fish took it on the wing, a foot above the surface. Why that cast and none of the countless others, nobody will ever know. Instantly he felt the barb. Not fright, but fight, was what it brought out in him.

Out of the water he rose like a rocket—out and out, and still there was more to him, no end to him. More bird than fish he seemed as he hovered above the water, his spots and spangles patterned like plumage. I half expected to see his sides unfold and spread in flight, as though, like the insects he fed upon, he had undergone metamorphosis and hatched. His gleaming wetness gave an iridescent glaze to him, and as he rose into the sunshine his multitudinous markings sparkled as though he were studded with jewels. At once weighty and weightless, he rose to twice his own length. Then, giving himself a flip like a pole-vaulter's, down he dove, parting the water with a wallop that rocked the pool to its edges.

The next moment I was facing in another direction, turned by the tug of my rod, which I was surprised to find in my hand. Nothing remotely resembling his speed and power had I ever experienced in my fishing. Nothing I might have done could have contained him. It was only the confines of the pool that turned him.

Straight up from the water he rose again. Higher than before he rose. It was not desperation that drove him. There was exuberance in his leap, joy of battle, complete self-confidence, glory in his own singularity. Polished silver encrusted with jewels of all colors he was, and of a size not to be believed even by one who had studied him for weeks. I believed now that he had taken my fly for the fun of it. I was quite ready to credit that superfish with knowing this was the last day of the season, even with knowing it was his last season, and of wanting to show the world what, despite age and impairment, he was capable of. Reaching the peak of his leap, he gave a thrash, scattering spray around him. In the sunshine the drops sparkled like his own spots. It was as though a rocket had burst, showering its scintillations upon the air.

Another unrestrainable run, then again he leaped, and for this one the former two had been only warm-ups. Surely he must have a drop of salmon in his blood! Up and up he went until he had risen into the bright sunshine, and there, in defiance of gravity, in suspension of time, he hung. He shook himself down his entire length. The spray that scattered from him caught the light and became a perfect rainbow in miniature. Set in that aureole of his own colors that streamed in bands from him, he gave a final toss of his head, breaking my leader with insolent ease, did a flip, dove, and reentered the water with a splash that sent waves washing long afterward against my trembling and strengthless legs.

"Dummy!" cried the boy on the bank. "You had him and you let him get away!"

# Epilogue

Even so worldly a man as Jonathan Swift could write late in life, in a letter to his friend Alexander Pope, "I remember when I was a little boy, I felt a great fish at the end of my line, which I drew up almost to the ground, but it dropped in, and the disappointment vexes me to this day." Sick with disappointment at losing my once-in-a-lifetime fish, I was sure I would never get over it.

But now I wonder, would I really rather have that fish, or a plaster replica of him, hanging on my wall than to see him as I do in my memory, flaunting his might and his majesty against that rainbow of his own making? Many times, when I was low in spirits, I have rerun that vivid footage photographed by my eyes and printed upon my mind, and been cheered, been glad that that was my last view of him. He is the one fish of my life that has not grown bigger in recollection, the one that needs no assistance from me.

Fishing stories always end with the fish getting away. Not this one. This, reader, has been the story of a fisher-man who got away. For old One-eye made a changed man of me. No fish since him has ever been able to madden me again. I have hooked and lost some big ones in that time, but to each and all I have been able to say, "Go your way. I have known your better, known him well, and there will never be his like again. You, however big you may be, are a mere minnow compared to my Moby Dick."

*The Spawning Run*

The Itchen, the Test, the Frome: the fabled chalk streams of south England, where Dame Juliana Berners and Izaak Walton fished—here I am in the middle of them, it's spring, the season has opened, and I'd might as well be in the Sahara. Even the Piddle, known also as the Puddle —the brook running through the farm here—holds good trout. I have seen them hanging in the shallows above the millrace, resting from their run, reaccustoming themselves to fresh water—for these will be sea-run trout, gamest of them all, returning to spawn: broad in the shoulder, deep in the belly, spotted like the gravel of the stream bed so that at first you don't see them, only their rippling shadows on the bed. The personal property, every one of them, of Mr. "Porky" Mitchell, the meat-pie king. Eighty-five hundred pounds sterling he paid for the fishing in three miles of the stream for ten years. So Tom Mears, my landlord, tells me. I stroll over daily to watch these trout. They congregate below the signpost which reads STRICTLY PRIVATE FISHING, just downstream from the stone bridge with the weatherworn cast-iron plaque threatening transportation to Virginia to anyone found defacing it. Mr. Mitchell's water bailiff watches me.

*Dorset, May 13*

The Anglo-Saxons are anglers. Here on Sundays queues
of them with cane poles and minnow pails line the banks
of the quarter mile of public water. In and out among
their lines one of Her Majesty the Queen's swans and her
cygnets glide. The serenity is seldom disturbed by anybody's catching anything.

Nowhere is the class division more sharply drawn than
in the national pastime. "Fishing in Britain," says the
pamphlet sent me by the British Travel and Holiday Association, "falls into three classes: game, sea, and
coarse." Read: upper, middle, and lower. Trout taken
from the public water here must be returned; they are
the property of Mr. Mitchell that have strayed. Only
coarse fish may be kept by the coarse.

Discussed fishing with my new friends at The Pure
Drop.

"Pike season don't begin for another two months, but
there's some fair fishing round and about for roach,
dace, tench," I'm told.

I remember reading those names of English fish in
Walton, but what they are I don't know. They sound
"coarse."

"It's trout I'm talking about," I say.

I get the look I've seen them give those who frequent
the Saloon Bar, where the same beer costs tuppence
ha'penny a pint more than it does here in the Public Bar.

Bill Turner, speaking for them all, says, "Trout, is it? Ah, well, I wouldn't know, not being a toff meself."

*Dorset, May 15*

While watching the fish in the millrace today, I glimpsed something go through that looked like a torpedo.

*Dorset, May 16*

Immoderate people, the British, especially in their pastimes, their reputation to the contrary notwithstanding. Take my new friend Dr., which is to say Mr., M.

M. is an authority, perhaps *the* authority, on the long-term effects of prisoner-of-war-camp diet on the male urinary system. On this important and insufficiently heeded aspect of war, M. has testified as an expert at war-crimes trials and in many veterans' disability-pension-case hearings. This, however, is a study which M. has taken up only in the last few years, and which he pursues only out of fishing season. He is retired from practice.

He retired and came home from Africa to London three years ago, then moved down here, where he has the fishing on Thursdays and Fridays on a half-mile beat on the Frome, and Mondays, Tuesdays, and Wednesdays on a three-quarter-mile beat on the Piddle, sublet from Mitchell the meat-pie king. Saturdays he plays the football pools.

I met M. in the farmyard yesterday afternoon when my wife and I came in from our bike ride over the heath. He was wearing waders and was busy rigging up a bamboo fly rod. I watched him do it. He jointed the rod, first lubricating the male ferrule by rubbing it on the wing of his nose, attached the reel, drew the already greased line through the guides, attached a leader (a "cast" they call it here) with a deftly tied central draught knot, opened a fly book, and selected a fly. Holding it between thumb and forefinger, he said—his first words to me—"What fly is that?"

I took it from him. I had tied the pattern. "I don't know what you may call it here; we would call that a Gold-ribbed Hare's Ear where I'm from. It's a number fourteen," I said.

He reached into the trunk of his car (the "boot" they say here) and took out another rod. He jointed this rod, put on a reel, threaded the line through the guides, and handed it to me.

"You'll do," he said. "Come along."

We went past the old gristmill and under the railroad trestle and across the meadow to where his beat of the river begins. A slow, flat, winding, and narrow stream the Piddle is, nowhere more than ten or twelve feet wide, though just as deep, and choked with water weeds that twine snakily in the current. Along its banks not a tree or a bush to interfere with casting.

We fished for an hour, or rather I fished: M. sat on the bank, smoking his pipe and watching. I do not like to be watched while I fish. In fact, I cannot fish if I'm watched. Cannot even cast my fly properly. And I felt bad that he was giving up his sport, especially knowing how costly it was. He refused to fish, however. "I do it every day," he said. "I want to see you catch something." I caught nothing.

After an hour he announced that it was time for tiffin. I tried to decline half his tea, but when he said that if I did not share it with him he would eat none of it either, I said I would share it with him. So I had half of one of Mr. Mitchell's pork pies, half a cucumber sandwich, half a banana sandwich, and a cup of tea. Afterward I accepted a fill for my pipe from his tobacco pouch. While we smoked, M. told me about himself.

Upon finishing his residency in tropical medicine, he got married, went on a fishing honeymoon to Ireland, returned to London, where he set his wife up in a flat in South Kensington, and shipped out to Nairobi. There he spent the next twenty-five years, returning home on three months leave every year to fish, and to see his wife. Once in that time he came back for an entire year. He had come into a legacy of three thousand pounds, which he spent on salmon fishing in Scotland. Best year of his life. If he should ever win a pot in the football pools, it's what he would do again. His period of service in Nairobi concluded, he came home three years ago, gave up the flat in London, and brought his wife (their grown son was now out in Ottawa) down here and bought his fishing. On this beat here he had killed six so far, this early in the season, the biggest one thirty-two pounds.

"A thirty-two-pound trout!" I exclaimed.

"No, no! Not trout. Salmon."

Now I know what that shape was that passed through the millrace yesterday, its dorsal fin out of water like a periscope.

This evening, telling Tom Mears about my day, I learned why M. did not fish while I was fishing. Here in England when one buys a beat on a piece of water, or subleases as M. does from the meat-pie king, one not only buys a specified number of days of the week, or half-days, one also buys a specified number of rods. What M. has is one rod for his days on his beat. Should he bring along a guest, he may not fish himself. I won't be taking up his invitation to go with him another time. In fact, I must give up hope of fishing in Britain. It's too complicated.

*Dorset, May 17*

So much for yesterday's resolution. I was at my desk this morning when I heard Tom call up from below, "Bill? Come down! Something here I think you'll want to see."

On the bricks of the back court, at the feet of a man in waders, lay the biggest fish I have ever seen. Silver, sleek, shaped like the fuselage of a jet plane. Its jaws were bared in a ferocious snarl. I had never seen one before, but I recognized it.

"Yes, that's a right nice cock salmon. Should run to about forty pounds, maybe forty-five," said the man in waders.

I stretched myself out on the bricks beside the fish. We were just about a match.

And from there I lay looking up at Mr. Porky Mitchell with envy and class hatred.

*Dorset, May 19*

"Scotland," said Tom. "There's the place for you. Up there they've got fishing hotels where you can buy rights by the day or by the week."

"Too far. Too expensive."

"Wales, then. Be there by afternoon."

Wales . . . The Severn. The Wye. The Usk . . .

*Dorset, May 20*

In the county town of Dorchester—Thomas Hardy's Casterbridge—where I went today to get myself outfitted with fishing tackle, I parked my car in the municipal lot.

"Enjoying your holiday over here, are you, sir?" asked the attendant as he copied onto my ticket the number of my Virginia license plate.

"Very much, thank you."

"First visit to Dorchester? Perhaps I can tell you some of the sights to see."

"Very kind of you. As a matter of fact, I've been here before."

"What! Here to Dorchester?"

"Why, yes."

"What would ever bring you back a second time?"

"Well, what has brought me back several times is my interest in your great man, Hardy."

*( 5 7 )*

"Mr. Hardy, is it? I knew him well. I was his driver."

"His driver! Were you really? You fascinate me!"

"Do I then? Well, so I was! Yes, Mr. Hardy had one of the very earliest automobiles in Dorchester. A fine big Daimler it was, the kind they don't make anymore. I used to run him up to London every month. We did it always in under three hours. Loved speed, he did."

"Loved speed? Now I should never have expected that!" (He used to get about the town on a tricycle.)

" 'George, faster!' he would say. 'George' (that's me) 'faster!' Ah, he was a fine man, and when he died he remembered me in his testament. I keep a photo of him here in the hut."

"Do you! Well, that is wonderful! You must cherish a very tender memory of him."

"I do. I do. Be glad to show it to you, if you'd care to see it."

"I'd love to see it!"

The photograph—framed—bore only a faint resemblance to Hardy. I said, "This doesn't look much like other portraits of him I have seen."

"Oh, you're wrong there, sir. I knew him well and that's caught him, all right. A speaking likeness, that. Yes, yes. Built some of the very finest houses in this town, did Mr. Hardy."

I knew that Hardy had spent a long apprenticeship as an architect, but it seemed hardly the thing to remember him for. "What's more important," I said, "he wrote some of the best novels and some of the most beautiful poems in the language."

"That will be the brother," said the parking-lot attendant. "It's Mr. *Henry* Hardy we're speaking of, the building contractor. Ah, he was a fine man, and it's a pleasure to talk to you about him."

My tackle consists of my rod: a two-handed ten-foot secondhand Farlow which looks as if it has caught a great many fish; line: oiled silk, torpedo-head taper, size FBG; two hundred feet of backing, thirty-pound test; reel; hobnailed hip boots; two dozen gaudy big double-hooked salmon flies; gaff; two books on the salmon, his habits, and how to catch him. Or rather, no. One does not catch a salmon. One kills a salmon. The distinction resembles that preserved in English between the verbs "to murder" and "to assassinate": ordinary citizens are murdered, leaders are assassinated. So with the King of Fish. He is not caught, like your perch or your pike or your lowly pickerel. He is killed.

Mr. Porky Mitchell's peculiar word is now explained: salmon, male and female, are called cocks and hens, I learn from my books. The salmon appears to be a very odd fish.

*Ross-on-Wye, May 21*

In the spring a salmon's fancy also turns to thoughts of love. Not a young salmon's but an old salmon's. And not lightly. With the single-mindedness of a sailor returning home after a four-year cruise without shore leave.

The salmon is anadromous. That is to say, he leads a double life, one of them in freshwater, the other in salt water. His freshwater life may be said to be his private, or love life; his saltwater life his ordinary, or workaday life.

The salmon reverses the common order of human affairs: a lot is known about his private life but nothing at
all about the rest. We get the chance to study him only
when the salmon is making love. For when the salmon,
aged two, and called at that stage a parr, leaves his native
river and goes to sea (to be a smolt until he returns to
spawn, whereupon he becomes a grilse), nobody, not
even Professor Jones, D.Sc., Ph.D., Senior Lecturer in
Zoology, University of Liverpool, whose book *The Salmon*
I am reading, knows where he goes or how he lives,
whether in the sea he shoals together with his kind or
goes his separate way, why some stay there longer than
others, or why some return home in the spring and others not until the autumn. He disappears into the unfished
regions, or the unfished depths, or both, of the ocean
and is not seen again until—it may be as little as one or as
much as four years later—impelled by the spawning
urge, he reenters the coastal waters and the estuaries and
up the rivers to his native stream like some missing person returning after an absence of years from home.

Nothing of what the salmon does in the sea is known,
only what he does not do: namely, reproduce himself. He
cannot. For his mating and for the incubation of his
offspring, fast-flowing freshwater is required. And he
can't, or won't, or at least would a lot rather not spawn in
any but the same stream in which he himself was
spawned. This may be far inland, perhaps deep in the
mountains of Wales, and he, when he begins to feel the
urge, may be in the Baltic Sea—in tagging experiments
salmon have been tracked as far as sixteen hundred miles
from their native streams. No matter—home he heads,

and, what is even more remarkable, he knows how to find his way back. He does it, they think, by smell.

By 1653, when Walton published *The Compleat Angler*, tagging experiments had already shown that salmon, if they can, return to their native streams to spawn. Walton writes,

"Much of this has been observed by tying a *Ribband* or some known *tape* or *thred* in the tail of some young *Salmons*, which have been taken in Weirs as they swimm'd toward the salt water, and then by taking a part of them again with the known mark at the same place at their return from the Sea . . . and the like experiment hath been tryed upon young *Swallowes*, who have after six moneths absence, been observed to return to the same chimney, there make their nests and habitations for the Summer following: which has inclined many to think, that every *Salmon* usually returns to the same river in which it was bred, as young *Pigeons* taken out of the same *Dove-cote*, have also been observed to do."

Since Walton's time, much thought and many ingenious experiments have sought answers to the questions, why and how the salmon does this. Memory? Instinct? The "conclusion" of these, up to now, is Professor Jones's hypothesis that each river has its characteristic odor, and that throughout the period of its wanderings in the sea the salmon retains a memory of, one may say a nostalgia for, this odor. Neither Professor Jones nor anybody else knows how the salmon finds and follows this scent through hundreds and hundreds of miles of salt water. This smell Professor Jones supposes to be a complex one, composed of many things, chemical and physical, owing to the different substances dissolved in the water, and it is this complexity which makes the scent of each river unique and unmistakable to its salmon off-spring. One is asked to imagine the salmon working its way past tributaries where the scent is almost but not quite the one it is seeking, like the hero of Proust's *Remembrance of Things Past* almost succeeding but repeatedly just failing to recapture the sense of happiness that came to him momentarily with the taste of the *petite madeleine* dipped in tea, until finally the flavor reminds him of when he last tasted it and his mind is flooded with recollections of his childhood vacations at his Aunt Léonie's house in Combray.

Salmon do have a very fine sense of smell. Migrant salmon on their way upstream have been seen to shy and scatter when a bear put its paw in the water above them. Also when a very dilute solution of the odor of the human skin was put in the water above them. And they do not respond in this way when the odor introduced into the water is not one they associate with one or another of their natural enemies. So their sense of smell is not only sharp, it is highly discriminating as well.

Say that he is *my* salmon, the one I am hoping to catch —kill, that is—a native of the parts I am headed for, a salmon of the River Teme, in mid-Wales. Through the sea he will have swum at speeds—this too established by tagging experiments—of up to sixty-two miles per day. He will have come, as I have just done, up the Bristol Channel. Off Cardiff he will have gotten his first whiff of freshwater; there the River Taff empties into the Channel, and there he will have rested for some days or even weeks, not from exhaustion, but because too sudden a change from salt water to fresh brings on a shock that can be fatal to him. Then past the Usk on his left, the Bristol Avon on his right, both redolent of the scent he is seeking, but neither just quite the thing itself. At Aust Ferry instead of the Wye he will have known to take the Severn, and to keep on it, ignoring hundreds of tributaries large and small, until just below Worcester, coming in from the left, is that waft which to him is like none other in the world.

The average salmon lives seven years. Thus a year in a salmon's life equals ten years in a man's life. Suppose a man left home at twenty and was gone for forty years, wandering as far as sixteen hundred miles away, and then at sixty he walked back without a map and with nobody along the way to ask directions of, no signposts to guide him, no landmarks: this would be about comparable to the salmon's feat in finding his way back to his native river to spawn. Add obstacles in his path in the form of falls as much as twelve feet high, not to be bypassed, to have to leap.

The salmon is named for his salient characteristic. *Salmo*, from the Latin, means "the leaper," and comes (as does the word "salient," by the way) from the verb *salire*, to leap. People came and watched and wondered at the salmon leaping in Walton's time, and they still do.

"Next, I shall tell you," Walton writes, "that though they make very hard shift to get out of the fresh Rivers into the Sea, yet they will make harder shift to get out of the salt water into the fresh Rivers, to spawn or possesse the pleasures that they have formerly found in them, to which end they will force themselves through *Flood-gates*, or over *Weires*, or *hedges*, or *stops* in the water, even beyond common belief. *Gesner* speaks of such places, as are known to be above eight feet high above the water. And our *Cambden* mentions (in his *Brittannia*), the like wonder to be in *Pembrokeshire,* where the river Tivy falls into the Sea, and that the fall is so downright, and so high, that the people stand and wonder at the strength and slight that they see the *Salmon* use to get out of the Sea and into the said River; and the manner and height of the place is so noticeable that it is known far by the name of *Salmon-leap.*''

At a pool in Ross-shire, according to Professor Jones, salmon have been seen making a leap of eleven feet four inches vertical, and he calculates that to do this the fish must have been moving at a vertical speed of twenty miles an hour as they left the water at the foot of the falls. We saw nothing so spectacular as that; but we joined a small crowd of people gathered on the bank of a river this afternoon and watched salmon leaping a falls about six feet high, and their determination and their strength and their grace, their hardihood even, as they hurled themselves at what seemed an insurmountable obstacle, some of them repeatedly falling back as time after time they just failed to clear the top, drew cheers from all of us who saw it.

It may live as long as nine months while spawning, but the moment it reenters freshwater the salmon has eaten its last bite.

Salmon fishing, Professor Jones—himself no angler, he tells us—observes, is a sport for the well-to-do. While my wife went inside to check us into the hotel, I insinuated my VW between two new Bentleys parked in the court. An incensed peacock was pecking at himself in the hubcap of one of the Bentleys with brainless persistency. When he had obliterated with his spittle the rival in that hubcap he spread his tail proudly and went strutting to attack another Bentley hubcap, passing up those of my VW with lordly disdain.

This hotel of ours, patronized by Bentley owners, with peacocks to decorate its stately lawns, winding, as the brochure puts it, among the lovely valley of the Teme, surrounded by thirty-five acres of parkland and enchanting gardens, is a nineteenth-century reproduction of a fourteenth-century Italian villa, with loggias and campanili, called The Redd. That is not a Welsh word, nor, as one might think after driving, as we did today, through Fforest Fawr, a quaint old spelling of "red." One who is up on his salmon lore, as I am fast becoming, knows that a redd is a salmon's nest.

"They won't be biting tomorrow," said my wife on her return.

"What?"

"The fish. Won't be biting tomorrow."

"How do you come to know that?"

"Learned it the first thing. Old gentleman just inside

the door was banging a barometer on the wall. Seeing me he burst into a broad frown and said, 'They won't be biting tomorrow.' So that's the outlook, my friend."

"Fellow guest?"

"A sample. Others coming out of the woodwork. This is going to be fun."

"Fishing," said mine host, Mr. Osborne, "is with artificial fly, strictly."

It may be that he says the same thing in the same tone to his British guests as well, but I thought I detected a pointedness in the way he said it to me. Turning inside out the pockets of my chinos, "Haven't got a worm on me," I said. Mr. Osborne was not amused. Maybe not convinced.

We stood on the flagged terrace overlooking the valley a hundred and fifty feet below, the top of a great pine level with our eyes. Below us spread a meadow of vivid green, its pile as regular as wall-to-wall carpeting, grazed by a herd of red Hereford cattle. At four o'clock in the afternoon the river was shadowed by the mountain rising directly behind it. Small pastures and hangers of dark trees dotted the mountainside, and scattered small gray stone farmhouses, low to the ground.

"Still time to have a try at it if you'd like," said Mr. Osborne. "On the house. Go down and have a look at the big pool just there. That was Major Butler's beat today, but he's come in already, having killed a twenty-seven-pound cock. There's more where that one came from."

I went down through the enchanting garden. The rhododendrons, laid out in a maze and growing twelve feet tall, were in full bloom and murmurous with bees. The garden path ended at a five-barred gate. Attached to its right-hand post and swinging at a right angle to the bars was a low-hinged gate at the top of the long flight of wooden steps leading down to the water. A woman in a tweed suit and wearing a felt hat stood at this gate, her back to me, watching something below so intently that I had to hem and then hem again and finally to say, "Excuse me, please." She turned then, slowly, not startled, for it was plain to see that she had heard all my little signals, and gave me a smoldering look. I am writing this before going to bed, but it is not because of what came later that I say it: her look was smoldering. She was deep in reverie. And yet she was quite aware of me. Aware of and quite disdainful of me, and, far from embarrassed and trying to hide the mood I had surprised her in, she seemed to flaunt it before me. I have seen such a look in women's eyes before, both hot and haughty—newlyweds often have it: *I have been aroused, yes, but I've got my man, I'm not for you.* Now, however, I am, perhaps, letting myself be influenced by what came later.

Halfway down the steps I met a man coming up. We brushed in passing, so narrow was the way. But I did not see his face nor think to return his "Good afternoon" to me until it was too late, still burning as I was from the woman's look.

Above the pool the water was fast and broken, but at the pool it broadened and deepened and flattened out. Above the still surface of the pool hovered a mist of mayflies performing their nuptial flight, rising and dipping like swallows at evening, the females dropping to the surface for an instant to deposit their eggs, others, their mating and with it their brief lives over, falling spent to the water on outspread wings. The faint, barely audible sound, as of a bubble bursting, which a dimpling trout makes as it sucks in a fly, was multiplied so many times it sounded as though the pool were at a slow boil. Then as I watched, trout, mostly small, began to leap for the hovering flies, rising straight out into the air and straining upright on their tails on the surface of the water like trained puppies begging. Then I heard a wallop and a heavy splash and out of the corner of my eye saw spray and then saw rings rippling outward in circles that rapidly covered the entire pool from bank to bank. I took the steps up three at a time and, flinging open the gate, nearly hit in the back the man I had met going down. He was talking to the woman. Neither of them took notice of me.

On my way downstairs in the hotel, rod, gaff, fly book in hand, I met my wife.

"How does it look?" she asked.

"Scary. There's one old sockdolager in there that if I should hook him is liable to pull me in and chomp off a leg."

"I'll come along and protect you," she said.

"Come on then! Because they're not going to be biting tomorrow."

We went down the path toward the gate. Nearing it, I saw something that made me take my wife's elbow and steer her aside and hustle her down an alley of rhododendrons until we got where I felt I could safely speak. I said, "Go quietly out there and look down that way and come back and tell me if you see what I think I just saw."

When she finally tore herself away and came back to me, my wife said, "If I hadn't seen it for myself—"

"I still don't," I said.

But another look convinced me.

"Right up there against that gate," I said to my wife. "In public. In broad daylight."

"Not fifty yards from the hotel," said my wife. "All rooms booked."

"Standing up," I said. "Fully clothed."

"I don't believe it either," said my wife. "I'd better take another look to convince myself."

"You've looked your fill already," I said.

"Do you suppose," said she, "that they're married?"

"To each other, do you mean?"

"Can we get back to the house that way around the bushes?"

"We're not going back to the house."

"What are we going to do, watch?"

"Wait."

So, me thinking of all those fish on the rise and especially of the one that made that mighty wallop, those tidal waves, we waited. I timed them quite generously, I thought, then I went and peeked around the rhododendrons. They were at it still. I rejoined my wife, who was beginning to find my role in this highly comical. That hatch of flies would soon end and with it the evening rise. Why was I being so discreet for two such flagrant fornicators? Taking my wife by the hand, I strode boldly out and down the path. The man's back was to us, hers was braced against the five-barred gate. He was hunched low, of necessity, and over his shoulder her face was visible, her head thrown back and her eyes closed. At the stage of

( *69* )

his work, or rather his pleasure, to which he had arrived, or was arriving, he was oblivious to our approach. I observed in passing that he was gray-haired and getting bald on the crown, and also that rings glinted on the fingers with which she clasped him to her, one of them a gold wedding band. I opened the gate narrowly—there was not room to open it wider—and my wife passed through. At that moment the lady opened her eyes and looked over her partner's shoulder and, seeing me, smiled like a cat being stroked and then let her eyes close again. I squeezed through the gate and went down to the river, where I caught nothing.

Before dinner, to the bar (club license, membership open to guests upon payment of nominal subscription, good for length of stay) for a drink and curious for a closer look at our country copulatives of the afternoon. Passing the various tables and overhearing the conversations was like walking down an English street and hearing every house's telly tuned in on the same channel. Remarks sometimes rather muffled coming through thick military-style mustaches. "Jock Scott. Twenty-pound gut. Let it go past his snout, then lunged at it. Straight upstream taking the line clean down to the backing. Thought for a moment I'd foul-hooked him." Most of the gentlemen had dressed for dinner, the ladies all wore dinner gowns. Men in their sixties, women in their forties.

We never did see our siren of the garden gate again, nor did we recognize her partner (whose face neither of us had seen) until, on our way in to dinner en masse, my wife nudged me, nodded and whispered, "There. There's our man. I'd know that back anywhere." She had certainly spotted him. He could have been thus identified for arrest. But though unmistakable from the rear, Holloway, as he is known to all, or "poor Holloway," or "poor old Holloway," seen from the front, even allowing for his advantage of ten years over the rest, he being not much beyond fifty, looked as unlikely as any of them to be the Priapus we had seen perform earlier in the day. He was low-built, balding, and gray, as I noted earlier, getting paunchy, and, except for the ruddy tip of his nose, pallid in complexion. Nor did he look to me as if he quite belonged to those well-to-do whom Professor Jones says salmon fishing is the sport of. The guests of this place all know one another, being regulars who return year after year with the fish, and Holloway is treated by all as an old companion and equal. But I sensed that he was not. Between them and him I sensed a subtle but essential difference. Like the difference between one of Fortnum & Mason's old customers and one of its old salesclerks.

Wondering what sort of place this was where such a thing could happen as we had seen in the garden this afternoon, I played with the notion, whether he might not be on the payroll, like the tennis and riding instructors—an unadvertised attraction, of course: the salmon for the gentlemen, he for the salmon widows—until, as we were rising from our tables at dinner to leave, I saw him do a thing which, while it confirmed my suspicion that he was not to the sporting classes born (and one does not belong unless born to them), strongly suggested that he was not a member of the staff: he took from his blazer pocket a ball-point pen and on the label

*( 7 1 )*

of his wine bottle drew a line to mark the level of his consumption.

I forgot to note that he was unaccompanied and dined at a table for one. He was the only gentleman who dined alone, though some ladies did. These, I'm told, are widows—some of them quite youngish widows—who since the death of their angler husbands return regularly to The Redd for their holiday out of loyalty to their memories.

Even in Britain, where it is much more plentiful than it is in most countries, fresh salmon sells at the fishmonger's for fifteen shillings upward a pound. To quote Professor Jones, "The days are long past when apprentices in Britain petitioned against being given salmon to eat more than twice a week. The eating of salmon in Britain is now a luxury." And that fifteen-shilling salmon on sale at the fishmonger's is commercially caught salmon, from the coastal trawlers' nets. What a pound of salmon costs the sportsman who, like Mr. Porky Mitchell, has leased a beat on a river, or one who has traveled to Wales or Scotland and put up at some place like The Redd, and who may go for years without even hooking a fish, it is not possible to calculate: it must come close to the cost of those hummingbirds' tongues served at the feasts of the Roman emperors.

So when our fellow guest, Major Butler, instead of having that twenty-seven-pound cock he killed today boxed in ice and shipped home, as he might have done, had it served with his compliments to his fellow guests for dinner this evening, I thought this was a very generous gesture on his part until I tasted it. Salmon in Britain is poached ("in great numbers," runs the joke) in milk. The taste is describable. Poached milk.

At the table next to ours, with his lady, sat the old gentleman my wife met first, the one banging the barometer in the hall and predicting, "they won't bite tomorrow," and after dinner we four drank coffee together in the lounge. Each spring for forty-two years, with time out for two wars, Admiral Blakey has left the deep salt sea with the salmon and followed them up the Teme to The Redd, though for the last three of those years, on doctor's orders, he has not fished. This he tells us with quiet pride. But his wife: her smile looks forty-two years old. A navy widow for most of the year, then on her holidays a salmon widow for forty-two years. I am reminded of the latest bit of lore I have learned from Professor Jones: "Those female salmon which for lack of opportunity or other reasons do not spawn, and which ultimately reabsorb their genital products (which fill their entire body cavity), are called *baggots,* or *rawners.*" I know I shall never cast fly over water again without seeing again in memory Mrs. Blakey's baggotty smile, and feeling a twinge of complicity.

It was Holloway who led the general male exodus to bed following the nine o'clock news on the telly. They had had a strenuous day on their beats (Holloway had had on his, I could vouch), and must be up and out early for another one tomorrow, besides, "We're not as young as we were, are we, Tom?"—one of those remarks which you know the first time you hear it you're going to be hearing again, often. Many of them needed to be awakened from their armchairs and sent off to bed by their wives. Not Holloway, the first to retire, who has none.

Watching him go, the Admiral shook his head so many times I decided he too had been behind a rhododendron watching this afternoon's tryst at the garden gate.

"Poor old Holloway," the Admiral at length sighed and said. It was then that I learned the name. "Poor bugger. You've got to admire perseverance like that."

I evinced interest.

"Fishes here. Fishes below here. Fishes above here," said the Admiral, sighing and shaking his head. "Fishes the Usk. The Severn. The Wye. Twenty years he's been fishing and never has caught a fish yet. Now that takes character. That is what I call sportsmanship. I mean to say, we're here to fish not to catch fish and all that—still, twenty years! I've been a keen angler in my time, but I do not believe I could have carried on with no more encouragement than that. Ah, but you should see the poor fellow on his beat! Can't handle his rod. Never knows where his fly will light, or if it will—he's got it caught in the trees more than he's got it in the water. Slips and falls while he's wading at least once a week and comes in half drowned. Comes down with the grippe—that Teme water's cold this time of year—and we—the women, that is —have to take turns nursing him. I don't know how many times he's hooked himself on his back-cast and had to be taken to the surgeon to have the fly cut out. Nasty thing, a three-ought Jock Scott in the earlobe. And yet the man carries on and keeps coming back for more. Actually seems to enjoy himself here. Always cheerful. Always hopeful. Jolly good sport about it, too. Takes any amount of ribbing and takes it with a smile. Not many like that. It wants pluck."

"Never married?" I asked.

"Oh, no. No, no. Confirmed bachelor."

Though his days on the stream are over and he will never cast a Jock Scott again, the Admiral retires, at his wife's reminder, at half past nine. I last see him giving the barometer a final bang, then going slowly up the stairs shaking his head. Shortly afterward the bar comes alive for the night and Holloway is down again in time for the first round, the only unattached man. And while the veteran brothers of the angle alone upstairs in their beds sleep the simple sleep of Father Izaak Walton, poor old Holloway reigns over their wives like a pasha in his harem, or like a cock salmon among the hens on the spaw—

The scream of a woman being murdered was what made me break off. I thought at the time it was the scream of a woman being murdered. Now, five minutes later, I don't know what to think. For I was alone when I dashed into the hallway in my pajamas, except for Holloway, also in his, who, in tiptoeing from the door of his bedroom to that of another one not his, gave me a wink in passing from which I inferred that he was not going to the aid of a lady having her throat slowly slit.

*Wales, May 23*

The woman screamed all night long at irregular intervals of from a quarter to half an hour, stopping only at daybreak. She was not being murdered, then, only tortured. Yet at breakfast this morning none of the other men (we anglers breakfast while our wives are still in bed) indi-

cated by word or look that he had heard anything unto-
ward in the night. They can't have slept through it. Impossible. Is this something known and accepted by all the
regulars, one of those things one doesn't speak about?
Would it not be in bad taste of me to mention what
everyone else overlooks? Can poor Mr. Osborne, like
Jane Eyre's Mr. Rochester, have a lunatic earlier wife
attached to the wall by a chain somewhere in an outlying
wing who howls by night? If so, I wouldn't want to be the
one to draw attention to it.

I felt conspicuous enough already, dressed as I would
dress to go fishing back home, in old blue jeans, a blue
work shirt I once wore to paint a red barn, and my Brook-
lyn Dodgers baseball cap, while my fellow guests wore
Harris Tweed jackets, drillcord riding breeches, tweed
hats from Lock's, and neckties.

After breakfast—eggs with salmon—we drew lots for
our beats on the river. It had begun to rain in the night
and so we all set off in rain gear—I in my plastic mac—
over our waders and hip boots, and with our pipes
turned down. I speak not only for myself when I say that
our turned-down pipes, with rain dripping from them,
perfectly symbolized our spirits. A north wind was blowing, and "when the wind is in the north, then the fisherman goeth not forth"; Admiral Blakey, with forty-two
years of barometer-banging behind him, had foretold
that they wouldn't be biting today; and the rain was coming down in spouts. Some of us might have turned back,
but for the presence of Holloway in our midst. That
shamed us for our faintheartedness. Gaff in hand, like a
bishop's crook, he set an example for anglers everywhere

to follow. If he, with his dismal record, could carry on undismayed, we could, we must.

The rain had washed all the hubcaps clean and bright and the peacock found himself surrounded this morning by fresh rivals.

One fishes for salmon in waters one may oneself safely drink, waters of the clearest crystal—when not in spate, that is. For the salmon is the most fastidious of fish and does not tolerate the least pollution. His sensitivity to human wastes and to the wastes of manufacture kills him, or else drives him away in disgust.

The Teme is a spring river. That is to say, its salmon return to spawn in the spring. Other rivers are fall rivers; their salmon return in the fall. But all salmon spawn in the fall, including those that come back into the rivers in the spring. And while they wait, some of them for up to nine months, they fast.

Can it really be true that salmon, such voracious eaters in the ocean, once they reenter freshwater, fast? Fast absolutely? Fast to the death? All salmon? All salmon fast, absolutely, and all but a few of them fast to the death. Not much is certain about this little-known, though much-studied fish, but that much is. Never a trace of food has been found in the dissected insides of one, not even one known to have been in the river for periods of up to nine months. People have always found this hard to credit, and it was once widely believed that none was ever caught with food in its stomach because they vomited on being hooked. Not so. They quit eating.

Then why will they—sometimes—strike at a fisherman's fly? Or a shrimp (prawn, they say here)? Or a fly tied to imitate a prawn? Or a minnow? Or a spinner made to imitate a minnow? Or a gob of worms on a hook? Why, indeed? To this, the oldest and most intriguing question about the salmon, you will not find the answer even in Professor Jones's book (about which I am beginning to feel as the little girl felt about the one she was assigned to review, and reviewed so pithily, to wit: This book tells me more about penguins than I care to know). Professor Jones speculates that it may be done out of irritability, and anyone who has ever seen a salmon (I am thinking now of the male salmon) taken from the spawning bed can easily see why he should think so. The salmon at this stage looks irritable. In fact, he looks downright ferocious, deformed by his single-minded obsession with sex.

What does the salmon live on? Love: that's the obvious answer. But he's not living, he's dying. This is going to be the death of him. He's eating himself alive: all that stored-up deep-seat fat, and not just fat: muscle, too. As he lies in the pool doing nothing, not even eating, from March until September, his idle mind on evil thoughts, his disused alimentary organs shrink and shrivel and practically disappear to make room for the gonads that swell and swell and swell until that is all he—or she—is inside. Meanwhile the silver sheen he came in with from the sea turns dull, and his meat turns red and kipper. The male grows a growth, called a kype, on the tip of his underjaw, forcing it away from the upper one, which also develops a hook, giving to his expression a rapacious snarl.

When the time comes for the salmon to spawn—when the female is "running ripe"—after a brief courtship in the quiet of the pool, they move upstream into the swift water. It is there that the eggs must be laid because they require for their incubation constant percolation of the water through the gravel surrounding them in their redd.

It is as impossible for a salmon as it is for you or me to tell whether another salmon is a male or a female just by looking. For much of their lives they don't care. When the time comes to care, the salmon have a way of telling who's who, or rather, who's what. A salmon sidles up to another and quivers. If the other fish quivers in response then it's a male like himself, but if it turns over on its side and begins flapping its tail on the river bottom, then it's a match.

When she is ready to spawn, the female salmon begins "cutting." That is, flapping her tail against the river bottom so hard she digs a hole in the gravel. With her anal fin she keeps feeling the hole until she is satisfied with the depth of it. When she is satisfied with it she crouches over the hole. Thereupon the male salmon joins her. He draws alongside her without touching. He begins to quiver eagerly. She gapes. He gapes.

For lunch today my wife was served *croquettes de saumon.* I had one of my old friend Mitchell's pork pies in a box put up for me by the hotel. For me, Admiral Blakey's glum prediction proved accurate and I returned fishless and as wet as a fish myself. But for two of my fellow guests, I heard with an envious heart, a game smile, and a sinking appetite, the day yielded salmon of large size.

*Wales, May 25*

Again all night long every few minutes that woman screamed, and again we were the only ones to notice it. Only long familiarity with it can explain the self-composure of our fellow guests. That, or the well-known British self-discipline. As for me, I don't think I could ever get used to it. It curdles my American blood. The first time it happened I bolted from bed and into the hall again. I was still there listening for it to come again when poor old Holloway emerged from his room and went tiptoeing past in his pajamas. He gave me his wink, and, in my amazement, I believe I may have returned it.

The mating of salmon, concluded:

It is concluded, all but. That was it. A union without contact between the partners, a crouch, a quiver, a mutual gape. It not only doesn't sound like much fun, from the human point of view; when you remember what a long way they've come, past what snares and ambushes, over almost insuperable obstacles, how they have gone hungry and grown disfigured, and knowing as you do that it will prove fatal, it seems pitifully unworthy of the trouble. A cheat. There is worse to come.

Friends, if you have tears prepare to shed them now. I know I nearly did when I got to the chapter in Professor Jones's book in which in cold ichthyological prose he relates the betrayal, the ignominy which now overtakes this grand fish.

For the sake of this moment the salmon has swum

maybe fifteen hundred miles through nobody knows what perils of the deep. He has—and he is one of the few that have—eluded the trawlers' nets and the fishmonger's cold slate slab, or, more ignoble end still, the cannery. He will not have come this far without having felt the barb and fought free of some of the many Jock Scotts and Black Doses and Silver Doctors dangled temptingly before him. He has leaped twelve-foot-high falls. He has survived gill maggots, fin worms, leeches, boils, white rot, white spot, gill catarrh, fungus, carp lice, sea lice. For this he has fasted, for this he will die. Now he is about to achieve fulfillment of his desire. The female has finished her cutting. With her anal fin she has felt out the redd and found it satisfactory. He now hangs alongside her, quivering eagerly. She crouches. She gapes. He gapes. She sheds some of her eggs, about nine hundred of them. Now begins for him the release of some of that pent-up milt which in two ripe testes fills his entire body. And from out of nowhere, more often than not, some impudent little Holloway of a parr darts in and discharges his tuppence worth! This little delinquent may be no more than four inches long. *He* has swum no seas. *He* has leaped no falls. *He* has foiled no Englishman armed with two-handed rod of split bamboo. He has been nowhere, done nothing, cheeky little imp. Yet this little love-thief, this mischievous minnow scarcely out of his caviarhood, has just cuckolded a cock salmon some two hundred times his size, right under his nose, so to speak, and has cheated him of his paternity as well; for puny as they are, they are potent, these precocious parr.

But then the old cock was once a parr himself and

played the same trick on his elders and betters in his youth.

After shedding her eggs the female salmon moves a little ways upstream and begins cutting another redd. She is killing two birds with one stone. For the gravel raised in the cutting of this new redd is carried downstream by the current and covers the eggs she has just deposited.

Back at the hotel, today for lunch there were *timbales de saumon.*

*Wales, May 27*

The mystery of the woman who screams in the night is solved. My wife finally mustered the courage to speak of it to one of the other ladies. It's the peahen. It's the mating season for them, too, and peahens, it seems, do that at this time. My God, said my wife, what does her mate do to her to make her scream like that? Or not do to her to make her scream like that, said the other lady, vain, self-infatuated creature; had you thought, my dear, of that?

And so life for a salmon begins not in but under a river, where, along with eight or nine hundred of his brother and sister caviar, his mother has buried him. That will have been in the fall. Next spring he hatches out, though remaining inside the redd.

At first the infant salmon is nothing more than a drop of egg yolk with a tail and a pair of bug eyes. This little tadpole is called an alevin.

If he is not found and eaten by another salmon or a trout or washed away in a spate of the river or stepped on by a cow or a wading angler, the alevin, after about a month, by which time his egg sac has been consumed, comes out of the redd into the river a proper little fish, a fingerling or a fry, at which change his actuarial table dips even more sharply. For now he is the prey not only of his cannibal kin and of his cousins the trout, but also of pike, perch, chub, eels, ducks, swans, herons, and cormorants, and of droughts, for the fingerling is even more sensitive than he will be when he grows up to any rise in the water's temperature.

When the young salmon grows to be longer than a man's finger then he is no longer a fingerling. He is then a parr—here in Wales, a sil; in other localities (I am indebted to Professor Jones for this list of delightful names): a pink, a samlet, a peal, a branlin, a skegger (so Walton called them), a locksper, a skirling, a laspring, and a samson.

It's about this time that a salmon finds out whether it's a he or a she. If a she, there is nothing to do but be patient and wait; if a he, then the fun has begun, at the old cocks' expense.

The salmon remains a parr for two years, spending the whole time in his native pool or near it, growing to be about four or five inches long and to weigh as many ounces. Then the salmon goes to sea, a smolt now. After just one year there it may be a foot and a half long and weigh three pounds or more. If it stays there four years it will come back four or five feet long and weighing forty or forty-five pounds. The salmon is a grilse when it returns to spawn, a kelt after having done so.

Thus one salmon in his time plays many parts, his acts being seven ages: egg, alevin, fingerling or fry, parr, smolt, grilse (cock or hen), and, last scene of all, which ends this strange eventful history, kelthood and mere oblivion, sans teeth, sans eyes, sans taste, sans everything.

Unless it be a hen and she turns out to be an old maid and then she has another: baggot, or rawner.

Lunch today: *quenelles de saumon.*

*Wales, May 28*

Every time I'm just about to doze off to sleep the peahen screams. What can he be doing to her?

In the evening, after dinner, before trooping off to bed, we anglers attend to our tackle.

Rather than disjoint our rods at the end of the day only to have to joint them again early on the morrow, we stand them jointed in a rack inside the ground-floor gentlemen's loo (as it's called here), to the right just inside the front door, opposite the barometer. There too we leave our gaffs and our rain gear, our muddy boots and waders, and there after dinner we go to get our reels and unwind our wet lines and hang them out to dry overnight. The open but covered loggia provides an ideal place for this, and we stretch them between brass hooks in the wall. Then those—and I am one of them—who favor knotted tapered leaders (or casts) over the knotless ones sold by the tackle shops, convinced that they sink better—and a leader must sink, for otherwise it casts a shadow, and nothing frightens a fish like a shadow—those, I say, who think as I think, sit snipping from their spools lengths of monofilament nylon of graduated gauges and joining them together with good blood knots pulled tight. Meanwhile, others of us tie flies out of feathers and fur and tinsel. This done, we hone the barbs of our hooks, which from striking against gravel and stones in the stream all day have become blunted. Many a good fish has gotten away thanks to a blunt hook, and it is Admiral Blakey's judgment that the logbook (more on this later), in which not once in twenty years does Holloway's name appear, might tell a different story if instead of making a bloody fool of himself among the ladies after dinner he spent his time sharpening his hooks. Then we oil our reels and we patch any holes or rips in our waders and boots and then we yawn and we recall the strenuous day we have had on the beat and tell one another that we must be up and out early for another one tomorrow and we remind ourselves that we are not as young as we once were and we excuse ourselves to the ladies and then we go up to bed.

Today for lunch there was *soufflé de saumon*.

*Wales, May 30*

There is a gap of a day in my diary.

I came in wet and fishless late yesterday afternoon, to find in my bed, where she had spent the day, going without lunch, my own salmon widow. The mood of the place and the season was upon her. On my approaching near and giving a quiver, she responded by showing a readiness to spawn. Indeed, she was running ripe; as for me, I grew a kype on the spot. We passed up supper, fasting instead, and came down late this morning, feeling and looking rather kelt.

If a wink can be said to be broad, Holloway's was to me at cocktail time this evening.

Is it a leftover bit of old sympathetic magic—drink your enemy's blood, eat his flesh, and thereby acquire the power to think as he thinks before he thinks it—that lies behind this unbroken diet of salmon?

*Wales, May 31*

Three years have gone by since Admiral Blakey last felt the thrill of a taut line, and for the last couple of years before that his catch was small as the limit of the reach of his arm was exceeded by progressive farsightedness, and the growing smallness of fishhooks' eyes forced the old angler to set forth in the morning with his Jock Scott tied on his leader for him and to have to abandon his sport and trudge home if through misadventure he lost it and could find no younger brother of the fraternity along the stream bank to tie on another one for him.

Now that his angling is ended, the Admiral's evenings, like the Admiral's days, are spent in catching, or rather recatching, fish in memory. Admiral Blakey's memory for fish is naturally retentive, and this is in contrast to his memory for any and everything else. His wife must prompt him whenever he tries to recall any of their children's Christian names, but he can and, what is worse, does tell you the weight of, down to the odd ounces, and the weather, wind, and water conditions attendant upon the killing of every fish he ever killed in his life. And you can be man or woman indifferently for the Admiral to tell you this; he no more knows the sex of his listener than a salmon past quivering knows who, that is to say what, he is communicating with. The man's talk, like the menu of this hotel, is always the same. He has caught a lot of fish in his time, and has more stories to tell about them—and the ones that got away—than a hen salmon has eggs.

The Blakeys have four children. He had a little trouble recalling exactly how many there were of them, but she reminded him with such positiveness I could not but think the number corresponded to the number of their conjugal embraces, lifetime. Despite myself, under the influence of this place, I tried to imagine one of those embraces. The most I could conjure up was something with about as much intimacy as that between the cock salmon and the hen. I pictured the two of them lying side by side without touching, and after a while gaping together.

I could never in the course of our acquaintance— short, to be sure, though it got to seem very long before it ended—form any image of the admiral in Admiral Blakey. Here was a man who had risen to a post of supreme command in a profession fabled in story and song, and it all seemed to have passed over him without leaving a trace, supplanted by the sport he had pursued. He never reminisced about his naval adventures, his imagery was not drawn from ships or the sea, his talk was as un-nautical as a cotton farmer's. He had but his one

topic, and had I had the rights of those bygone apprentices, I should certainly have petitioned against being
served it more than twice a week. True, I had my chance
to study Admiral Blakey only while at The Redd during
spawning season; of what he is like during the rest, which
is the greater part, of the year, I know no more than any
of us knows of the salmon's life in the sea. He may get it
all out of his system during his one month here and on
leaving have no more interest left in angling than a kelt
has in sex, for all I know about it. If this be so, however, I
fear it may leave the old gentleman quite spent, with no
topic for talk at all, and to this fear I am prompted by the
unbroken silence which at table, as well as at all other
times, reigns between him and his wife.

The Admiral's memory for fish, as I said, is naturally
good. But in telling my wife that the wind was south-
southwest at seven miles an hour, the barometer at 29.44
inches and rising, the water low and clear, that he was
using a 2/0 Durham Ranger on a ten-pound gut when at
4:42 p.m., June 10, 1929, after a fight lasting twenty-one
minutes, he killed a hen salmon measuring thirty-four
and one half inches and weighing thirty-two pounds, six
and three-quarter ounces, the Admiral is assisted in the
details by a promptbook here in the hotel. This docu-
ment, in eighty-nine volumes, one for each year going
back to 1881, is a record of every fish ever caught here by
the hotel's every guest, with all attendant circumstances.
This is the book in which, guest though he has been for
twenty of those years, poor old Holloway's name never
once appears, and neither will poor old Humphrey's, it
begins to seem pretty certain. These volumes provide
the Admiral his reading matter. He spends the day por-

ing over them and chuckling to himself, and he is only too happy to share his pleasure with any lady who happens along. In the current one, kept not in the bookcase along with the rest but on a table in the salon, I had seen, despite all my contrivances not to see them, my more fortunate—more skillful, should I not say?—fellow anglers taking turns making their entries for the day while digesting their salmon in the evening.

This evening I was perusing the volume for 1934, marveling again at the British national sense of honor that would entrust the keeping of a fishing log to the fishermen themselves, when my wife got off the Admiral's hook and he joined me.

"Nineteen thirty-four!" said the Admiral, and over his watery eyes spread that mist of happy recollection which the mention of any of the last forty-two years excluding the very last five can produce. "The eighteenth of June 1934! There's a day I shall always remember, and yet you won't find it noted in the book there. I'd drawn number six as my beat that day. A rainy day it was, barometer at thirty inches and steady, the wind out of the west at nine miles an hour, gusting up to fourteen. My rod was a Leonard, thirteen feet long, mounted with a 6/0 Hardy reel. My line was a King Eider silk, backed with three hundred feet of thirty-pound backing. My cast tapered from .060 inches in the butt to .022 in the tippet. I was fishing a 2/0 Silver Wilkinson, having observed in the river quantities of chub minnows which that pattern in that size most closely imitated. It was precisely twelve noon by the clock in nearby Llanblfchfpstdwwy church tower when I got a strike that very nearly tore the rod from my grip. This fish behaved in a most uncommon manner from the start. As you know, Humphrey, once hooked, a salmon can be generally relied upon to run in the direction in which he invariably faces owing to rheotaxis, also known as rheotropism, namely, upstream. This fish never once made an upstream run; he went steadily, and at a steady pace approximating that of the current, downriver. Within moments he had taken my line and three quarters of my backing. I put all the pressure on him I dared, giving him the butt of the rod and straining the gut to just under breaking point. There was no turning or raising him. Straight downriver hugging the bed he went as though determined to get back into the sea. I could regain not an inch of my line and I dared not let him have an inch more than he had already. There was but one tactic to adopt: wade with him downstream keeping pressure on him constantly until he should tire. We were, as I said, near Llanblfchfpstdwwy church, on beat six, and the time was precisely twelve noon. At half past two we passed the ruins of Cwffd-nant-Bwlch Abbey, and I still had regained none of my line. This of course had taken us through beats seven, eight, and nine, where in succession my good friends the Reverend Smythe-Prestwick, may he rest in peace, Colonel Watson and Mr. Finchley, had very obligingly withdrawn their lines and themselves from the water to allow my fish and me to pass through. Though my rod was bowed into a hoop, the fish swam on untiringly. I began to think perhaps I had foul-hooked him. We went by and through the villages of Mmfcwmmr, Upper Llndwrtfyndd-ar-y-bryn, Lower Llndwrtfyndd-ar-y-bryn, and Bwlch-ddû, and were passing the 23rd Royal Welsh Fusiliers—that's a pub—some five miles from our point of contact, when at last I felt him begin to weaken. I now began to reel in steadily, and within another half mile I got my first sight of him. Or rather, them. For to my astonishment and delight, I discovered that I had got on not one but two large fish, one to each of the fly's two hooks. A most uncommon occurrence even in the life of a very experienced fisherman, and so I resolved to have them mounted, side by side and cheek by jowl, sharing the fly. At last I brought them to gaff, and at seven thirty-four p.m. I lifted from the water the biggest pair of waders I believe I ever saw in my life. I said to myself at the time that the man who came out of them would scale sixteen stone. And I was proved right when two days later my good friend Colonel Watson, fishing beat number two, hooked him on a 4/0 Black Dose.

At dinner this evening, or rather at dinner's end, Holloway, after marking the label of his wine bottle, came over to the Blakeys' table.

"Well, Admiral," he said, with a wink at me over the old angler's head. "Well, Mrs. Blakey. It's been lovely seeing you both again. Lovely. I shall look forward to seeing you both again next year. Good-bye."

"Good-bye," said the Admiral.

"Good-bye," said Mrs. Blakey.

"He's going, then, is he?" said the Admiral, shaking his head sympathetically at Holloway's departing back.

"No, dear. We are."

"Oh, yes. To be sure. So we are."

*Wales, June 1*

Fishing demands faith. Faith like Saint Peter's when the Lord bade him cast his hook into the water and catch a fish for money to pay tribute to Caesar. To catch a fish you have got to have faith that the water you are fishing has got fish in it, and that you are going to catch one of them. You still may not catch anything, but you certainly won't if you don't fish your best, and you won't do this without faith to inspire you to do it. You won't approach the water carefully. You won't study the water carefully. You won't cast carefully. You won't fish your cast; to do this, patience is required, and patience is grounded on faith. You won't fish each stretch of the water thoroughly before giving up on it and moving to the next stretch. The satisfactions of a day's fishing are deep; and just as deep on a day when you don't catch a fish, but unless you keep faith that you are going to catch a fish that day, then fishing seems a waste—a waste of time, money, effort, and most depressing, a waste of spirit. Faith and faith alone can guard the fisherman against a demon of which he is particularly the prey, the demon of self-irony, from acquiescence in the opinion of the ignorant that he is making a fool of himself. Few things can make a man feel more fully a man than fishing, if he has got faith; nothing can make a man feel more fully a fool if he has not got faith.

After nine days of fishing the Teme without once getting a nibble I had lost my faith. Not my faith that there were fish in the river. They were there, all right. With my own eyes I had seen, and with my own knife and fork had eaten, a miraculous draught of Teme fishes. The fish were there; I had lost my faith that I was going to catch one of them, and my cup of self-irony ranneth over. I cast and I cast and I cast again with that big heavy rod, I beat those waters until my wrists swelled and stiffened and ached me all night long while that peahen screamed, and I marveled how Holloway could make shift to keep at this drudgery even as a camouflage to the pleasures he returns here to possess himself of.

Then this afternoon, defeated, deflated, and dejected, heedless in my approach, clomping along the bank in my heavy, hobnailed boots and casting my shadow I cared not where—the first shadow I had been able to cast since coming into Wales—I came to a bend in the river where the undercutting of the bank by the current made a pool and into this pool I did not cast my Green Highlander, I dismissed it there, with leave to go where it would on its own; I didn't care if I never saw it again.

The big fly lighted at the head of the pool near the opposite bank and quickly sank. Absently I watched the line swing out into the current. I saw it stop. I was hooked on a snag. In my mood this was all I needed and, lowering my rod, I grasped the line to break the fly off, disjoint my rod, and go home. But I was using a heavy leader, one bigger in the tippet than any leader I had ever used in my trout fishing back home was in the butt, and it would not break. I gave another angry yank, whereupon my line began to move. I thought I had dislodged the snag from the riverbed and was still hooked to it, until I reflected that an object dislodged from the riverbed would move downstream with the current, not upstream. I had had a strike and had struck back without even knowing it, and had hooked the biggest fish of my life.

I reeled in the slack line and raised my rod. He was still on. His run was short. He had gone to the bottom to sulk and I could not budge him. When I put the butt of the rod to him and saw the rod bow and heard the line tighten and felt his size and strength, a sense of my unworthiness came over me and I was smitten with guilt and contrition.

I didn't deserve to land this fish. Fishing without faith, I had done nothing as it ought to be done. He had hooked himself—I just happened to be holding the other end of the line. I pictured him lying there on the riverbed in all his unseen silvery majesty. How mysterious and marvelous a creature he was! I thought how far he had come to get here and of the obstacles he had braved and bested. While keeping pressure on him with my rod held high, I thought of the towering falls he had leaped, driven by the overmastering urge to breed and perpetuate his kind. And here I was about to kill him before he could achieve the hard-won consummation of his desire. It was the King of Fish I was about to assassinate. I felt like a cur.

How often in books published by the most reputable houses, with editors who verify their authors' every assertion, had I read with soul dilated of one of that greathearted breed of dry-fly ascetics who, every time he caught Old Methuselah, the venerable yard-long brown trout of Potts's Pool, put him back—until under cover of darkness one night a clod armed with nightcrawlers and a clothesline unblushingly yanked Old Methuselah out and brained him with a car jack and the magic of Potts's Pool departed forever. I said to my soul now, I won't gaff him. A fish as noble as this deserved a better end than poached in milk or jellied in aspic and garnished with blobs of mayonnaise. I could see myself already, this evening at the hotel, smiling a wistful smile when my fat and fish-fed fellow guests commiserated with me on my day after penning their entries in the logbook. For when I had fought the fish into submission, when I had mastered his valiant spirit with my own even more valiant one, when he turned over and lay floating belly-up at my feet, I would carefully extract the hook and hold him right side up and facing into the current until he got his breath back, and then I would bid him go, finned friend, go, my brother, and do not slink in shame, go in pride and intact, gallant old warrior, go, and eschew Green Highlanders.

I would like hell.

I sometimes return a little fish to the water, but I leave it to those knights of the outdoors who contribute articles to the sporting magazines, and who catch so many more of them than I ever will, to put back big ones.

I raised my rod so high it quivered; still the fish clung stubbornly to his spot. Every once in a while the fish would give a little shake of his head, transmitted to me through the taut line, as if to test whether he still had me hooked. I held on. He would let a minute pass, then would wallow and shake his head as if he were enjoying this. It was like having a bull by the ring in his nose and being afraid to let go of it. At one point, resting one of my wrists by holding the end of the rod between my legs,

I had a moment of wild wonder at myself, at the question I had just asked myself: Did I really want to catch a fish this big? Heretical thought for a fisherman; yet I could not relate this to fishing as I knew it. I was used to exulting when I netted a fourteen-inch trout weighing a pound and a quarter. Now my hopes had been overfulfilled. Truth was, I was scared of the sea monster that I had—or that had me—on the line and couldn't get off.

After fifteen minutes my fish began to move. The drag on my reel was set to just under the breaking strength of the leader, yet he stripped line from the reel with a speed that made the ratchet buzz like a doorbell. I was not wading but was on the bank; now I began to run along the bank—I should say, I was dragged along it. When he had gone a hundred and fifty yards upstream—with me giving him precious line at one point so I could negotiate a fence stile, then sprinting, in hobnailed hip boots, to regain it—he braked, shook his head, then turned and sped downstream a hundred and fifty yards, taking me back over the fence stile. I still had not seen him, and the slant of my line in the water told me I was not going to see him for some time to come. He was deep, hugging the river bottom.

For forty-five minutes he kept this up—I clambered over that fence stile six times from both directions—growing an inch longer and a pound heavier in my mind —my wrists, too—each minute. When he quit it was not gradually, it was all at once, as if he had fought with every ounce of his strength and all his determination up to the very end. I stepped into the shallow water at the edge, and, gaining line, began reeling him toward me. Even his unresisting weight strained my big rod. Ten feet from where I stood his dorsal fin broke water. It was three feet back from where my line entered the water, three feet back from it his tail broke the surface. My mouth was dry with desire. I gaffed him. Or rather, I made a pass at him with the gaff, nicked him, he turned, lunged, and was gone. The line snapped back and wound itself around the rod like a vine. My leader had parted at one of the blood knots I had so tightly tied. There was something detestable in the very shape—curly, coiled, kinky—of the end I was left holding. Imagine a pig the size of a penny and he would have a tail just like that.

I smiled wistfully, all right, that evening at the hotel when the others, penning their entries in the logbook, commiserated with me on my day.

*Ross-on-Wye, June 2*

At lunch today—*mousse de saumon*—Holloway drained his bottle of wine. He is moving on farther upstream for his annual stay at another fisherman's hotel to try his rotten luck there. Poor old Holloway! You've got to admire perseverance like that. We also were leaving this afternoon, also leaving behind in the logbook no record of our stay. But, with the wind east-southeast and the barometer at twenty-nine inches and falling, using a Green Highlander on a 2/0 hook, I had had one get away that would have gone to thirty-five—what am I saying?—forty-five pounds! Up to the end Holloway was still trying. He will be making the spawning run up the Teme and stopping at The Redd again next spring, his twenty-first. The last I saw of Holloway he was teaching a willing pupil, young Mrs. Bradley, whose old husband drew a rather distant beat on the river this morning, a lesson in the gentle art of angling. Which, as Walton's Piscator instances in support of his contention that ours is an art of high esteem, was how Antony and Cleopatra also whiled away their leisure moments.

And the poor salmon, on whom love seems so hard— do all of them die after spawning? Nine tenths of them do; of those that survive it, nine tenths are hens. Professor Jones offers no explanation of why so many more of the males die than the females. At the risk of anthropomorphizing, I would suggest it's from shame at being so often and so openly cuckolded by those pesky parr; except that there is no evidence to indicate that the cock salmon know anything more about what is going on right under their own tails than the anglers did who came to angle for them at The Redd. The widowed hens return, the way we have just come today, to the sea, and there grow fat and sleek and silvery again and then return to spawn another time. Some durable old girls make it back twice more. A few old rips make it back three more times.

# Cast and
# Cast Again

**1**

"Be at number 15 Place Vendôme Monday morning 9:15 sharp," the wire read.

Number 15 Place Vendôme is the address, in Paris, of the Ritz Hotel, where, two days earlier, my wife and I had met the owner, Charles Ritz, and had promptly earned his disapproval of our fly-casting techniques. Not that we put on a demonstration for him there in the bar of his hotel. Indeed, I really wanted to talk to him not about fishing but about the literary associations of the Ritz—so very rich in them—and about one in particular. But when I asked Charles for his recollections of Marcel Proust, who for years dined there nightly, he said, "I may have seen him. He was another flyswatter." That was Charles's name for anybody who was not a fly-fisherman. I dropped the subject. He then got it out of us that we did not practice the technique of fly-casting he prescribes in his book *A Fly Fisher's Life*. We did it wrong, then, and, provided we did not turn out to be too old to learn, he was determined to teach us the right way.

So his wire was not an invitation but rather a summons, a command, and we were there exactly on time. However, at half past nine we were still sitting in

*( 1 0 1 )*

Charles's car with him and his chauffeur, waiting. For what, we were not told.

Presently there appeared on the Place, headed our way, a short, slight, bespectacled young man dressed in knickers, a bulky sweater, and a tweed cap, carrying large canvas bags slung from both shoulders and, over one shoulder, a bundle of fishing rods in their cases.

"There's my boy," said Charles.

This was the beginning of my acquaintance with Pierre Affre, a little man with a big ambition, in fact an obsession, a man in a race against time and against many other men in quest of a prize for which all of them, as nobody knows better than Pierre, were probably born too late.

That morning at the casting pool in the Bois de Boulogne, beside the old disused live pigeon–shooting stand, Charles Ritz almost ruined my fly-casting, such as it is. Just watching him cast was enough to discourage me. Then over eighty (but still square-shouldered and erect as a drill sergeant) he could lay out a hundred feet of line with a light rod, softly and with perfect aim, and make it look as easy as swatting a fly. Swiss, Charles had the precision of timing of one of his country's many-jeweled watches. He had perfected his own method of casting, had baptized it with a name, had made a religion of it and had become a zealot in preaching it. After one hour of his coaching I could no longer cast my own way, and it was plain to me that to master his I would have to be born again. Charles then left me to practice while he turned his attentions to my wife.

Behind Charles's back I reverted to my old bad habits,

hoping to regain a little self-respect. After a few minutes I was again casting about as well as I ever had; a few minutes was all it took to cast as well as I. Pierre Affre joined me and, in English, said quietly, "You should not listen to Mr. Ritz. You cast far enough to catch fish. He wants everybody to be a tournament champion. Do it your way."

I complimented Pierre on his English. It was strongly French-flavored, but he was not just fluent in it, he was voluble, he was fairly bursting with it. It was hard to believe that he had been speaking it for only one year. He had dropped Russian, in which he was quite far advanced, to study it. I, who have been a professor of English in my time, found his motive for learning it unique in my experience. "I had to," he explained. "English is the language of fly-fishing."

Pierre had rigged up the battery of rods he had brought along. These were prototypes, not yet production models, from the factory of Pezon et Michel, which he and Charles together had designed. They were now to be tested.

Of Pierre Affre's ability with a fly rod perhaps no more need be said than that for eight of his twenty-eight years he had been the fly-casting champion of France, and has won medals as his country's entrant in international tournaments. That day in the Bois de Boulogne what I was shown as he and Charles Ritz cast side by side resembled nothing so much as a duo sonata—music without sound—rendered by an old maestro and his prize pupil. What many people can do, those two were doing as few people can, or ever have done. Just to cast a fly rod is not very hard, but the difference between competence at it and artistry is about the equivalent of the musical comb compared to the violin. Measured against either of those virtuosi, my motions in doing it were those of somebody beating a rug, while each cast of theirs had the finesse, the assurance, and the dispatch of a diamond cutter splitting a stone. Between the two of them there was that sense of shared pleasure and a common bond that chamber music players have, the young man honoring the old one, he finding in his young friend a continuity that would last after him.

On our drive back to the Ritz I discussed with Charles a project I had in mind. I was thinking of giving myself a fishing holiday in the spring, hoping to pay for it with an article, and I had just decided where I would like to spend it. I had been tempted by Montana's Madison River, with its giant rainbow trout, its majestic mountains. I had considered Maine's Moosehead Lake, famed for its landlocked salmon. Yugoslavia, with its big brown trout, had lured me. But really my decision had never been finally in doubt, as I now realized.

We stopped at an intersection to let a frail old man cross the street. "In a few years," said Charles, "I'll be like him. An old flyswatter."

I continued. It was glorious scenery I wanted, it was an elusive fish, it was tradition and lore, and it was comfort —someplace where there was a nice little hotel, preferably one with a proprietor who was himself a keen fisherman. So I had decided to come to Paris and stay at the Ritz and, in that pleasant stretch of the Seine that runs from the Quai d'Orsay past the Tuileries and the Louvre, under the Pont Neuf, alongside Notre Dame, to the Pont Sully, try for that rare fish, the *gardon*. Rare, that is to say, in those waters—as any tourist can tell you who has hung over the parapet and watched a Seine fisherman at his sport; the common roach, contemptibly common every-where else in Europe but there. Along the banks of what river in the world was there more of interest and beauty to see? And what fish inspired more devotion in those who fish for him with so seldom a reward? Charles was enthusiastic, and he promised to mount the *gardon* I was hoping to catch, all three inches of it, and hang it on the wall beneath the giant swordfish which gives its name to the Espadon grill at the Ritz. He was even willing to risk my one misgiving: that when you find a nice little fishing hotel and write about it and put it on the map, you spoil it.

I never went on that trip and Charles never became an old flyswatter. Within months he was dead. It was I who broke the news of his death to Pierre, who was off in the wilds of Iceland at the time, fishing for salmon.

Pierre lived on the same métro line, Pont de Neuilly–Vincennes, as we. When it came time to say good-bye at the Tuileries station that morning, we decided to walk on together to the Palais Royal. There we found we still had more to say to one another, so we walked to the Louvre. We wound up walking Pierre home to his apartment on the Left Bank, near the Mint. He had the day off, and there were things he wanted to show me.

Pierre lived, like a character of Balzac's, surrounded, almost swamped by, the paraphernalia of his idée fixe.

Fishing rods in sheaves were stacked in every corner of his three rooms. Reels lay everywhere. Tents, camp stoves, backpacks, axes, were piled in the middle of the floors. Books and magazines, all devoted to fishing, were stacked against the walls. A tabletop was heaped with correspondence from fishermen and conservation clubs.

I was shown all his treasures. Bamboo trout rods as wispy as magicians' wands, salmon rods the size of vaulting poles: each one—and there were dozens—was taken from its case, jointed, tested, appraised. One-of-a-kind reels that never went into production or had been specially made for presentation to a champion caster or a legendary fisherman. Flies tied by famous tiers containing feathers from exotic birds now protected from the threat of extinction. Books long out of print with engraved, hand-colored plates. The talk, not always about fishing, was unflagging. We finally parted early the next morning.

By then I knew such out-of-the-way things as how to masturbate a prize bull for the purpose of artificial insemination, and that the human race owes it to the life-work of a certain Miss Rothschild, of the banking family, that fleas, so important to us because they carry some of our most dread diseases, have at last been classified. Fleas are classified by the shape of their penises. I also knew by then all the latest about the Atlantic salmon in its long, losing battle for survival.

Pierre—Dr. Affre—knows these things because he is a veterinarian. Throughout our first evening together, friends of his kept dropping in to have their puppies examined, inoculated against distemper. On a trip to the toilet I found a convalescent hawk in his bathtub. Pierre's doctor's thesis was written on the Atlantic salmon.

In France, as elsewhere, veterinary medicine can be a very lucrative profession. Pierre could, if he would, earn a great deal of money at it, for he is brilliant, tireless, able and willing to take jobs which other vets turn down, such as vaccinating large herds of cattle—hard and often dangerous work—or night duty in animal hospitals. Pierre does not enjoy operating on house pets, for it is monotonous and unchallenging; he would prefer to do research. But that does not pay. If he is to have the money which his expensive sport requires, he must treat sick cats and dogs. Even so, Pierre always has, as he, making one of his rare mistakes, puts it, "few money." The reason for this is that no sooner does he get a little in his pocket than he throws up his job and is off to Scotland or Canada or Iceland in quest of the trophy salmon that swims continuously in his thoughts. Pierre is free to travel, being single. "The girls, they like me," he says, "until I take them fishing." He has no intention of getting married, for that would tie him down, nor does he wish to bring children into a world like this, where, by the time any son of his were grown there will be no more salmon left to catch. That, as regards his favorite fish, is Pierre in his black mood; he can be, the very next moment, just as intemperately optimistic.

It was the same year—his twentieth—in which he won his first national fly-casting championship that Pierre caught his first salmon. Until then his fishing had been for small game. That year, in a truck borrowed from his father's plumbing business, he went to the Pyrenees. There, in the Gave d'Oloron, he caught one of the few salmon remaining in that river which had once abounded in them. It was an eighteen-pounder. Pierre paid for the trip by selling the fish. Unlike America, most European countries, including France, permit the selling of game fish, and salmon is everywhere high-priced. It grows more so with each passing year. In that economic fact lies Pierre's hope and his despair, the latter of which gains upon the former with each passing year.

The large photograph on the wall of his apartment of Pierre bringing that fish ashore is that of a man who has found his fate. It might be his wedding picture. Sad if so, because of the salmon's uncertain future.

When they are young and fancy-free, fishermen play the field, angling for anything, pleased with whatever they get. Their hearts are not yet in it. But waiting for each and every one of them is *his* fish, and each species—the ones really worth fishing for, that is—demands the undivided attention of a jealous woman. Just as wedding bells break up the old gang, so do the individual species of fish—even different methods of fishing for the same species. Freshwater fishermen and saltwater fishermen belong to different races. After that great division, the myriad subdivisions begin: fly-fisherman, spin fisherman, bass fisherman, trout fisherman, muskellunge fisherman, striped-bass fisherman, bonefisherman: they belong to separate nationalities, speak diverse tongues. Of all fish, the one Pierre Affre fell for at first sight, hook, line, and sinker, is the most beleagured, the most exacting, the most finical, and, though she seldom comes across, yet she must be kept in the style to which she is accustomed.

\* \* \*

Pierre did not fit my notion of a salmon fisherman, not in any way. He was too young, not rich enough, too high-strung, too lively minded, and he was French. That France produces few salmon fishermen is perhaps best shown in the fact that, possibly excepting Denmark and Holland, no nation has so thoroughly destroyed its once great salmon fishery with so little public protest. As to disposition, salmon fishing requires rather a phlegmatic one, the opposite of Pierre's excitability and restlessness. Patience is not, despite the popular notion, required in all fishing; in salmon fishing it is. Patience, perseverance, indeed doggedness, and a low expectation of reward.

A salmon fisherman ought to be British, and he will want to be upper class. Success as a salmon fisherman depends little upon skill, as does trout fishing; it depends instead upon luck, which is to say upon the size of the fisherman's bankbook. The rod with the best, which is to say the costliest, beat of the river, the one who can rent it at the height, which is to say the costliest time, of the season, is the one who will catch the most and the biggest fish. Far better, of course, not to have to bother with renting a beat, picking a time. That is why many of those thinking of going in for it seriously have arranged to be born Scottish lairds with twenty or thirty miles of prime water flowing through the estate. Having lacked the foresight to provide for that, you must work very hard, or at least very profitably, and invest wisely, and save, and you will still do well to wait until after retirement, when your pile has been made and you have got time on your hands. Much time is needed, for, as any gillie will tell you, "One catches a salmon very seldom, sir." He will also tell you the story of the gentleman who, at the end of his week's fishing, points to his single salmon and says to his man, "George, that fish cost me two thousand pounds." To which George replies, "Jolly good thing, then, you caught only the one, sir."

Moreover, salmon fishing is a sport traditionally reserved not just to rich men, but to gentlemen. To this most exclusive of clubs, with its unwritten but rigid code of conduct—like the British Constitution—one is, of course, born. A gentleman, when he goes fishing, dresses for the occasion. He wears a jacket and a necktie. These will not be new, neither will they be shabby. The jacket will have come from the right tailor, the necktie will be regimental or old-school. A gentleman fishes for the salmon with the fly, always with the fly. He does not scorn, because he does not deign to notice, the parvenus, continentals, and colonials who have come lately upon the scene in ever-increasing numbers and who dress otherwise than he, nor does he insist that everyone fish always with the fly. Indeed, pickled prawns are what he rather expects of the low- and the foreign-born.

A gentleman fishes determinedly and then, at a fitting hour of the day, he as determinedly quits fishing and turns to other pursuits and pastimes appropriate to his station. Tea, a drink at the bar in congenial company, a leisurely dinner, then coffee, brandy and cigars, a game of bridge, a nightcap. He makes no unseemly haste to be on the water in the morning merely because he is spending a few hundred pounds a day to be there. A gentleman is not—need it be said?—a fishmonger. His catch goes as gifts to his friends. When a gentleman catches nothing—

which is very often the case—he conceals whatever disappointment he may feel, and no gillie would ever dare presume to cross the social gulf that separates them and sympathize with him for his bad luck. He is not new to this, he would have you know. He has generations of not catching salmon behind him. Fishing for him is a pastime—or is it even that? Is it not rather a class obligation—like grouse shooting? Certainly it is not a passion. Gentlemen do not display passions.

Pierre Affre is the son of a plumber, the grandson of small farmers. He must earn his living, and his consuming passion for salmon fishing leaves him little time to do it. The river he, along with millions of others, lives on was once a salmon river, believe it or not, but was now little more than a common sewer, poor even in three-inch *gardons*. Always with "few money," and in competition, for a steadily dwindling salmon population, with those with lots of it, what hope has Pierre got?

"I have a secret weapon. It is, that I am not a gentleman," says Pierre with a very French, very republican, knowing little smile.

Already I had felt pity for a man with many years ahead of him, incapable of self-deception because he was an authority on the subject, falling in love with that desperately endangered species, the salmon. If his sport was dependent upon the continuation of the genus *Gentleman*, then I felt even sorrier for him. What pollution and hydroelectric dams have done for the salmon, inflation, taxes, and death duties have done for its traditional enemy-conservationist. It would be a toss-up, which of the two is more threatened with extinction.

( *111* )

* * *

The winter following Charles Ritz's death, Pierre went back to school, to the Pasteur Institute, to study epidemiology. Weekends he spent in the field trapping wild ducks in a project to determine their role, if any, in spreading, through their migrations, human influenza. Very interesting, very unremunerative work. When spring came Pierre had even fewer money than usual. Meanwhile, there were early signs that this might be a good year for salmon. The netters—curse them!—were taking fish high upstream in the Loire. A few had been caught on rods in the Allier, deep in the Auvergne. The latest issue of *Trout and Salmon* reported good catches on the Scottish rivers.

His studies over, Pierre went to work. Weekends he put in ninety-six-hour, round-the-clock stints at the animal hospital. He telephoned an estate agent in London. Available, owing to late cancellations, were a week on the River Spey, a week on the Tweed, and a week on the Tay. He had fished the Tweed but never the other two, both of them among the world's most famous. The price was, as such things are reckoned, reasonable, and for good reason: The spring run of fish would be about over, the fall run not yet begun. Eternal question for the salmon fisherman—the one, that is, who has to ask how much it costs: whether to go when it is less expensive, knowing you will catch fewer fish, or to gamble on an expensive stay with better chances of a good catch? Pierre believes that the best time to go fishing is, as somebody once said, when you can get away. He rented all three beats. I went along, feeling as though I was, in a way, keeping my date with Charles Ritz, after all. A young Frenchman and an aging American, both out of the peasantry and still not very far out, both politically progressive, both drawn to a snobbish, anachronistic, upper-class British blood sport. . . .

**2**

"Lower Floors" is the beat of the River Tweed just upstream from the ancient town of Kelso. Along with a great deal more of the river, it is the hereditary property of the Duke of Roxburghe. It takes its name from nearby Floors Castle, the duke's seat. Floors Castle is said to have exactly as many windows as there are days of the year. That is, architecturally, its one distinction.

On this Saturday afternoon in June the duke's herds and the duke's flocks were seeking shade beneath the duke's oaks in the duke's meadows from—I almost said, so extensive are his grace's holdings, the duke's sun. The one thing he was wanting in was salmon in the water we were renting from him.

We had fished since break of day, pausing only briefly for a picnic lunch on the riverbank. Rather, Pierre had paused only then; I had stopped frequently to rest. Wading the rock-strewn river tired me. So did casting my long rod. Long for me, that is to say. It was of graphite, the lightest of rod-making materials, a one-handed one of ten feet weighing just over four ounces. To the gillies this was small and they were sure it would barely kill a trout, never a salmon. They were wrong; with line enough on the reel, it would have killed a whale. What it could not do was cast as far as the long two-handed rods common on the salmon rivers of Scotland.

Pierre's was one of those rods, fourteen and a half feet long and so heavy I could hardly heft it. Pierre was even slighter of build than I, yet while I often tired from casting my light rod, he cast his big stick daylong, from dawn until deep in the night, stopping only occasionally to change flies. He kept in training to retain that championship title of his.

Never cautious in wading the river, Pierre had grown totally heedless in pursuit of the fish that continued to elude him. Though he offered as little resistance to the current as I did, what a contrast the two of us were! To steady myself and feel ahead of me for pockets and holes in the riverbed, I carried a staff. I inched along. I always waded upstream, never downstream, where the current could so easily buckle your knees, sweep you off balance. Pierre, without any staff, bounded in any direction as though he were jogging on a track.

Now, in midstream, almost up to his armpits in water, he was casting all the way to shore. To first one shore and then the other, switching the rod from hand to hand, as powerful and as dextrous with either. He was casting the full length of his line and doing it with a rhythm as though he were spring-wound. No metronome could have been more methodical. When his cast was fished out and he raised his rod to commence a new one, the length of line that was drawn from the water seemed unending. As he took a step downstream to his new position, the line straightened behind him and there it hung momentarily upon the air. At precisely the instant when the maximum power had been flexed into the rod by the rearward pull of the line, it was brought forward. Out rolled the new cast to that length which no amount of seeing it could lessen my amazement, my awe. Pierre was proof that size, strength, had nothing to do with casting. It was timing, mastery of the rod's own rhythms and inherent power, as a tiny jockey masters a huge horse. Not an inch of the water fished by Pierre went unfished. Watching him, I understood the value of what Charles Ritz had tried to impart to me. The satisfaction one might take in casting well even when the fishing was poor.

You have got to be a very good fisherman to count on yourself always to catch fish, especially when the stakes are as high as they are in salmon fishing. Pierre did count on himself, and he had good reason. In other years he had sometimes returned from Scotland to Paris with so many fish that, after selling them to the specialty food-shops in the rue du Faubourg St. Honoré, he not only paid for his trip, he made a good profit on it. Even in the worst years he had always managed to catch enough to defray a large percentage of his expenses. That was how to be a salmon fisherman without being either a gentleman or an industrialist. To do it you had to fish hard and well. Pierre fished well always, and he liked nothing better than to fish hard. This year, after two weeks, one on the Spey and one here on the Tweed, fishing as well as ever and even harder, he had two small fish.

I had watched him grow grimmer daily. As soon as he was up each morning he looked outside, then made a face. Another bad day: sunny, warm, still. This was supposed to be Scotland! Where was the rain, the wind, the cold—salmon-fishing weather? He had remained polite with me, but in his eagerness to be always on the water he had grown increasingly impatient with the time I took eating, drinking. The food in our hotel was excellent—not to mention the single-malt whisky. The difference in our ages Pierre could not accept. We must be on the river even before the gillie got there and until long after he had left. What need had we for a gillie? If I was uncertain which fly to use or where to fish, just ask him. In fact, we had fished now with every fly in our boxes. Which we used seemed not to matter.

Despite all this bad luck, and despite his constant burden of knowledge of the salmon's weekly-worsening plight, Pierre remained undaunted, finding always in a new day, in fresh, unfished water a spring of hope. "There is always tomorrow, Bill," he would say. Or, "There is still the Tay. A whole week on the Tay! Let us not be discouraged." Then, his trust betrayed, he would say, "No fish are here." It takes a very self-confident fisherman to say that of a body of water, sure that if there were fish he would catch them. Had it been any but Pierre, I would have said a fatuously self-complacent fisherman.

"Then let's not waste our time. Let's take the day off. Go sight-seeing. Catch up on some sleep."

"No! Never! We try again."

Pierre is like the inveterate gambler who says he knows this crap game is crooked, but it's the only one in town.

\* \* \*

Not only was the fishing different, many things in Scotland were changed, just in the year since Pierre was last there, and many of the changes were traceable to the same cause. The narrow Scottish roads, all built years ago, were clogged with tractor-trailers, including the huge tandem ones from the Continent. Scotland was now a rapidly expanding market for Britain's partners in the EEC. To remedy the congestion, new roads were under construction everywhere and old ones were getting lanes added to them. Ancient, narrow, arched stone bridges were being bypassed for new ones, with scant consideration being given to the well-being of the river. To me, who grew up in Texas in the thirties, a time of both boom and bust, there was something familiar in the air of today's Scotland: overlaying the smell of poverty so old and so pervasive it had become the way of life, the heady new smell of crude oil. Scotland, for so long to England what the American South had been to the North, neglected, exploited, was now spending the money from its North Sea oil without waiting to count it.

Every tourist is a Tory, it has been said. But in his opposition to the changes taking place in Scotland, Pierre was no tourist, he was an adopted son. To Scotland he turned as surely as its salmon return there to complete their life cycle. The Scots are a very patriotic people, but none among them, not even those in the kilts of their clans, loves the country more than Pierre. The advent of progress and prosperity which they so uncritically welcomed could not but worry him. Scotland had been one of the salmon's last remaining European retreats. Spain had sacrificed hers to the demand for more kilowatts: hydroelectric dams blocking the fish from their spawning grounds. The Irish Anglers' Association had recently petitioned their government to desist from the hypocrisy, indeed, the outright deception of advertising the country's fishing as a tourist attraction. Irish fishing, once so fine, was a victim of that long-impoverished and backward country's rush to industrialize. People have always been eager to change fishes into loaves.

North Sea oil now. One more enemy to add to Pierre's already long list. The dams, the Danes, the diseases, the seals, the offshore trawlers, the inshore netters, the poachers, the polluters: the salmon has many enemies. As an authority on the subject, Pierre knows them all; as a fisherman, he feels them all. The salmon's enemies are his enemies. To have so many is disheartening. They disperse a man's anger without diminishing it; they dissipate his energies. Too many fronts to have to fight on all at once. This very week in Berlin smoked salmon was selling in the shops at fifty-six dollars a pound. Much as he would love to have some himself to sell in that market, Pierre knows that such prices are the most serious threat of all to his beloved salmon. Who would not like to have some to sell in that market? When a commodity becomes that precious it is impossible to enforce laws regulating its harvest. Patrolmen and wardens who try to do so are sometimes killed. At stake is money big enough to make men desperate.

Add to the ominous signs of progress in Scotland the worrisome number of Common Market anglers, especially French, we had encountered. Knowing them well, Pierre does not trust them. Few fly-fishermen among them, few gentlemen. They do not take it in sporting spirit when they do not catch fish, lots of fish.

The kind of fisherman Pierre admires and likes to share the waters with was perfectly exemplified in Mr. Robinson, our fellow guest at the hotel in Kelso. A regular there, Mr. Robinson, now in his sixties, has been coming to the Tweed from his home in Yorkshire since he was a boy. He is a gentleman angler of the old school, a breed less and less often to be met with. He dresses the part. He keeps gentleman's hours. He does not greatly deplete the stock of fish. Mrs. Robinson is my source for the information that, in fact, he never catches anything. Does Mr. Robinson let a detail like that spoil his sport? Mr. Robinson understands that catching fish is as incidental to fishing as making babies is to— The thought completes itself.

Noticeable by their absence from the hotel are younger replacements of Mr. Robinson. All the anglers here are his age or older—some much older. Indeed, of some of them one wonders how on earth they manage to keep upright in the currents of the river. To be a salmon fisherman takes money that most young men have not got. It bodes ill for the salmon, already with so few friends and protectors, that it has got no more than it has among the younger generation of these isles, its traditional home. The salmon, even as it disappears itself, has come to represent a passing way of life. The hotel, a monument to the fish, looks now like a period-piece stage set. It might have come from that recent exercise in nostalgia for the Edwardian era, the TV serial *Upstairs, Downstairs*. Salmon fishing has, indeed, always depended upon a privileged class, one which diverted itself with the

traditional British field sports, and, thus, upon an under-
privileged class, one willing to work for wages that
helped subsidize those enormous, lofty-ceilinged salons
and corridors, those gracious, sweeping lawns and well-
tended gardens, those leisurely, big meals, and do it with
a cheerful servility which few young Britons feel obliged
to evince any longer.

Salmon fishing goes on in Scotland, the demand for it
is as great as ever even as the quality of it declines. Vying
now for the available beats, and pushing the prices beyond what all but a few of the British themselves can
afford, are big-businessmen on holiday from Germany,
France, Belgium, Switzerland—Arab oil sheikhs will
come next. Practical men, they want results—not understanding that fishing, as done in Britain, is the most
impractical pursuit known to man, with salmon fishing
the most impractical kind of all. When traditional methods fail to produce these results, they have no patience
with tradition. Pierre is, of course, right: English is the
language of fly-fishing, as it is of cricket, golf. The sport
was born here, developed not just its vocabulary but its
character here. Continental fishermen cannot understand the mystique of the fly. On the Continent the spinning rod and reel—those great levelers—are universal.
There can be no doubt that they are more killing. Why,
in Britain, should the fly be prescribed, hallowed, sacro-
sanct? The Frenchman who comes to fish here regards
this as another quaint British eccentricity. He regards
their disdain of prawns for bait with the same amused
contempt as he does their avoidance of snails as food.
The thing is to catch fish, *n'est-ce pas?* What does it matter
how? And if you are paying what you are for it—that is to

say, being held up by these oh-so-refined and sportsman-like British—then you do not want to return home empty-handed to a wife and friends derisive enough already about your spending all that money on your sport.

I had watched Pierre hook and catch his two fish, a nine-pounder and a fourteen-pounder, and the evident conflict of his feelings made me wonder why he persisted in it. He had progressed to a point where just to catch a fish was little, if any, pleasure to him. To be driven relentlessly by his passion, to fish with such intensity, to go unrewarded for days on end, to betray his principles and equate himself with those he despises by stooping to the use of prawns, then finally to feel a pull on the line, wait out the breathless moments before striking, and then to know at once that this was not even remotely the one he was after but only another fish. Today over lunch on the riverbank he had revealed to me what it is that keeps him going, the source from which he draws his faith. It is founded upon myth and mystery.

We fish for salmon in fresh water, but, as Pierre reminded me, that is not its element, that is merely its cradle and its grave. Its adult life is lived in the ocean. We know—the Danes, with their depth-sonar devices, solved the age-old secret, and then greedily began to slaughter all the fish they could—whereabouts in the ocean the salmon go after leaving their native rivers. But how long have we known that? A mere decade. What other secrets, just as old, just as fundamental, do the salmon still keep from us? How can we be sure they all go to those waters off the coast of Greenland? Even that oldest of our known "facts," that all salmon return to the rivers of their birth to spawn, do we really know that for certain? Our ignorance of the ocean and the vast variety of life in it is as vast and as deep as the ocean itself.

"We are so sophisticated now," said Pierre. "We smile at tales of sea serpents and at the people who believed in them. Now modern historical research has discovered old records, many of them, by witnesses who could not have known one another, in different languages, telling of sightings in the same area and at the same time, ships' logs, passengers' diaries, all describing the same thing. Something phenomenal.

"How little—*pouf!* nothing!—we know about the ocean!" He pronounces "ocean" in the French way, with three syllables. "We only begin now to know how deep it really is. What is in those depths? What species unknown to us, what specimens? Go to your Museum of Natural History in New York and see the giant squid. Enormous. You cannot believe. And the label tells you, this is an immature one! Until recent times the coelacanth was known only in fossils. Thought to be extinct for millions of years. It was in the ocean all the time. If it has survived, what else? The record Atlantic bluefish is thirty-two pounds. I myself have seen the people on the Mediterranean coast of North Africa catch much bigger ones daily and carry them home to eat. There was that friend of Hemingway's, a fishing companion, I cannot remember now his name. He tells in his book of a time when he caught an immense tuna, a new record fish without doubt, and how, after a fight lasting all day and into the night, the great fish, maybe three thousand pounds, surfaced, beaten at last. Then out of the water came a creature that eat the great tuna for bait. Something no line ever made could hold. The world-record salmon is seventy-six pounds. But Calderwood writes of seeing one taken by poachers in Devon that weighed over one hundred. Perhaps somewhere in some depths of the ocean, beyond reach of the trawlers' nets, their depth-sonar machines . . ."

Listening to this, I thought, poor Pierre, disloyal to all his scientific training, betrayed by his longing to catch a prodigy into believing that such prodigies exist. A graduate in veterinary medicine, years of studying zoology, embryology, comparative anatomy, and his love of fishing has made him as credulous and superstitious as a savage. And then I thought, maybe his is the true scientific personality. Maybe they are not the hardheaded, empirical-minded skeptics we others think they are, but instead romantic souls, dreamers, believers, not doubters. They must believe in unexplained phenomena, undiscovered species, places still unvisited on the globe, a permanent frontier, life on Mars, must believe not in man's capacity eventually to master all knowledge, but in his everlasting incapacity to do so, must believe in mystery, in, if you will, magic—for if everything were known, explained, classified and catalogued, there would be no scope for them.

Nightly I had seen Pierre spend minutes gazing up at the huge mounted salmon which hung on the wall in the hotel lounge—as does one in every fishermen's hotel in Scotland—as though in reverence to his deity, his totem. The one here was forty-five pounds—a thing so incongruous, so outsized, as to bear only a forced resemblance to its species. It was like something to be seen at a freak show. Pierre could stand looking at it for minutes at a time—until his reverie was interrupted by the inescapable intrusion of the plaque. This said that the fish was caught as long ago as 1902. The painful thought crossed Pierre's mind that he had been born too late, into a world inimical to the fish he worships, a world so greedy for their flesh that it kills them before they can attain their maximum size.

I asked him, "If you should ever catch a salmon like that, one over that magical mark of forty pounds, what then? Would you be content to quit?"

In his mind Pierre saw himself hooking, fighting, subduing, netting the prize of his long, arduous quest. "Yes! Let me catch him, and then . . ." And then "quit" with all its dreary implications sank into his consciousness. The thought was desolating, inadmissible. "Well, if there is a forty-pounder waiting for me, then maybe there is a fifty-pounder. Who knows, maybe even . . ."

If such a fish as Pierre dreams of exists anywhere in today's world, it is not here in Scotland, nor in Iceland or Canada; it is in Norway. Pierre knows that. Every salmon fisherman knows it. The world record, for rod and line, that seventy-six pounder, was caught there, and fish of forty pounds and over—a few—are taken yearly. Why, then, do not all salmon fishermen rush there? Because not all of them have the ten to twelve thousand dollars per week that prime salmon fishing in Norway costs— though enough of them do have that there is a waiting list. To save money enough to go to Norway is not possible for Pierre. Probably it never will be. Not that he cannot earn that sum. He can. But to do so he would have to stay at home and not go fishing at all for longer than he can bear.

It is past ten o'clock. Silence, but not darkness, has fallen with the coming of the northern night. The birds are roosting, the sheep and the cows are still. Against the sky loom the dark, irregular ruins of Kelso Abbey. A last light goes out in Floors Castle. As though awaiting that signal to begin its poaching, an otter slithers silently down the bank to the river.

A tiny, lone figure surrounded by water, supperless Pierre fishes on in the bright Scottish summer night. He will fish until the stroke of midnight, when by Scottish law all fishing must stop for the Sabbath. His cast is fished out. He begins his lift. Up comes the long rod, a glint of moonlight on its arc. Out of the water comes the long line, scattering droplets that glisten phosphorescently like the tail of a meteor. It straightens rearward in a tight loop, pauses, then starts its forward trajectory. Forgotten are the countless casts that have preceded this one fruitlessly. This could be the one.

# The Rigors
# of Bonefishing

Fishermen, like fish, are divisible into three classes: freshwater, salt water, and anadromous—those who are partly both. I am a freshwater fisherman, and strictly with a fly. My territory is also restricted. Never far-ranging in my fishing, I have grown still more sedentary with time, until now, like an old trout that in order to conserve motion has narrowed its feeding range to about its own length, I confine myself to the streams within easy reach of my home in upstate New York. And when the streams congeal with ice and the trout lie dormant beneath it, my fishing urge lies dormant, too, beneath a thick coat of cold indifference.

Recently, however, at just that time of year, I felt a yen like that which at a certain moment in its life comes to a salmon, which until then has never known any place but its native stream nor ever before felt any desire to leave it. Why it wants to leave now and where it wants to go the salmon does not know, but a restlessness takes hold of it and a craving for the taste of a thing it has never tasted. What the salmon suddenly craves is salt water, and suddenly so did I.

The salmon, when it leaves home to go to sea, does not know where it is going; I did. Into my mind had come visions of coral islands and unpeopled sandy strands, of cloudless skies and sparkling clear blue water and palmettos waved by warm winds: a picture by Winslow Homer of the Bahamas—which was as near to seeing those islands as I had ever come. I knew, too, which variety of fish I was going after. I longed not to match strength with a marlin nor to play tug-of-war with a tuna. Those are in the heavyweight division of fishing, and I cannot make the weight. I longed to pit myself against the wary and elusive bonefish. The bonefish: "Small, but, pound for pound, the gamest fish that swims," I had read in a book. Myself, I am so built that I too must fall back upon that phrase "pound for pound" when making comparisons.

Going fishing always entails buying some tackle. As I was going into strange waters after strange fish, I required a whole new outfit. I had been warned not to take my irreplaceable Payne rod. The first bonefish I hooked would surely break it, I was told. Although it whetted my desire to hook a bonefish, I disbelieved that. More persuasive was the warning that salt water would corrode the guides and rot the wrappings of a bamboo rod. I bought myself a thing the length of a flagpole, and about as responsive, made of fiber glass—something I had always sworn never to be caught beating my wife, much less fishing, with. For this rod I bought a suitable reel, one made to withstand the corrosion of salt water and big enough to hold a flyline the thickness of a clothes rope plus two hundred yards of strong backing, for fully that much, I was told, was needed to contain the hooked bonefish's first surge for freedom. I bought four-dozen big flies that looked as though they had been part of a shrimp cocktail, a dozen coarse leaders, and a pair of sneakers. I boarded a plane in New York City that flew me to Palm Beach, Florida. There the next morning I took a light plane to the small island called Deepwater Key off the easternmost tip of Grand Bahama Island.

The first difference between trout fishing and bonefishing is this: trout fishing is done alone—that, for me, is its main charm; in bonefishing one is never alone. Flying in low to land, I had seen from the plane that with its maze of waterways, its countless mangrove swamps and small uninhabited islands, all alike, all devoid of features, this was a place in which a stranger could never find his way alone; and I remembered that in those Winslow Homer watercolors of fishing in the Bahamas there is always on board the boat a native guide: black, barefooted, tall, lean, youthful. My guide was Otto Pinder: black, barefooted, and lean, but sixty-three years old. Alone together in a small skiff day after day for the next two weeks, Otto and I were to get to know each other pretty well.

Our being both only children and both stepfathers—information which Otto got out of me before we even left the dock—established for Otto an important likeness between him and me. I came away after two weeks with him still unsure how many Otto had been stepfather to; the number was always growing. His second wife had brought him eight, but Otto had not stopped there; over the years Otto had adopted children with both hands, and on my last day with him he let drop the fact that he had raised Armand, another of the guides, "from a kid." Otto had the easy, almost promiscuous paternalism of all the out-islanders, but Otto had it for anybody who came along. He had fathered nobody, and yet—or maybe, and thus—Otto treated everybody as though they were his children. He more or less adopted me.

One fishes for bonefish in a bonefish "flat": a stretch just offshore of an island or a mangrove swamp, in the sandy bottom of which live the clams and the crabs that bonefish feed upon. On the flat the guide poles the skiff, but some of the flats are as far as ten miles from the camp; for getting to them the skiff is powered by a twenty horsepower outboard motor. Otto used all twenty horses all the time, regardless of the wind, the tide, the visibility, or the shallowness of the water. That first morning, after leaping away from the dock, we skimmed over the bay and entered a broad tidal creek bordered by mangroves. The tide was on the ebb, the water lying low over the pale sand. Through the clear colorless water the green water of the channel wound like a creek within a creek. The zigzagging of the channel was as frequent as the folds of an accordion, yet Otto took each turn at full speed. At each swerve the boat leaped clear of the water and smacked down again, and we were soon drenched with spray. When we arrived at my first bonefish flat, Otto's cutting the motor plunged us into a silence so intense it pressed upon my eardrums.

Never, not in the remotest, spring- and snow-fed, rock-bottomed mountain stream, had I seen water so clear. All that lay below it was exposed to view as in a well-kept home aquarium. Here and there on the bottom were patches of sparse, low-growing grass, but for the most part the blond sand was as barren of growth as a desert. Starfish lay spread upon it and big black sea urchins with long spines. These were like cacti, and contributed to the odd sensation of looking at a desert under water. The water was like the heat waves that shimmer above the desert sands.

"Are you a much experienced bonefisherman, sir?" Otto asked.

"The only bonefish I have ever seen is the one hanging above the bottles in the bar at the camp," I replied.

"Um-hum. Vell, vile ve look for vun, I vill tell you a little bit about bonefish." This substitution of *v* for *w* and *w* for *v* is not owing to any German blood in Otto, as his given name might lead one to suppose. Otto is purest African, and this way of talking is not peculiar to him. All the out-islanders do it.

Otto has guided many fishermen, some very knowing ones, some famous ones, and while poling them silently over the bonefish flats he has picked their brains. Add what Otto has gotten from them to what he has acquired through his lifelong and keen observation, and what Otto does not know about bonefishing nobody knows. There are some things even Otto does not know.

From Otto I learned that the bonefish is a strange and still mysterious creature. One reason for this may be that interest in the bonefish as a game fish is still comparatively new, and studies of its habits and its life cycle go back not very far. Less is known about the bonefish than about any other game fish. What is known sets the bonefish apart as solitary and strange. The bonefish has no close relatives; it is the only member of its family. Unlike most fish, which bury their eggs in the waterbed, bonefish lay eggs which float upon the surface of the water. They broadcast their milt at large upon the surface to find and fertilize the eggs. The eggs become larvae, and the larvae do a most unusual thing, something that in the entire animal kingdom must surely be unique: Before growing bigger they first grow smaller. The bonefish larva, in turning into a fish, shrinks in the course of some ten days from a length of three inches to less than an inch. Where these miniature bonefish then go is a mystery, but they leave the flats in which live the things that adult bonefish feed upon and do not return until they are a foot long and weigh about a pound. Where and how the bonefish spend their time while attaining that size is not known, but they are never caught any smaller than a foot long. And now for the strangest thing of all. This has not been proved, but the authorities believe that bonefish are all born female, then at the age of about five years they all turn into males. Bonefish of the size caught by anglers never have any roe in them.

To set my hook when a bonefish took it, I would have to strike hard, Otto told me. For the bonefish has a mouth like that of no other animal. The top and bottom of it are covered with innumerable little round glassy beads; they look like seed pearls, and they are harder than pearls. With these the bonefish can crush the shell of a clam.

The bonefish is called in Latin *Albula vulpes:* the white fox. Foxy it is; that I was to have proved to me on my first day of bonefishing. It was to be a while before I would have a chance to verify its color.

I have been poled by a Venetian gondolier twice Otto's size and half his age, but the gondolier did it less smoothly, less quietly, and he panted more than Otto did in poling me over the bonefish flat. Meanwhile, though I did not know this at the time, what Otto was mainly doing was not poling the skiff nor instructing me, but watching for the signs by which, to a practiced eye, bonefish give themselves away.

"You hear that bird crow just now?" Otto asked. I had heard, for it was the only sound I had heard yet. It was a cackle issuing from the mangroves that puzzled me because I had never heard its like before. "A bonefisherman alvays likes to hear that sound," said Otto. "That's the marsh hen. It crows three times a day, at the turning of the tide. It is on a turning tide that bonefish come in from out in the deep vater to feed. You see on the bottom those little mounds of sand? See on the tops of the mounds a little sprinkling of bluish-colored sand? That bluish sand comes from underneath and is thrown up by a clam digging in there. Bonefish root vith their snouts for the clams in the sand."

It was a perfect day for fly-fishing, with hardly a breeze to interfere with casting, the water as smooth as a fresh coat of varnish. But Otto suggested that I begin by catching my first bonefish on the spinning rod he had brought along, using live bait, a shrimp, so as to know what to expect when my second bonefish made its first run for freedom. It is this initial run for which the bonefish is famous. The bonefish does not grow big; three to five pounds is the average size, an eight- or nine-pound fish is a big one, anything over that is a trophy. Nor does the bonefish ever, or hardly ever, leap when hooked. But it makes a run so powerful that it must be experienced to be believed, and when it does it must be given its head. Otto had seen fishermen lose their flylines to their first bonefish. Now, I have a fly-fisherman's disdain of spinning rods and reels (make a fisherman out of *any*body), and my feelings for live bait are those of a rabbi for pork. But I was new to this; best listen to the counsel of an old hand.

If there were any bonefish in that first flat, Otto did not see them, so we took another fast boat ride to another flat. In an hour's poling and peering we found no bonefish there either, so we rode to another flat. I began to see what the succeeding days were to show me a lot more of: that one must hunt for bonefish, and that it is grueling work.

Hard on the poor guide, you mean, who must pole the boat? But for the fisherman sitting on his cushioned seat with a cold bottle of beer in his hand while being poled about waiting for the guide to spot a fish and show him where to cast—pretty soft compared, for example, to clambering about in the cold currents and among the slippery rocks of a mountain trout stream. It is not like that. If he is to succeed in doing what he has come all this way and is spending all this money for, the fisherman does not sit, he stands in the bow, rocking with the motion of the boat and using muscles to keep his balance that he is not used to using and which after just one day of this are not going to allow him to sit, all the while intently watchful, scanning the water which even through Polaroid sunshades glares at him steadily. For although he will seldom if ever succeed in seeing a bonefish before it has been seen by the guide, he must see it no less than a split second after, because the time he has in which to make his cast is about equal to that which a hunter has in getting off a shot at a flushed grouse. Similar to that in another way, too. For just as the hunter shoots not at the bird in flight but at where the bird will be, so the bonefisherman casts not at the fish but at where the fish will be.

"Cast, sir! Cast!" said Otto. He pronounced it *kyahst*.

I could see nothing to cast to.

"There! Abouty fifty feet at two o'clock. Big fish!"

How, in that water where at that distance the least thing was visible, could I not see a big fish? This was the first of many, many times I was to ask myself that question. My vision, though not what it used to be, is not all that impaired. Yet I was, and so I stayed all the time I was in the Bahamas, bonefish-blind. I could see everything else in that crystalline water but what I was there to see: bonefish.

The fish that Otto saw that first day were not schooling fish but cruising fish, in singles and in pairs. I had to lead them with my cast as a wingshot must lead his bird, and this I had to do without seeing them, or having seen them too late. If my bait landed behind them, they went on their way. If my bait landed too close in front of them —and too close was anything under fifteen feet—it spooked them. *Then* I saw them! Then their dorsal fins broke water and went cutting through it at a speed which made me disbelieve my eyes. Only once did I see a bonefish clearly. Him I saw approach my bait and shop all around it, and I saw him shake his head as he spurned it.

I was not disappointed not to catch a bonefish my first day. I would have been disappointed if after coming all that way to get there I had caught a bonefish on the very first day. The bonefish is renowned for its wariness, its cunning. To console me for my failure, Otto, at the end of the day, reminded me of this, and offered his explanation for the bonefish's intelligence.

"Vunce," said Otto, "I fish a gentleman he say to me, 'Otto,' he say, 'vat makes the bonefish so smart?' I say to him, I say, 'I vill have to tink about that a little vile.' I tink, and here is the answer I made to him—you tell me if you tink it is a good vun. I say, 'Vat makes the bonefish so smart is, the bonefish he don't associate vith no dumb fish. He associate only vith bonefish, and, you know, sir, they all wery smart.' "

On our second day we saw no bonefish at all, so although the day did not pass quickly, I shall pass quickly over it. But first this observation:

The fisherman models his disposition upon that of the fish he is after. Or maybe the fisherman chooses to fish for the fish whose disposition matches his own. The salmon fisherman's doggedness in casting repeatedly into the same pool to tease or to provoke the fasting salmon into striking his fly resembles the salmon's doggedness in leaping falls and surmounting obstacles in the sexual single-mindedness which has brought it back from the sea to its native river to spawn and die. The trout fisherman's stealthiness in approaching the stream, his deliberation in the selection of his fly and his delicacy in its presentation, make him a reflection of the trout, so finicky about its food, so cautious in rising to it. The bonefisherman soon finds himself tense and watchful and jumpy as the bonefish is. The bonefish comes inshore when the tide is low to feed on clams buried in the sand of the bottom, and there, when the water is shallow and most transparent, the bonefish is most exposed to its enemies: sharks, barracuda, and bonefishermen. Consequently the bonefish is always alert, skittish, quick to take alarm and flee at the slightest disturbance in the water or in the air above the water. The guide must pole the skiff noiselessly, and must spot the fish before being spotted by the fish, and the fisherman must be able to see the fish as soon as it is shown him by the guide. I came in from my second long day of standing in the bow of the boat with the bail of my spinning reel kept always open and the line draped over my fingertip waiting for Otto to say, "Cast, sir, cast about fifty yards at three o'clock," and my shoulders were aching and my neck stiff from the hours of strain and tension. Hours of scanning the water, the dazzling, empty water, never daring to relax my watch, and continually, almost constantly, imagining that I had seen a fish when I had seen only a ripple in the water casting its shadow on the sand or the shadow of a needle-fish or a barracuda or merely a patch of waving weeds or one of those spots of bluish sand thrown up on the mounds of pale sand by the burrowing of a clam.

In the first flat we fished on our third morning Otto saw a "mud." A mud is one of the things the bonefish guide is on the lookout for, one of the signs by which bonefish give themselves away. When the bonefish root for clams in the bottom they stir up the pale yellow sand and the darker bluish sand and the water becomes discolored. It turns a milky pale green, the color of absinthe when the water is added.

A mud quickly settles and the water clears, so to see one is to know that bonefish have been there shortly before. Which, however, does not necessarily mean that they are still in the vicinity. They may have seen you.

Otto grew tense and watchful, and even quieter with the boat than usual. After a moment he pointed. I saw, ahead of the boat about fifty feet away, what looked like four young plants sticking out of the water, shoots just putting forth their first pairs of leaves. Only the leaves were the color of polished silver.

"Bonefish," said Otto. "Tailing."

Without a sound he poled us nearer. In the clear water I saw the fish standing on their noses on the bottom, waving their forked tails as though to keep their balance. I saw all four, as though on a signal, drive their noses into the sand up to their eyes. A moment later all four tails gave a wag of pleasure.

I cast, leaving open the bail of the spinning reel, and as rapidly and as silently as he had poled us near, Otto poled us away. When he stopped the boat I closed the bail of the reel. A moment passed, then I felt a tug at my bait so sly I barely felt it. But Otto had seen it, and he said, "Hit him!" I struck, and nothing happened: that tough mouth. "Hit him again!" said Otto. I struck again, and I thought that with my very first one I had hooked a trophy bonefish, for with incredible speed the line cut through the water, not stopping until it was two hundred yards from me. Few things, I know, live up to their legend, but my first bonefish did. As it paused to rest at the end of its run, I realized why the bonefish fights the way it does. In the flats where it feeds and where it is fished for there are no holes to dive into, no objects to hide among or wrap the line around—except mangrove roots, and

Otto has placed us between the fish and the mangroves—so what the bonefish does is run, fast and far.

Three more long rapid runs my bonefish made, then after a couple of circles around the boat it was finished. The bonefish fights hard; for that very reason it fights not very long, and many are dead from exhaustion when brought to the net.

"About three and a half pounds," said Otto when he lifted the fish into the boat. Amazing that a fish no bigger than that should possess such strength!

Just as it feels on the line, even a small bonefish looks big. It is a powerfully built fish, round and thick throughout its length, shaped for speed, with big fins and a big tail, and its scales are hard and as closely shingled as a coat of mail. It looks as if it had been chrome-plated. I was now able to judge the color of *Albula vulpes*. That is a misnomer. It is not white. It is the color, or noncolor, of a mirror in bright sunshine. In the glare of the Bahamian sun, fresh out of water and with its living gleam still on it, it shone like an uncirculated coin and could be looked at only by squinting the eyes.

I had another one, as like the first as two new nickels, within five minutes more. Otto had seen a mud about fifty yards away at three o'clock, and although he had not seen the fish, there was something to his eye which told him to tell me to cast to it. My bait was taken before it had time to sink to the bottom.

The bonefish is too bony to be much good to eat, I am told by those who have tried it. Otto, however, laid claim to my two, and after displaying them to the other anglers and the other guides on coming in, took them home with him for supper that evening. Fish is brain food, they say, and if you want to be smart enough to catch the smartest of fish, you must eat him, no matter how bony he may be.

I had caught my first bonefish and everybody was glad —everybody except me.

I did not want to seem proud, so I accepted the congratulations of my fellow guests at the camp, and I did not want to hurt Otto's feelings nor wound his professional pride, so I accepted his congratulations; but I felt I had still to catch my first bonefish. The two I had caught did not count. They were caught on a spinning rod using live bait. That hurt my pride.

But while better casters than I—and their name is legion—might have been able to cast a fly in the wind that had come up in the night and was still blowing that fourth morning, I knew without trying that I could not. Not that it mattered, for we saw no fish to cast to that day.

We did see some bonefish on the fifth day, but the wind was still blowing, stronger than ever, and none was biting. On the sixth day, still windy, we did not see any. I think that was the way it was, but maybe it was the other way around. The days have all run together in my mind— remembering the heat of the sun, the heat from above and the heat coming up off the water, the hours of standing in the bow of the boat being poled over the countless flats all alike, I should say the days have melted together in my mind. Anyhow, some days we saw fish and some days we saw none, but on no days were we catching any.

Some mornings we went all the way out to Bimini—not the better-known Bimini that lies between Florida and Andros Island, but another Bimini—Otto's favorite fishing grounds, though for me as unproductive as all the others we tried. With nothing much to rise above, the sun rose early and was high in the sky, and hot, by the time we went, facing it, out Rumer Creek. Among the mangrove roots herons stalked. A flock of buzzards hung motionless high overhead. Once, in Rumer Creek, the tide high and the water mint green and faceted by the breeze so that it sparkled like cut crystal, porpoises frolicked alongside us for a way, arching themselves out of the water like cats asking to have their backs stroked. Sometimes our careening through the water would bring to the surface a needlefish, and then we saw a sight that must be seen to be disbelieved. Adam, in naming the creatures of the world that God had given him dominion over, was at his very best in naming those of the sea; the names are all so apt, so descriptive. So without further description from me: A needlefish would appear on the surface of the water standing upright on its tail and would walk in a straight line—"hop" would express it better—for as far as fifty yards before sinking out of sight. Or sometimes the needlefish would perform for us its other stunt. Instead of walking on the water on its tail, it would bound across it on its belly, leaping high into the air and touching down again as frequently as a frightened rabbit touches earth, and bounding again off the surface as though the water were as solid as earth, and again for distances of up to fifty yards.

Then past August Key, with Water Bush off to our right, and out into open water, past Fish Mangrove and then, a long time after, past Tom's Point, then between Bimini Point and Bimini Rock we would ease into a flat and cut the motor. Otto would take up his pole, I my rod, and, he at his post in the stern, I at mine in the bow, we went silently up the scalloped edges of a cove, past mangroves strung with brown seaweed like rotted fishnets, searching the water, and seeing nothing. Or rather, seeing lots of things. Seeing staghorn coral, brain coral, sponges, purple sea fans, sea urchins, sea cucumbers, starfish, sand dollars, conch of every kind, the kinds identified for me by Otto: helmet conch, emperor conch, queen conch; seeing scallops, auger snails, winkles— even a cowrie, rare in those waters. I saw needlefish and houndfish, sharks of every kind, barracuda. Sometimes would come undulating along on the top of the water, soft and shapeless as the *mother* that floats on top of vinegar, a stingray. To its back would cling a pilot fish, too lazy to swim for itself.

Often during those long, empty stretches of time I asked myself what was I doing there? What was a halfway intelligent man doing there in that heat and glare wearing out himself and a poor old overworked not to say overaged guide in the idiotic pursuit of an inedible fish costing hundreds of dollars per useless pound? I went on asking myself that, but I left Otto out of it after this: on the morning following our longest, least rewarding, most exhausting day yet, I said to Otto that I would bet he had slept soundly the night before; I had. He had, too. But only after, dissatisfied with the results of our day together, taking his rod and fishing late into the night. No, he had not caught anything.

Each evening at the clubhouse bar I was asked by my fellow guests how my day had gone, and when I told them, was given their sympathy and assured that tomorrow it would be different. Maybe I am being mean-spirited and ungrateful, maybe I am judging them as only I myself deserve to be judged, but I do not believe that the sympathy and encouragement they gave me was altogether unselfish. It was not I but themselves they were trying to cheer up, for the sight of me depressed them, jinxed them. I don't blame them. Nobody loves a loser.

To fill in those fruitless, monotonous long stretches of time I took the Lord's advice to his fishermen disciples Simon and Andrew to become fishers of men, and angled for Otto.

Much of our talk was about fishing. An amphibian himself, coming on land only to sleep, Otto fishes three hundred days a year. Which, he calculates, reckoning what it costs those like me who come to the camp as paying guests, makes him the richest man he has ever known, and Otto has known some very rich men, who, however, can do what they and he like best to do at most only a couple of weeks each year.

"Your married voman she sometimes say to you, 'You talk too much about fishing?' " Otto asked me. "Mine, she vake me up vun night and say, 'Otto, you been talking in your sleep. Know vat you say? You say, 'Cast, sir, about fifty feet at vun o'clock.' "

Otto was born and has lived all his sixty-three years in McLean's Town, the waterfront hamlet of some three hundred people, most of them children, across the bay from Deepwater Key. He is the grandson of a slave brought from Africa to the out islands. He does not know his ancestral name. "My gran'," Otto told me, dropped his title. His slavemaster bearing the title Pinder, my gran' took that for his title."

The men of McLean's Town are all fishermen. Otto has been on some sort of boat all his life. When he was a young man, before the trade was ruined by greed, he was on the sponge-fishing boats. During the twenties he was on rumrunners going into the Florida Keys. He has served on commercial fishing boats and on private sport-fishing yachts. And in between cruises he has fished commercially on his own through the years.

At an age when most men begin to think of retiring, or certainly of curtailing their activities to match their diminishing strength and their failing faculties, at fifty-two, Otto took the most strenuous job he had ever had, and the one requiring the keenest eye: He became a bonefish guide. Though Otto made it look easy, poling the skiff over the bonefish flats is not easy, it is hard work even for a much younger man than he was when he began, certainly than he is now. I was to have an opportunity to learn how hard it was.

Otto's way with a boat was masterly, so was his way with a boat under outboard motor power, masterly—and absolutely destructive. It was as if, conscious that he had less time left him to bonefish than did the other guides, he was in a hurry all the while. Motion sports, as I call them—and I sneer when I say it: moving one's body from one place to another, riding up a mountain in order to slide down it again, bumping over snow or over waves in order just to do it—have always seemed to me mindless: transportation without destination, sensation without sense. But sitting up front in the skiff with that elderly daredevil Otto at the throttle, skimming—when not crashing—over the clear water of the Bahamas, I began to feel that motorboating, if only I lived over it, was rather fun. Our combined weight, Otto's and mine, was about two hundred and fifty pounds soaking wet—as we always were within moments of leaving the dock—and this light load, combined with Otto's natural inclinations with a boat, gave us an advantage over all the rest: we left them sitting. Swerving and heeling in following the channels, occasionally digging one through a sandbar with the propellor (I was told by the camp mechanic that Otto wears out two boats, four motors per year), Otto had me doing a sort of sit-down rhumba, my shoulders twisting one way, my hips another, and the rest of me still another; meanwhile he sat as though glued to his seat, the filter of a filter-tip cigarette clenched between his teeth.

If I marveled—and sometimes shuddered—at Otto's mastery of a motorboat, I marveled, purely marveled, at his outdoorsmanship, at his knowledge of and at-oneness with his world. The land there was as flat as a map, with no landmarks, and each place looked the same as all the others. The islands and the mangrove swamps were thrown down upon the water like the pieces of a jigsaw puzzle just emptied from their box and waiting to be put together. Yet Otto not only knew every island and islet, every creek and creeklet, he had a name for each. He was modest about this knowledge. A few years ago, he told me, the government sent a team of surveyors to make a "fresh" map of the place. They asked at the camp who was the most experienced of the bonefish guides to show them their way around. They were told that all the guides knew their way around, but that if they wanted the one who had taught all the others, they wanted Otto. I said,

"Yes, surely you must be the one who knows these waters best." Otto replied, "David [another of the guides] he knows them as *vell* as I do. But David he was born August of the year I vas married the first time in October, so I know them *longer*." Otto knew the tides to the minute each day and just what kind of tide was needed to get us to a certain flat, fish it, and get out again. He knew wind and weather. He knew the birds and their calls. Above all, he knew the creatures of the sea, knew them as though he himself had created them and given each its name. In water dancing over bright sand that dazzled the eye and was filled with things that looked to me as much like a bonefish as a bonefish does, Otto could spot a fish at a hundred yards and tell you within half a pound its weight. He could see fish or he could see a ripple on the surface which to me looked merely like a gust of wind rippling the surface, and know that it was not the wind but a school of fish, and while they were still invisible to me, say how many fish were in the school.

Otto, like all the other natives, believed that whatever lived on land or flew or swam was to be killed and eaten. He was a great killer of turtles. He ate all fish and all shellfish. A few years ago he had eaten a barracuda that poisoned him. He nearly died; all his hair fell out. But he still ate barracuda. He is the only man known to Gilbert Drake, the camp's owner, ever to eat a pelican—which prompted from me the predictable remark, "I wonder how the helican?"

From a lifetime of gripping a boat pole Otto's thumbs were twisted out of shape. His bare black feet were gnarled and knobby and the nails were cracked and splitting like the horns of an old steer. His scrawny shanks looked as though they had been charred in a fire.

I often wonder why I persist in going fishing. After twelve days of standing in the bow of the skiff I was no longer able to account for it at all. My luck is consistently bad, and even when I have a rare good day I question whether the rewards are worth the effort. Most fishermen do not like fish—to eat, that is; I do, but it is an appetite I am seldom able to satisfy. More often than not, when I go fishing, something awful happens to me. Nothing had on this trip and I was down to my last day. But the day, like the Ides of March, had come; it had not gone.

"Today," said Otto, when I met him at the dock, "to-day, sir, ve get vun. Maybe two. Today is going to be different. You'll see."

I tried my best to look encouraging. I had gone past disappointment myself, and now I was concerned only that Otto not have another bad day.

I had long since given up carrying the fly rod. The wind whistled, screamed, howled—on two days it had been such that I stayed in camp and on the second of those days everybody, even the most determined and hardiest, which is to say, the eldest, of my fellow guests stayed in camp because the guides all refused to take them out, so in two weeks I had never even jointed my fly rod and I was to bring it home, along with its reel, line, and four-dozen pink shrimp flies, unused.

We went out to East End, eight miles from camp. We saw bonefish at once, many of them, but they were all in a rush to get somewhere, and always going into the wind, so that a cast meant to land in front of them always landed behind them instead, and so spooky were they that a cast landing anywhere within thirty feet of them scattered them like water dashed on a hot stove.

But at least we were seeing fish, even if, by noon, we still had not caught any, and while we ate our lunch at anchor, the wind died, the water smoothed as if an iron had been passed over it, and our hopes rose.

"You see," said Otto, looking skyward, "somebody up there knows it's your last day."

We finished lunch quickly, eager to get fishing. Otto yanked on the motor cord. The motor gasped. Otto yanked again. And again. And again.

An hour later Otto was still yanking the cord, though by then it was Otto, not the motor, doing the gasping; the motor made no sound at all.

The lagoon we were stalled in was about three miles wide. A large island separated it from the open water. It was the open water we must reach if we were to be seen by another boat; here we might stay forever. In the skiff was a second pole. I took the shrimp off my hook for the last time and threw it in the water and laid my spinning rod in the bottom of the skiff.

It was then that I learned what hard work poling a skiff —even poling half a skiff—was. Within minutes I was panting for breath. And this was what Otto, an old man, and far from a big one, had been doing for me for the past two weeks—what he did three hundred days of the year! With my help, or possibly despite it, Otto got us across the lagoon and around the point of the island at six o'clock that evening.

We poled to shore and dropped anchor. I supposed we

were going to spend the night on the island and that in the morning the camp would send out search boats for us. If they found us and got us back to camp by noon I could still catch the biweekly plane to Palm Beach. If I missed that plane, I would have to put in four more days bonefishing.

Otto had a plan. Gilbert Drake, Junior, was out this way today with a party fishing for permit off the barrier reef in his big motor launch. They would stay out late. Otto would now build a bonfire, and on his way in Mr. Gil would see the smoke, come to investigate, and tow us home.

I sat in the skiff while Otto went ashore. There was a narrow beach and I waited for Otto to return to it carrying driftwood. He was back at once, empty-handed. His arrival coincided with a crackling that broke out behind him. No flames were visible in the glare of the dying sun, but billows of smoke soon were. Otto had set fire to the island, and it was a big island, as I was to see later, on being towed past it. The crackling mounted and a gust of heat swept over us. We poled quickly away from shore, and still more quickly.

And suddenly all around us the water was alive with bonefish. Frightened by the noise and the smoke and the heat, they were heading out to sea in shoals. As I stood leaning on my pole panting for breath and watching them swim past in their hundreds, I heard Otto, though he spoke in a mere murmur—much as he must have done in the dream from which his married woman had waked him—say, "Cast, sir. Oh, sir, cast."

# Great Point

When the alarm clock went off at half past four I was awake and waiting for it, wishing for it, the nightlong, fitful southwest wind having made my sleep fitful—that, plus my anticipation, mixed with some misgiving, over the coming day. The place was Nantucket, the month September, the day the last one of my two weeks stay on the island.

Disgruntled with freshwater fishing, with drought and pollution and crowds on the streams, I had heeded the advice given me by a famous fisherman, since dead, and had turned to the ocean, expecting to find it teeming with trophies and to have, if not all of it to myself, at least a sizable private portion of it. During my time on Nantucket I had seen a great many more fishermen than fish. The striped bass and the bluefish had shunned its accessible shores. In the tackle shops, fishermen reported daily on conditions at Surfside, Smith's Point, Tom Never's Head, and the story was everywhere the same: high tide or low, daylight or dark, using this bait or that: nothing.

Such conversations, however, often ended on a note intriguing to a newcomer like me. "Catching them out at Great Point," one man would observe with a sigh. To which the other man would give a snort and say, "Oh, sure! *There!*" After that, there was nothing more to be said, it seemed. I ventured a time or two to wonder aloud, why not try at Great Point, then, if that was where the fish were? What I got by way of reply was the dampening look of an old salt for a rank apprentice, of an islander for an off-islander.

Now, surf casters are men of stamina, rugged and adventurous, ready for anything. Theirs is not a gentle and contemplative recreation. They rise in darkness, drive distances, fish in the worst weather. Of all the many subspecies of fishermen, they take the greatest risks; in fact, they are downright reckless, even foolhardy. Numbers of them, breasting the breakers, invading the surf, seeking to extend their cast a few feet to reach a school of feeding fish, are swept to sea and lost each year, leaving widows and orphans to mourn them. What was there about Great Point that deterred these? That it stuck, on its narrow spit of land, five miles out into Nantucket Sound, I could see on the map; but surely that was not enough to account for its being avoided, despite the known presence of fish there, by those oldtime surfmen whose scuttlebutt I overheard at Bill Fisher's Tackle Shop, Nantucket's fishermen's fo'c'sle. The mystery in which they wrapped the place made more to the matter than that. Meanwhile, who were those fools who rushed in where others feared to tread, the ones who were out there catching the fish?

These questions were to be answered today. I had been joined on the island by my friend, the dauntless Al Clements, a man whom nothing can discourage or deflect, or even distract, wherever there is water with possible fish in it. Al would stop at nothing—knowing this was the cause of my misgiving, and my anticipation. He had come in his four-wheel-drive Scout—the indispensable conveyance for the trip to Great Point. Now as I dressed in the predawn darkness to the lost-soul wailing of the wind, I felt a bit like Melville's Ishmael, accosted on another Nantucket morning by Elijah, crazed survivor of a voyage aboard the *Pequod* with that maniacal fisherman, Captain Ahab: "Shipmate, have ye shipped in that ship? Have ye signed the articles? Anything down there about your soul?"

Today's Nantucket fishing fleet is not square-rigged whalers with longboats on davits ready for lowering at the cry of "Thar she blows!" It is an even more numerous fleet of four-wheel-drive vehicles bristling at all times with surf rods the length of harpoons, ready-rigged for the signal which sweeps over the island with the wind, "Bluefish in!" You see them landing off the ferryboats from Hyannis, bouncing over the cobblestones of Main Street, parked outside the A&P, the rods riding flat in racks on the roof or else upright, like lances, in a row of sockets bolted to the front bumper so that the riders look through them as through bars. In the darkness of early morning and early evening, from May to November, they ply the sand-swept island roads bound for the beaches. For although the books tell you that bluefish are mainly daytime feeders, the ones that vacation around Nantucket have not read the books, they are as independent and set in their ways as the islanders themselves; they dine at dusk, they breakfast by the light of the moon.

It was dark but moonless when we set off that morning

from Madaget, at the island's westernmost tip, with Al, pipe in mouth, at the wheel. The treeless, featureless, flat landscape might have been the sea and we in the cabin of a boat. We were to traverse the length of the island. A strong starboard wind opposed us as we tacked toward Nantucket town. Sanguine as always, Al said, "Today, Bill, we're going to kill them." Doubtful as always, I grunted.

Our course took us around the town and out west toward Siasconset. We veered from that route shortly to go northwest again, toward Polpis. Long, narrow, nearly enclosed Nantucket Harbor accompanied us off our port side.

At the coastal settlement of Wauwinet the paved road ended. It seemed that the world ended there. We stopped and got out and, by flashlight, in a hurricane wind, deflated our tires. For not even a four-wheel-drive vehicle, not even in low-low gear, can get through deep sand with its tires inflated. We reduced the pressure to ten pounds per square inch, making certain by the gauge that it was the same in all four tires. The least imbalance —as little as a pound's difference—can cause one wheel to dig into the sand and spin uselessly. You do not want to be stuck on a narrow beach with the tide rising or a line storm coming on. A fisherman-conscious community has provided an air compressor and hose at that jumping-off place for the use of those returning from the Point and resuming the paved road—a reassuring thought, one that I, buffeted by that wind and blinded by that darkness, grasped at uncertainly but eagerly.

There we left behind us the last lone human habitation and entered upon the spit. Instantly we learned why all but the most determined—some might say, the most demented—fishermen avoid Great Point. It was as though we had launched in a small craft upon a stormy sea and in a raging gale.

On either side of the narrow spit of land, which rose barely above water level, the ocean heaved and swelled. The spit seemed to undulate upon it. Running more or less down the middle of this ribbon of sand was a road of sorts—a track about as permanent as the wake of a boat. Ruts made in it by previous cars lasted no longer than a trail in water, buried within minutes in drifts, dunes, waves of sand. You had to cut your own path through them. No caution could be observed, for to pause was to sink, so we went at breakneck speed—I know of no stretch of road anywhere which restores that tired expression to more vivid life. As in a small boat at sea, we pitched, we tossed, we yawed, we swerved right and left, almost plunging into the water on one side of us and the next moment into that on the other side, we rolled, we crested and bottomed, we were jolted in all directions, now against the roof and now against each other. His pipe removed from his mouth for safety, Al clung to the wheel. I clung, when I could, to my door handle.

Twenty minutes the five-mile trip took; it seemed longer. After about the first mile of it I began to laugh. I was laughing at my own madness in going to such lengths in pursuit of fish. After that, I laughed because I did not know what else to do. Finally, I laughed because I was enjoying myself. So was my friend. There comes a time in life when, because you are on an adventure, even an uncomfortable one, you enjoy yourself. It is not the old routine, whatever it may be, and there is no knowing how many more chances life will bring you to do something madcap. Living over just such experiences as you try to fall asleep at the end of yet another day, you are reassured that you have lived.

It was just over a year earlier, shortly before his death, that a world-renowned fisherman, Charles Ritz, had said to me, "Our kind of fishing, yours and mine, fly-fishing for trout and salmon, is coming to an end. The habitat of those fastidious fish has been tampered with too much. Their range has shrunk steadily, and, despite the efforts of a few concerned people, will continue to shrink. The future of sport fishing is in the ocean. Only it—up to now —has been big and mighty enough to withstand man's mistreatment of it." His prediction was being realized faster than he himself had foreseen, if my experience of the past couple of years was indicative. So, late in life, I had faced about and gone to encounter the ocean.

To get here I had come a long way—not in distance so much as in attitude, orientation—and I had arrived as ignorant as an immigrant. Born and brought up on the prairies, I had remained a landlubber. Oh, I had crossed the Atlantic more times than I could remember, both by boat and by plane; but once safely on either of its shores I had headed inland instinctively. No beachcomber I. That was not my element. So much water seemed too much for me. Now, a newcomer to it, I felt as though I were the first, as though I had discovered it. From this desolate outpost, in the nacreous light just breaking, it looked as though it were being seen for the first time, just emerging from the primal void.

A fierce wind was blowing—just how fierce we would learn when, battered and bruised from our wild ride, we stepped out into it. From off the Point it blew to sea laden with sand, a veritable sandstorm, making the waves look like windswept desert dunes. Arrested upon the wind, hundreds of gulls and terns hung low over the water, screaming incessantly. The waters off the Point—treacherous waters where many a shipwreck lies—matched the wind in their convulsions. Heaving and seething, hissing loudly, the waves dashed against the spit, each lapping higher than the last on the rising tide, each undertow capturing and carrying back with it more of the shrinking shoreline. They seemed at war among themselves, wave rearing and crashing against wave, roller chasing roller.

I was, of course, far from the first ever to see it. From this very island, so changed since his time, Herman Melville once looked to sea, and it looked the same to him as it does now to us—the only thing that does. Arresting thought! We have polluted it, depleted it, we have all but exterminated the leviathans Melville fished for in it, yet it endures, outwardly unchanged. Of nothing on land can it be said that we see it now as it has always been seen. The ocean withstands our imposition. In its ceaseless motion lies its permanence.

No wonder we invest it with prodigies, with sea serpents and monsters, for not even its real and observable wonders, its whales and its great sharks, its giant squid and octopuses, seem commensurate to its vastness, the mysteries of its depths, its tremendous pressures, its titanic moods. No wonder we fancy it to contain a Bermuda Triangle in which all who venture disappear never more to be seen, with a lost Atlantis, with legends such as the Flying Dutchman doomed to wander eternally over its wastes. The imagination is unmoored by it and drifts without landmarks on its limitless expanses, over its fathomless profundities.

Was it hereabouts, on Nantucket, perhaps, that Melville first had his thought: Meditation and water are wedded forever?

At first the doors of the Scout could not be opened. They were unlocked, yet they could not be opened. When finally one of them was, the wind took it, wrenched it half off its hinges, slammed it against the front fender and sprung it so it could not be closed again until after a visit to a body shop.

Outside, you could not see your feet; they were lost in the driven sand. It seemed that the entire spit, treeless, as is most of the island, was being blown away; we wondered whether by the time we were ready to leave we would be able to get back overland. There was no looking into the wind—no facing it, even. Wherever you were exposed to the blast, even on the palms of your hands, your skin smarted and stung. It was a moving wall. It doubled you over, knocked out your breath, rocked you on your heels. It threatened momentarily to blow just a puff harder and pick you up and hurl you out to sea. The sand filling it was coarse, all finer stuff having long since been winnowed out; rated as shotgun pellets, it would have been about number 9, the size for quail. With that blast you could have frosted glass, removed housepaint, scoured brick buildings, engraved—or effaced—tombstones. Luckily for us it was at our backs as we faced the water; otherwise we could not have fished. Had we had to cast into it, it would have flung our big, heavy lures, treble hooks and all, right back at us.

The sea surface erupted regularly in a fine spray as though a shotgun had gone off underwater. Then birds dropped to the water as though shot. They rose again with baitfish wriggling in their bills. An instant later the same spot erupted again, this time with heavier ammunition. Out of the water and into the air leaped fish a yard long, missile-shaped, metal-colored, glistening: bluefish of twelve to fifteen pounds. These it was that had driven the baitfish inshore and made them leap out of the water in terror and desperation. The baitfish drew the gulls and the terns. Now they were drawing other fishermen besides us.

Here was one of the differences I was discovering between freshwater and saltwater fishing. One of the principal charms of trout fishing, at least for me, is the solitude; one of my disappointments in it recently had been the growing crowds on my favorite streams. Now, expecting to find myself alone somewhere on the long Atlantic coast, I found myself on one of its most inaccessible points fishing in a crowd, at times even tangling lines with my neighbor on one side or the other, and finding this a key element of the excitement. There were times when every man on the beach was tugging at a rod bent —big and stiff as they must be to hurl heavy lures long distances—nearly double. To be one among them elevated the blood pressure—*not* to be one among them did, too. Then you cast even faster, even farther.

There was, I was learning, a pattern, a rhythm to waves —a different one each day, even at different hours of the same day, and even for adjacent stretches of the same beach. I was learning, too, that you must observe this rhythm and conform to it, else you may feed the fish instead of them feeding you. Even then you must be alert, for the sea is capricious and can slip in a breaker out of step. Already in my brief experience I had had unlooked-for ones take the sand from under my feet, drop me in a hole, sweep me up and draw me in.

That morning off Great Point it was twin breakers succeeded by the tow. In tandem they slammed the shore, then withdrew deeply to gather themselves for another assault. By waiting out the breakers, then sprinting after the tow, I could lengthen my cast by a good thirty feet. Then while my lure was still traveling I scurried up the strand, sandpiper-quick, to escape the incoming breaker, meanwhile leaving open the bail of my reel and letting out line. In effect, I was casting my lure in one direction and myself in the other. I had to propel myself backward, for the wind was not to be faced. Such was its force and the steadiness with which it blew that the sand was driven into everything. It grated in the gears of reels designed to keep it out. It spoiled a can of beer before I could down it. It had later to be shoveled from the Scout. I was to find on returning home after four hours exposure to it that my pants pockets contained enough to fill an hourglass. My hair and scalp could have furnished enough for several egg timers. Five showers later I would still be picking grains from my ears.

I would backpedal up the strand and retrieve my lure. That will sound like a leisurely enough exercise to someone whose fishing has been confined to freshwater ponds. In surfcasting to bluefish, using a big, long, heavy rod, a big reel and big, heavy plugs, you retrieve as fast as you possibly can. Seeing it done for the first time, you will think those maniacs on the beach reeling frantically away are trying not to catch fish but to rescue their lures from them. They are doing what you must do. When baitfish find themselves in the vicinity of bluefish they flee fast; your imitation baitfish has got to do the same. So you reel until you pant, until your hand is stiff, your arm trembling with the strain. And as soon as you have recovered your lure you hurl it back out as fast as you can get rid of it. As in all fishing, you will catch nothing with your bait out of water, but in fishing for bluefish you cannot rest for a minute. For, just as capriciously as they appear offshore, they are gone again. You fish for them while they are there, before they consume all the baitfish and depart. That does not take them long, for they are the most gluttonous of fish, equipped with a mouthful of teeth that could shred a truck tire. They will redden the surf with the blood of their prey. When they have gorged themselves they vomit and start all over again. Although it is grueling and you are aching all over, especially on Great Point, after that ride to get there, you are too absorbed to notice.

You crank as fast as you can, and with today's fast-ratio spinning reels each turn of the handle recovers a yard of line: that will give you an idea of the speed of your lure on top of the water. The first time it is stopped dead as though hooked to a pier you will have an idea of the speed of a big bluefish frenziedly on the feed in overtaking it. Casting a minute dry fly to a finicky, mistrustful, one-pound trout is no preparation for it. No caution in bluefish. They are greedy, undiscriminating, and seem never to have been warned against fishermen. My first one that day nearly yanked the rod from my hands.

The fish and I were both stunned and disbelieving to find ourselves connected by a line. He did not panic and bolt. He just stopped where he was like a balky mule with all four feet dug in. He was not to be budged from the spot where, mistaking it for another of the real thing on which he had been feasting, he bit my barbed lure and found himself being pricked and tugged at. I could feel his bafflement and indignation through the line. I could feel him toss his head as he tried impatiently to shake the hook. Then he made a run; the drag of my reel was loosened to give him his head. A hundred yards he went before I could rein him in. I was using twenty-pound-test line, and the odds were long that my fish weighed much less than that, yet, fresh-hooked and full of fight, he had the power easily to break the line. I lowered my rod tip and pumped. I gained line, the fish took it back. For a quarter of an hour this tug-of-war went on. At the end of it I was almost as spent as the fish.

I coaxed my fish in at last on an incoming wave and beached it. I knew not to put my hand in its mouth to free my plug. Those teeth. They can take off fingers. Nor did I pick it up by the tail while it was still alive. Bluefish are limber, able, like sharks, to bend double and bite you. I beat my fish to death with a billy club.

Unlike freshwater fish, solitaries that drive others of their kind out of their territories, saltwater fish school together. Where you catch one you are apt to catch more. Bluefish hunt in packs, like wolves. Sometimes these packs fill acres of water. (When that happens you are in for an added sensation, unless, as we had that day at Great Point, you have a steady, strong wind at your back: you can smell them. The smell is that of a ripe melon.) It was plain that we were into such a school, and, there being no legal limit on the catch of saltwater fish, nor any prohibition against their sale, as there is against the sale of all freshwater game varieties, fish were now accumulating on the beach behind each man. These were soon covered with sand. There was no time to put them away in cars, no time even to shoo away the gulls that alighted to peck at their gills.

The frenzy with which the fish were foraging was imparted to us. Add to this the pounding surf, the wind, the screaming birds, and now the sun rising red and swollen, possibly portending an early end to the fish's feeding and to our sport. Meanwhile, on every other cast you hooked one. You grew impatient with the time it took to subdue and land it before you could catch another. All were in on the kill. Down the line a man was setting his hook, another pumping his bent rod, another beaching a fish, another clubbing one. Seeking to cast farther, I stood in the surf now, wet to my chin. All caution was thrown to that wild wind. The teeming ocean was casting up its bounty to us. It was shortly to prove too much of a good thing.

I was trying to untangle a frantic tern I had caught on the wing. Beside me, Al was fighting a fish. I heard a twang, like the crack of a rifle, audible above the wind. When I had freed the bird I turned and found Al reeling in a slack line. It had broken and he had lost his fish and with it his lure and wire leader. A moment later the same thing happened to another fisherman. On my next cast it happened to me.

We tied on longer leaders. When, even with these, we lost lures, we reasoned that our lines were frayed on submerged rocks.

Our school of fish had multiplied and, their numbers goading them to competition among themselves for the baitfish, they were feeding more voraciously than ever. Baitfish exploded from the water. The birds collided with one another in falling upon them.

Now on every cast you hooked a fish, only to lose him. I watched one man alone lose what he told me were twenty-two lures, costing three to four dollars apiece. Such was the spell of the place, with the waves and the wind and the clamorous birds and the frenzied fish and the very frustration of it goading you on. The more of them you lost the more determined you were to land this one. And you would think you were going to. You would regain line, feel the fish tire, its will and its resistance weaken, walk it down the beach to somewhat quieter water. Then it was gone like all the others, taking with it yet another of your lures. There must be dozens of them out there by now with lures dangling from their jaws. Al had been cleaned out, was using mine, and losing them.

All were mystified by what was happening to us. It was the man at the body shop who later enlightened us. A native Nantucketer and a fisherman himself, he explained that our trouble had been simply too many fish. When a bluefish, one of a large school such as we had run into, is hooked, he told us, the others bite the line, the swivels, even bits of weed caught on the line, mistaking the motions these make in the water for those of bluefish.

By ten o'clock the other fishermen, out of lures, or of patience, or both, had departed, leaving the beach to us. Al had gone through his half of my lures; finally I lost my last one. We exhumed our fish, and I began to recover from the spell I had been under.

I was not sorry to quit, though I had had to be forced to do it. Only then did I realize how tired I was—contented but tired, and sore all over—and I had yet to scale, gut, fillet, and freeze my share of all those fish as soon as I got home.

And before I could do that, as I remembered only now, I had to make the return trip over that road.

*Bill Breaks His Duck*

Dear Al,

Had no chance to phone before we left on this impulsive adventure as you were vacationing on Nantucket.
Hope you had better sport with the bluefish there than
we've had so far with the trout of the River Itchen.

Impulsive, yet this trip actually began a year ago, in
Princeton. As a writer in residence at the university
there, I was required to give a public reading—one open
not just to faculty and students but to the townspeople as
well. These are usually rather sober occasions: stories
about the loss of childhood illusions or the miseries of
married life. I decided to try for laughs. I read my little
book *The Spawning Run*, which, as you know, though it's
really about sex, purports to be about fishing in Britain.
"The Itchen, the Test, the Frome, the fabled chalk
streams of south England, where Dame Juliana Berners
and Izaak Walton fished—here I am in the middle of
them, it's spring, the season has opened, and I'd might as
well be in the Sahara": those are the opening words of
the book, my lament that those waters are so exclusive,
so expensive as to be beyond my hopes of ever fishing

them. God himself, the saying goes, couldn't get a day on the Test.

At the reception following my reading a lady introduced herself, said she was the wife of a Princeton physician—English-born—that he owned, along with his brother-in-law, a mile of the Itchen, and that I was welcome to fish it any time I pleased.

During this past winter, looking over my tyrannical typewriter at the fields and drifts of snow outside, I daydreamed sometimes about that. Pure fantasy, of course. Then one day about a month ago, as we were having a preluncheon sherry, the postman brought a card from the lady saying that she and her husband had just returned from a fortnight's holiday on the Itchen, that the fishing this year had been uncommonly good, and hoping we would someday accept their invitation. Ah, if only! However, it would be a totally irresponsible thing to do. But it was pleasant to imagine, even to have a second sherry on. What a change of outlook that second sherry brought about! An opportunity to fish the Itchen, Izaak Walton's very river: it would be totally irresponsible to turn down a once-in-a-lifetime offer like that. I phoned a fisherman friend in New York, himself English, to ask what the fishing was like over there at the end of the season. Good, he said, and added, "If you're going to fish the Itchen, why not the Test as well? I've got a cottage right on the bank of it which you're welcome to."

We prepared ourselves by practicing casting on the lawn. We needed practice. As I needn't tell you, the fishing in our area has been so poor, what with our long drought, that we had given up on it. My casting had deteriorated through disuse and Dorothy had all but forgotten how. To my horror I found that she had reverted to the old bad habit of holding her casting arm close against her side (remember the now thoroughly discredited way they used to teach you by making you hold a book in your armpit as you cast?) and flexing her wrist rather than keeping it stiff and flexing her elbow instead. It took me until our departure date to break her entirely of that. Now here we are.

Trouble is, not only have we arrived in a dry spell and a heat wave but we're having to unlearn everything we knew about trout fishing and start all over from scratch. The way it's done here is as different from the American way as is driving on the left side of the road.

The cottage on the Test won't be ready for our occupancy for a few days yet; meanwhile we're staying in a country hotel a few miles outside Winchester. To get from here to our fishing we drive through the hamlets of Headbourne Worthy and Abbots Barton, Kings Worthy and Abbots Worthy and Martyr Worthy to Easton—place-names which you, with your reading in the literature of fly-fishing, will associate with Lord Grey of Fallodon and with the man who, if he didn't exactly invent the artificial nymph, certainly brought the use of it to the pitch of perfection: G.E.M. Skues.

Our first day of fishing was on a Sunday, and in the narrow lane leading from the village crossroads toward the river the only place to park our rented car was beside the churchyard gate. Made of local flintstone and built to last, St. Mary's, Easton, was there when William the Conqueror compiled the Domesday Book. It sits below the lane yet still overlooks the river, which here flows from east to west. That day it seemed hardly to flow. Following upon a month-long, unbroken dry spell, it was low and smooth and gleamed under the bright, clear sky as though it were frozen over. As we had been told there was no hatch of flies to be expected until late morning at this season of the year, we had arrived just in time for the sabbath services. We were jointing our rods and pulling on our Wellington boots preparatory to breaking the Eighth Commandment when the parishioners in their Sunday best came to the summons of the church bells. But we got no censorious looks from them. Maybe we were saved by our accents, colonial souls being lost beyond redemption. However, down on the river there awaited us a fishing catechism as strict as any church's. It was to be a series of Thou Shalt Nots.

You know how it is with us. Rod rigged, suited up, we go down to the water and study it for a moment, hoping to see fish on the rise and the hatch of flies the fish are rising to, identify the fly and match it with our artificial, or come somewhere close to a match. That's our hope but it's one seldom realized. Most days on our insect-poor mountain streams there are no flies to be seen coming off the water, no fish rising. I seldom see a trout —until one has seen me first and been spooked and gone dashing away in fright, not to feed on anything for the next hour. So when we study our stretch of a stream we are studying the water itself, its eddies and currents, pockets and pools, looking for likely places for a trout to lie. Then, there being nothing visible on the surface, we select a wet fly, or rather, since there's no knowing what the fish are feeding on, we don't select one, we take the first thing we find in the box, something flashy and attractive, bearing little or no resemblance to any known insect, wade in and start casting downstream, carefully covering all the water from bank to bank. Whoever did here what I have just described, standard American practice, would have committed four—no, five—no, half a dozen—unpardonable sins against the British code of trout fishing. By evening of the day on which he did it the fellow's notoriety would be such that he would probably not be served a drink in any pub in this valley. Certainly he would find no other patron willing to drink with him. For perpetrating just one of the infractions contained in the above, the aforementioned G.E.M. Skues, probably the best trout fisherman who ever lived, was forced to resign his rod on the Itchen after having held it for forty-five years.

Here every stretch of trout stream has its hut to shelter in from showers; at ours we were met that morning by Grant Wolstenholme and Pat Fox. Grant is the Brother-in-Law, the resident co-owner of our water, and Pat its bailiff. We paired off, Grant and I going one way to fish and Pat and Dorothy the other way. Too late, I noticed that the weeds as thick as fur through which our path wound were nettles. I was stung not only on both hands but right through my trousers.

At the foot of our stretch Grant and I stood talking. I took in the terrain and already I felt daunted by the obstacles to casting a line. The water was too deep to wade; besides, wading, even where possible, is something that isn't done here, presumably because it would make fishing easier. One fishes from the bank. Along each bank were footpaths four feet wide. Behind the one path stretched a barbed-wire fence. Behind the other path rose a wall of weeds eight feet tall. It would be possible to widen that path and by cutting back the weeds make casting easier, but whatever makes fishing easier makes it that much less sporting.

We talked on, Grant seldom looking my way but keeping his eyes always on the water, while he politely but positively laid down the rules to me. I began to wonder when we were going to start fishing. I didn't know this at the time, but we were fishing, doing it according to the custom of the country.

For here, Grant explained, trout fishing is "a waiting game." Here one casts only to a fish that one has seen. If in the course of the day one sees no fish, one goes home without having made a cast. The mere thought of casting to the water, blindly, at random, in hopes of connecting with some unseen fish, as we Americans do, is abhorrent to the English angler, disgraceful—about like cruising in the dark for a streetwalker. He waits and watches, and while he waits he faces, as fixedly as does the trout itself, upstream. He would no more think of facing downstream than a Muslim would pray to the west. Even to cast a glance behind him would be to invite a fate like Lot's wife's when she looked back at those sinks of iniquity, Sodom and Gomorrah. From all this it follows that on these waters the wet fly, the promiscuous, undiscriminating, chuck-and-chance-it wet fly, which is always cast downstream, is anathema. It was for using a sunken fly that Skues was banished from here. He fished the nymph, that transitional stage, neither wet fly nor dry fly, which represents the natural insect in metamorphosis from the one stage to the other on its way up from the stream bed to hatch on the surface and take wing, and he fished it most sportingly, always upstream and always to a fish he could have sworn in court that he had seen; still, it didn't float, and in those days of the dry-fly dictator-ship—1938—that damned it, and him.

The dispute between Skues and the dry-fly purists was Low Church versus High Church. In the end Skues won, posthumously, and fishing with the nymph is not just tolerated on the Itchen nowadays, it is widely practiced; but this is the only deviation from the dry fly permitted. That, I'm convinced, is because, once they had overcome their antipathy and tried it, the purists found that fishing with the nymph is not easier but rather harder than fish-ing the dry fly. That would make it acceptable. Leave it to the British to complicate the already oxymoronic sport of trout fishing—pleasurable frustration—with still more self-imposed handicaps.

Wild-sounding though my words may seem, I do not exaggerate the aversion felt by British anglers toward any method of trout fishing other than to an individual fish, upstream, and with either a dry fly or a nymph. That one does not fish for trout with spinning lures or with live bait is taken for granted, along with toilet training. This is not the law—there are few laws governing out-door sports in this country where fish and game are not common property but belong to the owners of the water and the land; it's a gentlemen's and sportsmen's code. It's not even written down. But then neither is the British Constitution, which works very well nonetheless.

The fish of the River Itchen are all wild fish, stream-bred. There is no stocking of the river, none of your pond-reared, liver-fed, put-and-take hatchery fish. And they are all brown trout—no rainbows, such as there are in the Test. Now, as any angler with the braces off his teeth knows, the rainbow grows bigger than the brown trout, is more colorful, and, once hooked, is a far more spectacular and tenacious fighter. But it's easier to fool, thus less sporting. Any salmon, I asked? A few. Every effort was made by the owners to keep them out, yet the odd one did manage to get in. Imagine regarding salmon as undesirable! I've known a good many trout snobs— I'm something of one myself; but for single-minded devotion to the fish, that takes the prize.

As if they had punched a time clock and come on their shift, trout began to rise, poking their heads and shoulders out of water. None before, now one minute later, here, there, and everywhere rose fish any one of which, if only we could have landed it, you and I would have sent to a taxidermist.

Grant picked a fly off the water. It was so miniscule I hadn't even seen it. I wouldn't have known what it was in any case; I have trouble enough recognizing my fellow-American insects. Grant identified it as a Pale Watery Dun. Then of this least of nature's creatures, but important to trout, to him and to me, he said, "Poor little thing! It's dead." Another person might have been amused at pity so incongruously misplaced but I had a moment's illumination, a sense of the oneness with his world which a dedicated fly-fisherman can feel.

The insect known as the Pale Watery Dun is imitated by the fly known as Tup's Indispensable, so called because it was originally tied with hair from the ballocks of a ram, or "tup." (See *Othello:* Iago to Brabantio, "Zounds! sir, you're robb'd; for shame, put on your gown! Your heart is burst; you have lost half your soul. Even now, now, very now, an old black ram is tupping your white ewe.") I turned out to have a Tup's Indispensable among my newly bought English flies. Grant found it for me and said, "Have at that fellow rising just there. I know him. He'll go four pounds."

"You have at him while I observe how it's done," I said. "I see that I've got a lot to learn."

Grant stopped tiptoeing along the footpath when he was still a good fifty feet away from the outermost rings made by the fish's latest rise and dropped to his knees. Fish fine and far off, yes, I thought, but must I cast that distance, clearing those weeds at my back, and onto this glassy water put down my fly within a foot of the fish so as to give it no more than a split second to inspect my offering and, on top of all that, do it on my knees? That, as I watched, was what Grant Wolstenholme did again and again, never once hanging up, and with such finesse that, although the fish never took his fly, neither was it put down in fright. If he couldn't catch that fish, what on earth was I, in my clumsiness, to do?

I said I believed I'd seen enough to go off and try on my own. Grant wished me luck. Between him and me I put three bends of the river so as to be out of sight.

I spied a fish on the rise, knelt, cast, and hung my fly in the weeds. In trying for that, my first fish, before putting it down, I lost half a dozen of my new flies in those weeds. Agrimony, they're called, and, often as it must have been made, the pun is irresistible: they are very agrimonious. In searching for my lost flies, I found, while getting stung all over by nettles, almost as many others left there by fishermen before me. Here that's part of the game and adds to the sport, as does hanging up on the barbed-wire fence, which, after giving up on the weedy bank and crossing the footbridge, I promptly did. "The riverkeeper's fly box" Pat Fox calls the fence, and says that by running it and harvesting its catch he can earn himself a quid on a good day. I could blame at least a part of my failure on my equipment. I had brought with me from home several rods but all were meant for casting to either bank from midstream of the narrow brooks you and I are used to. On Monday I went to a tackle shop and bought myself one eight and a half feet long. With the added length of this rod I'm not much shorter, when kneeling, than I am when standing.

That Sunday, discouraged, disgusted, stung and smarting from top to toe, I quit fishing and went off to see how Dorothy was making out with Pat. I came, unseen, around a bend and found him giving her a lesson in what I recognized from my reading as the steeple cast, with which to clear the weeds at her back. I departed, still unseen, after hearing him say, "The wrist: it's all done with the wrist. Now imagine that you are holding a book under your arm . . ."

All the best.

Yours,<br>Bill

cc: Nick, Ted, Bob

*Winchester, Hants., England*<br>*September 17*

Dear Nick,

We have now fished the Itchen every day for a week. The weather has remained dry and hot, the water low and clear. These fish have eyes in the backs of their heads, and are all the warier for having been caught and put back a dozen times, each and every one of them, so our time is spent down on our knees, among the nettles.

The fish are here, all right: big fish and plenty of them. When I say "big" I mean three, four, five pounds, fish the likes of which you and I are privileged to see maybe once in several seasons. And they feed. There is no point in getting onto the water before ten in the morning nor in staying on after four in the afternoon. Pat Fox tells me that when there is an evening rise at this time of year it's spectacular, only there never is one. Between those hours the fish feed freely, greedily. But on what do they feed?

Sometimes there is a hatch of flies thick enough to attract swallows—a hatch of swallows feeding on the hatch of flies. Yet to these not one fish rises. At other times I study the water to see what it is the fish are feeding on so voraciously, study the air above their stations, and not a fly can I see. They're nymphing, then. Feeding on insects just under the surface before they can reach it and hatch and take wing. But which pattern of nymph to try?

Nowhere have I encountered fish so particular. I now realize that to have any sport with the wild and wary trout of this river one must know thoroughly its insect life and the unfamiliar English flies that match the natural ones. In desperation I've tried some of the old reliable attractor patterns that, without imitating anything with a Latin name, just look irresistibly buggy and which often work so well for us: the Coachman, the Wulff, the Rat-face McDougall—all are scorned, even when, as seldom happens, you put your fly, tied to a leader fifteen feet long and tapering to a tippet of 6X, down on a dime.

Our take of the week: one fish between us. The only small one I've seen.

The weather has been against us but that's not enough of an excuse. The truth is, the Itchen demands and deserves far better fishermen than we are. Thoroughly beaten by it, I look forward to the Test, beginning tomorrow. What makes me think we'll do any better there? I'm encouraged by words of Pat Fox's. They weren't meant to be encouraging, they were meant to be condescending. "Mmh," he said dryly. "It's easy over there." I just hope that the scorn contained in that is abundantly confirmed.

Yours,
Bill

cc: Al, Ted, Bob


*Romsey, Hants., England*
*September 20*


Dear Ted,

No two trout streams are ever quite alike, yet when they're separated from each other by no more than a few miles you don't expect the differences to be very great, certainly not what they are between the Itchen and the Test. Water equally clear, equally cold flows in both over the same dense growth of watercress, starwort, ranunculus, mare's tail, crowfoot. Ducks nest, swans cruise on both—we have a resident pair just outside our cottage door. It's as obligatory on the one river as it is on the other to fish to a seen fish, upstream, and with either the dry fly or the nymph. There similarities cease. The differences between the two are in the attitudes and the approaches of the regulars who fish them. Those of the Itchen are Roundheads, those of the Test, Cavaliers.

For Pat Fox the Test may be easy—not for the likes of me. But it is easier than the Itchen. It's easier because, first and foremost, there are a great many more fish in it to be caught. There are more fish because, unlike the Itchen, the Test is stocked with hatchery fish, stocked heavily and often. These learn soon enough to earn their own living and to be wary of handouts, but they are never as farouche and unapproachable as stream-bred fish. And in the Test there are rainbow trout as well as browns. Rainbow trout are not fools, but they are naturally a bit more trusting and a bit less finicky than their European cousins. On the Test wading is resorted to only when there is absolutely no other way to reach a fish, but it is not totally forbidden. The killing of an occasional fish is allowed on the Test, thus not all become too experienced to be caught again, whereas on the Itchen each fish is put back, thereby adding another wrinkle to its brain and possibly to those of its offspring. In sum, the less puritanical, more relaxed and permissive approach along the Test allows some hope for a fair fisherman like me; the Itchen is strictly for experts.

We moved over here the other day. We're settled, several miles outside the town, in this little cottage on the bank of the river. Rods, rigged and ready, hang on a rack in the dining room, boots stand on the floor along with landing nets, wet socks dry on the rose bush outside the door. Reels and fly boxes and assorted gear litter all surfaces in the sitting room. The river is just fifty feet away. Downstream from us a few hundred yards there's an island of about half an acre in midstream. Footbridges link it to both banks. We've been invited by the owner to fish all her three miles. From down at the foot of this stretch, looking across water meadows in which Henry V assembled his troops before sailing off to Agincourt, you can see the tower and roof of squat old Romsey Abbey. Its bells peal to you as you fish the evening rise.

I believed it was impossible ever to get a rod anywhere on an inch of this river and already owners along it whom we've met have one and all invited us to fish their stretches. Our first day it was upstream from here, at Mottisfont, the setting for that excellent book, John Waller Hills's *A Summer on the Test.* The weather—which has since changed most decidedly—was still clear and hot then. So clear and so hot that the water bailiff, pulling a long face and shaking his head as he put us on our stretch before returning to his tractor, said, "I'm afraid you're wasting your time today, sir."

You know my dismal record well enough to know that were I to report catching the world-record fish it still wouldn't amount to boasting; it would just be luck. Well, that morning, fishing an English fly called the Beacon Beige, which I chose only because it reminded me somewhat of my old favorite back home, the Gray Fox Variant, before the bailiff had reached his waiting machine, on my first cast, I hooked a two-pound trout.

Fishing is the life and the talk of this valley and word of my prowess quickly spread through it. The bailiff reported to the owner of the water that this American bloke had hooked a fine fish on his very first cast on a day that defied the world. The supposition, which I did nothing to dispel, was that I could do it every time. The bailiff was equally impressed by the fact that I refused his offer to net and land my fish for me but insisted on doing it myself. The fact is, he was certain I was going to lose the fish and astonished that I didn't. I was determined to land my first English fish unassisted. Other invitations to show my stuff have followed this exploit of mine. In fact, we've been offered more fishing than we can do.

Herself caught something rare that morning—rare for us, that is. A whole school of fish were dimpling the water in midstream. Midstream there is far from shore, a long cast, but she laid down her fly in the midst of the commotion, hooked, fought, and landed a fish which, though it was the first of its kind we'd ever seen, we recognized as a grayling. It had that outsized purplish dorsal fin and its shiny scales were so perfectly regular and so metallic, it looked like the work of the Dutch silversmiths who make those articulated fish to ornament a table. Here grayling, so exotic to us, are anything but rare, they're common, and because they take the fly yet are not trout, they are a nuisance to the fisherman and are regarded as vermin. It was as good eating as it is said to be, though we could neither of us detect that scent of thyme from which its scientific name derives.

Yesterday—still clear and hot—we fished at Kimbridge, between us and Mottisfont, at the invitation of the owner. Buoyed by my change of luck, I found myself not only casting better but actually believing in the possibility that I might catch something.

As might be expected, a bridge crosses the river at Kimbridge. About a hundred yards below the bridge I spotted a fish rising regularly just off the opposite bank. So wide is the river there that wading is a must. It's not easy. The water is so choked with weeds, even though they are scythed down several times a year, as to make wading extremely difficult. The nearest I was able to get to my target would still have been too far away had I not had my new long rod. I cast to that fish without putting it down through seven changes of flies. The eighth, an Iron Blue Dun, was what it wanted, and I had the satisfaction of deceiving with a match of the hatch my first English trout. About two pounds and full of fight—a fish to make my season back home, here run-of-the-mill.

Later that day, upstream from that spot, just below the bridge where the river widens into a big pool, Graham Finlayson, taking pictures of me from the far bank, pointed to the water at his feet and held his hands two feet apart.

I yelled across to him, "I can't cast that far."

Graham spread his hands still wider, rolled his eyes, formed his lips into a silent whistle.

I couldn't even see the fish; there was no way in the world I could reach it. The distance was beyond my range. To complicate matters further, I would have to cast between two reeds sticking out of the water about a dozen feet apart. It would be about like kicking a field goal from your own ten-yard line. The length of float over the fish I would get before having to pick up my line to keep it from catching on the downstream reed would be measured like the faster shutter speeds on Graham's camera. However, nothing was to be lost by trying.

My first cast fell short. I expected that. What pleased me and encouraged me to try again was how little short it fell. My second cast was the best of my life, right between those two reeds, alighting in the innermost of the rings left by the fish on its last rise like a bullet in a bull's-eye. So amazed was I at the cast I'd made, I forgot my reason for making it and thus almost didn't strike back when the fish struck. A conditioned reflex took over for me and I was fast to one of the biggest, one of the fightingest fish of my life.

Either it had been hooked many times before or else it was hooked now for the first time ever—the memory of fear or the awful, unaccountable novelty of it: either could have explained the fish's explosive rush to escape. There was no restraining its first upstream run that emptied the reel of line down to the backing. But of that I had a hundred yards, so I didn't try to check the fish. I held the rod with both hands above my head and let it run, the farther the better. The expenditure of such energy would soon enough exhaust it.

As the fish rested from its initial run I surveyed our battlefield. The advantages were, as they always are, the fish's; one was overwhelmingly in its favor. Thick everywhere on the Test, the weeds here turned the water into a soup. The drought had lowered the water level so that they rose to the very surface, lush as the growth of a greenhouse. Upon such headlong runs as the fish's first I must depend, for should our fight last long it would take to the weeds as surely as a fox to earth and I be unable to budge it from its lair for fear of breaking my leader.

Never had I known a fish so game. Though I had yet to see it, I knew it was a big fish, but size alone could not account for this one's fierce resistance. That was indomitable spirit. Downstream and upstream, again and again it charged, and rather than tiring it seemed to gain mettle.

Joined as we were by the taut, throbbing line, the fish telegraphed to me its every impulse, almost its every thought. Mortal enemies we were, but lovers could hardly have been more closely coupled. Thus I knew when, having tried and failed to free itself by running, it resorted to another dodge. I felt its rise begin in time to lower my rod and give slack to the line. It broke the surface and climbed into the air, threshing, showering spray. A rainbow it was—my first. It was the phosphorescent red line down its length that told me unmistakably what it was. It stood upon the water like an exclamation point. A fish of four, maybe five pounds—decidedly one of the biggest I'd ever hooked.

Having tried running and leaping only to find itself still hooked, the fish wasn't long in doing the thing I dreaded. It dove for the weeds. I waded to it (easier said than done), made a pass with the landing net, but succeeded only in scooping up weeds. The fish bolted, then sounded again. How many times this happened I don't know. Sometimes there was not water enough to cover the fish's back, then it slithered over the weeds like a snake. Always it fought with undiminished resistance. I thought to deceive it into thinking it was now free and venturing out of the weeds on its own by slackening the line. This worked just once; the fish learned fast.

Our fight had taken us steadily upstream. Graham had followed, snapping away. He was counting on a successful outcome, a picture of me holding up my trophy. To disappoint him would double my own disappointment. But I was growing apprehensive. This must not be allowed to continue. By now the leader was surely fraying, it might soon break, the hook would have worn a tear in the fish's jaw and might soon pull out, or else might straighten. To prepare Graham for the worst, I yelled, "I just may lose this fellow."

For now the end, one way or the other, had come. Just below the bridge the fish had half buried itself in the tangle of growth on a cable stretched there across the river. It couldn't free itself, I would have to do it. I closed in.

There was no way to get the net under the fish and I knew that even now, spent as it was, it still retained a last reserve of power to call upon, a reserve which it didn't know it had but which the touch of my hated hand would spark. But a fish that brave I meant to put back anyway, after getting a picture of it; genes like those were a treasure to its kind, and the fish was drowning by the moment. I grabbed it and, sure enough, got what felt like an electric shock. The fish was gone, taking with it my fly. When I rose, defeated, I realized how tired I was.

"Lost it!" I yelled across to Graham.

"But you put up a jolly good fight!" That came not from Graham. It came from a party of four who had watched from the bridge. So absorbed had I been that I never knew they were there. They gave me a hand and I tipped my hat to them.

You know how, after a fight with a good fish, whether we land it or lose it, we always exaggerate the length of time we had it on the line. To Graham I said later, "It was probably nothing of the sort, but it seemed to me I fought that fish for fully a quarter of an hour."

"Twenty-two minutes," said Graham. "I timed it from start to finish."

Stopped on the road today to ask directions of a lolli-pop lady. A lollipop lady? One who halts traffic to let schoolchildren cross the road using for a stop sign a dingus the shape of a big red lollipop. I thanked her. "Pleasure, my angel," she said. A touch of old Hamp-shire, I'm told.

Yours,
Bill

cc: Al, Nick, Bob

*Romsey, Hants., England*
*September 25*

Dear Bob,

A party of fishermen, friends of our host, have been using the cottage this weekend as a base, a shelter from the rain, a place to have a drink. One young fellow came dashing in day before yesterday to announce that he had just seen the biggest trout of his life. It lay below the footbridge that spans the river to the island. We went down to have a look. It was a big fish and, had it been a trout, it would have been the biggest of anybody's life, but it wasn't, it was a pike. It lay in about three feet of water, looking as sinister as an enemy submarine lying in wait, and like a submarine camouflaged in stripes, green on green. I dutifully reported the fish's presence to the riverkeeper. These killers of trout are much hated by the owners of the water, who want the fishermen who lease rods from them to be happy with their catch. The keeper made several passes at snatch-hooking the fish with a spinning rod. He failed.

Yesterday, the weekend over, the party gone and with no trout anywhere to be seen, I thought I'd have a try for that pike. Dorothy accompanied me. The fish lay in the same spot, hadn't moved an inch. Using a Mepps spinner, I made a cast across stream and reeled it slowly past the fish. It struck. I struck back, hooked and in the same second lost it. I cast again instantly. Again the fish struck and this time it was hooked solidly. The rod was a small one, the line light, and the fight that ensued took me up and down the island several times before the fish surfaced. The net, a big one, hardly contained it. As I had come away from the cottage without my leaded "priest," I had nothing with which to administer the last rites. I was not about to try removing the lure from between those jaws. So, me squeezing the mouth of the net as tightly closed as I could and Dorothy carrying the rod, we got it home that way, she whooping the length of the path, "Hi hi! He he! Ha ha! Ho ho!" Twelve and three-quarter pounds it was and it had once been a great deal bigger. An old fish to judge by its worn and blunted teeth, one that had devoured many a trout and duckling. Once again word of my catch has spread through the valley bringing invitations to fish other waters and rid them of these predators.

In Winchester today made the obligatory pilgrimage to the cathedral. On the gravestone of Jane Austen, inlaid in the floor of the aisle, rested a bouquet of flowers fresh from a florist. To the sender, Jane Austen was as alive as ever in life, for on the card accompanying the bouquet was written, "In gratitude."

Then to the Walton chapel. "That miserable old pla-
giarist" he was to Skues (a lawyer by profession), but in
that sentiment Skues is almost as alone as he was in
fishing his nymphs in his time. To most of the brother-
hood their Izaak is more their patron than the sainted
Peter (he fished with a net) and, in 1914, the anglers of
England and America honored him with a stained-glass
window in the chapel of this great cathedral where he is
buried. Walton had two rivers in his long life, as he had
two wives. Of his rivers, the first was the Staffordshire
Dove, that of his old age (he lived to ninety) was the
Itchen, which flowed then as it does now just outside the
walls of the Cathedral Close. In the window's two portraits of him he is shown on the banks of the one and of
the other. It is worthy of note that in both he is doing
what English anglers in the course of a day's fishing do so
much of: not fishing. In the one he is reading and in the
other he is saying grace over his and his companion's
streamside lunch. You've seen sunlit, dewy mornings and
early evenings with the mist rising from the river when all
the world scintillates like stained glass. Perhaps Walton's
book has been a pleasure to so many because it was a
pleasure to him. In writing it, he tells us, he made a
recreation of a recreation.

Rain has set in as though to make up at once for the
long dry spell. Already in Devon and Gloucestershire
roads are flooded, impassable. Ordinarily, I'm told, the
white chalk hills through which the Test flows absorb
rain like a sponge and release it into the river slowly and
filtered clear, but this is too much too fast. This morning
the water had risen several inches and is rushing and

darkly discolored. It will be some time before a fish can be seen to cast to hereabouts.

Out by invitation to dinner last evening where the conversation turned to my native state. Said a citizen of this self-sufficient corner of the world, "Now, where *is* Texas?"

Yours,
Bill

cc: Al, Ted, Nick


*Romsey, Hants., England*
*September 30*

Dear Ted,

Kept indoors by pelting rain. On days like these, back home, you'd go fishing anyway if you'd come a long way to get to it, as we have, and your time was limited, as ours is. But you don't see any fish on days like these, and here, if you don't see fish you don't fish. So you stay indoors. At least, we do, though we see men whose one day of the week on the water it is stalking along the riverbanks and peering like hungry herons, oblivious to being streaming wet. And not just men. We share our home stretch here with two women who are the most fanatical anglers I've ever seen, and I've seen some fanatics. Of these two, both of whom answer to the same given name, one is as mad keen (as they say here) on the sport as the other. They've got a station wagon which must surely be used for fishing only: no one—no two—could possibly pack and unpack all they carry in it more than once a season. Anyway, they're here from morn till night—no time to unpack it. Out of it when they park outside our cottage and set themselves up for the day come half a dozen rods and reels, rain gear, walking sticks that unfold to become roomy canvas chairs, a camp stove, teakettle, landing nets, two dogs that accompany them in their fishing. Nothing deters these two, nothing daunts them, nothing tires them, and both are grandmothers more times than one. No matter how foul the day they are out till dark and then, even without a fish between them, they are sorry to quit. "Where are you going to be fishing today?" one of them asks me. "Fish? Today? In this?" I reply. "Oh, well, *we* are." The other day before they set off downstream to fish their way back up it I invited them to come in for a drink and a drying-out when they returned. The downpour was daylong. When they came in it was almost dark and they were dripping wet and their Wellingtons were caked with cow dung and I watched them through the window primping themselves before knocking on the cottage door, each in turn holding up a pocket mirror for the other to make her face. Said one, "We're exhausted and, as for me, I'm being very wicked. It's Sunday and I've got a husband and a son for whom I ought to have cooked dinner and today is the birthday of one of my granddaughters. But"—merrily—*"here I am!"*

Kept indoors by the weather, I've been doing some reading and it has changed my thinking about the regulations governing fishing here. They are not the arbitrary and snobbish refinements upon an already elitist code that I took them to be. Here they make sense. In fact, they are an admirable example of sportsmanship, consideration for others, and a farsighted effort at conservation—things which make sense everywhere.

Wading. It muddies the water and spoils the sport for the fisherman just downstream from you. Here in this small and thickly populated country there always is a fisherman just downstream from you. Until recently most of our American trout streams were never crowded enough to make this a consideration, but here they are—and they are getting to be with us, too.

Wet flies. To fish them is, in an arresting phrase of Skues's "to occupy a selfish amount of water." And they are less sporting. You will often read that, popular opinion to the contrary notwithstanding, fishing the wet fly is actually harder than fishing the dry fly, and no doubt it is easier to strike and hook a fish seen rising to your bait than to develop that sixth sense which tells you when to strike an unseen fish. But it is certainly true that casting the dry fly demands accuracy and delicacy whereas you just chuck the wet fly and leave it to the current, and it is true too that with the dry fly some closeness to matching the hatch is required, some knowledge of stream entomology, for then the fish has time to inspect your offering, while at something vaguely buggy moving rapidly underwater it must strike without time to reconsider the matter. And of course trout do ninety percent of their feeding underwater, only ten percent on the surface. Using the dry fly only is natural conservation of a limited resource.

Fishing only to a seen fish. The third and most different of the differences between us and our English cousins. Possible on these placid and pellucid chalk streams, rich in insect life, unadaptable to our fast and broken waters. But I couldn't have caught more fish casting wholesale than I've caught calling my shots, nor had

more fun doing it. Being more deliberate, less accidental, it's that much more gratifying. Studying your adversary individually, you get to know it better. It seems more
like *your* fish.

The Test has been the laboratory of fly-fishing. Not
much originated here but—excuse it—everything got
tested, and then hardened into intolerant dogma. It was
here that the wet fly was definitively dropped, or, to say
the same thing another way, that fishermen turned
around and faced upstream. It was here later—too late
for poor old Skues—that the long dictatorship of the dry
fly was overthrown and the nymph accepted. Many of
today's standard fly patterns were perfected on the Test.
Most of these things were done on one stretch of the
river, that belonging to the world's oldest and most exclusive trout club, the Houghton, in nearby Stockbridge.
This club was founded in 1822 and from the start its
membership has been limited to twenty-two. Members
and their guests have included Turner and Landseer,
who left behind drawings of theirs in the club's record
books. One recent guest: H.R.H. the Prince of Wales.
Tomorrow's guest: yours truly.

We drove over yesterday, met the keeper, Mick Lunn,
and were shown the clubroom. Entering this was the
angling equivalent of opening King Tut's tomb. The fur-
nishings were put in place on or shortly after the date of
the club's founding and never moved, neither subtracted
from nor added to, reupholstered or refinished, since
then. The leather of the armchairs is cracked and split,
and soiled by generations of hair pomade. Wine spilled
from toasts raised to Her Majesty Queen Victoria stains
and always will the carpet, which any ragpicker would

refuse. On the walls hang trophy trout not mounted but mummified. No one but the members knows what the dues are, but this sort of sanctified shabbiness is very expensive. The would-be member waits until a place among the twenty-two falls vacant. Today's oldest active member is ninety-three rising ninety-four.

Eight miles of the water the club owns. It is stocked plentifully with fish raised in their own hatchery under conditions as close as possible to the wild. An invitation to fish it is about like being presented privately to the queen. I'll let you know how we do. Oct. 1: Fisherman's luck. We were rained out.

Yours,<br>Bill

cc: Al, Nick, Bob

*Romsey, Hants., England*<br>*October 5*

Dear Nick,

Our stay here draws to a close; this will be my last communication. Seasons on fishing here are not fixed by law but by the riverowners. Or rather, by nature herself. It's getting to be spawning time for trout now, and time for men to turn their thoughts elsewhere.

But fishing goes on for a while yet—salmon fishing. Yes, there is something of a run of salmon in the Test, and here, in contrast to the Itchen, they are not discriminated against but made to feel welcome. Day before yesterday I was invited to try for one.

Picture not a rugged mountain tarn, nor a raging waterfall, nor a rocky, wind- and spray-swept estuary far from habitation. Picture instead a level lawn as carefully tended as a cat's coat. Three feet below the lawn the Test slips quietly by. Picture a house of the Edwardian era, reflecting in its sprawl and ease that era of peace and privilege, the last glow of empire before the sun began to set over it. Picture neat flower beds and barbered shrubs, thatched gazebos, close-clipped hedges, tile-topped ivy-grown garden walls, the roof a range of gables with out-croppings of chimney pots, a flower-filled conservatory.

I didn't catch my fellow guest's full name when we were introduced but it didn't matter, in moments we were Bill and Doug. Jolly nice chap. Suggested to me, who hadn't the foggiest, which fly to use, a Logie, and positioned himself on the lawn so that I was fishing ahead of him.

We were fishing downstream, of course, casting always the same length of line, enough to reach the opposite bank, and letting the fly drift with the current to mid-stream before picking up and casting again. When, having fished out a spot, Doug moved nearer me, I moved on, thus keeping the same distance between us. It was awfully generous of him to fish water I'd already fished through—generous or else he felt certain he could catch fish where I couldn't—something I was quite ready to grant.

We'd been at it no more than a quarter of an hour when I felt a fish mouth my fly. For once in my life I did something right. In Scotland years before I had lost my first and only salmon by responding to it like the trout fisherman I am: I instantly struck. It's what every trout fisherman does and in so doing, half the time, he pulls the fly out of the fish's mouth, the jaws of which, if it's a cock fish, are forced apart by the kype it grows at spawning time and can't be closed. With salmon you must overcome your every instinct and suppress that impulse, wait, let the fish turn downstream, then strike. Then you will hook it in the corner of its mouth. Remembering this, I let my fish send me four signals before I struck. Four. I had it, though as the sequel will show, God only knows why. But I did, and it was a good one.

We were not many miles from the mouth of the Test, and until the recent rains no fish had been running. This felt like one fresh in from sea, not one that had lolled about in a spawning pool for weeks, even months, eating nothing, growing lean and weak and debilitated by sex. This was a salt still randy and spoiling for a fight like a sailor just ashore. The rod I was using was not a light one but this fish put a deep bend in it. I needed both hands for the battle. Doug, of course, obligingly withdrew his line from the water. In fact, he got a landing net, and after a tug-of-war lasting ten minutes, laid out my fish on the lawn. Like all the fish of the Test with which I've now made acquaintance, whether passing or permanent, this one was game to the end. Gallant.

Now, a seven-and-a-half-pound salmon is not a big one, yet when it's your first you're pleased with it and with yourself, especially with gracious ladies on a lovely lawn to admire it and congratulate you. But a seven-and-a-half-pound rainbow trout *is* a big one, and that, on closer inspection, was what my fish turned out to be. With that you're more than pleased. It was a very silvery fish, with hardly any spots, and its red stripe was faint;

that was what had caused us at first to mistake it for a salmon.

I hadn't seen it, hadn't cast upstream, hadn't caught it on a dry fly. But, said my hostess, a fish that size was a cannibal, one she was glad to have out of the water, and for it any means was fair.

On hearing about it, one new friend of mine observed, "Bill has really broken his duck." It had to be interpreted for me, too. It's cricket talk, with "duck" short for duck's egg, or zero. Translated into baseballese it would be, hitting a grand-slam homer after a season-long slump at bat.

Doug had done a perfect job of netting my fish and over the drinks that followed I thanked him as best I could. He left for home earlier than we did and then I was able to learn from our hostess that the part of his name I hadn't caught was the title. It was "Lord." Not many can boast of having had a peer of the realm for his gillie. A sense of his lordship's sense of good form: "If you're going to poach, okay, but you've got to do it properly. The fellow who waits until the owner is in bed and then goes down and takes his fish, now he's what I call an honest poacher."

The English are surprised and skeptical when told that you find them to be a likable people, friendly and hospitable. (Some of them are not even entirely pleased. To a people long used to power and deference, being liked may seem uncomfortably close to cozying up, friendliness and hospitality virtues useful to those who in their station have need of useful virtues.) I'm reminded of the story about the two American ladies, strangers, forced to share a table in a crowded dining room. Said the one, "I can tell from your accent that you're from Boston. I've just been there for the first time. Before leaving Georgia I was told to expect to find Bostonians cool and un-friendly. It's not true. They were all just as nice as could be." Said the lady from Boston, "I am afraid you did not meet the right people." Thinking back as we're about to leave on the generosity and kindness to us of everyone here, I guess maybe we didn't meet the right people.

See you soon.

Yours,
Bill

cc: Al, Ted, Bob

# The Fishermen
## of the Seine

One of the sights of their city that has both amused and exasperated generations of Parisians, and tourists too, are the fishermen of the Seine. As long ago as the 1840s, Daumier caricatured them. One of his drawings depicting a fisherman buying a fish from a fishmonger is captioned, "Parisian anglers usually catch their best fish at the market." Ernest Hemingway, remembering his Paris of the 1920s, says that travel writers wrote about the men fishing in the Seine as though they were crazy and never caught anything. He says it was in fact serious and productive fishing. However, he has not convinced many people. The stereotype persists. It is not entirely without foundation.

On the Île Saint-Louis, just downstream from the house on the Quai d'Anjou overlooking the river in which Daumier lived and observed his fishermen, where the bank changes its name and becomes the Quai de Bourbon, any time between six and eleven in the morning, you will find a man of late middle age in freshly washed and ironed bright blue bib overalls, fishing. Well, you may and you may not. He was there every morning during my recent stay in Paris until the last day when I went to say good-bye to him and then he was not there. I am hoping that it is not that the booze had got him at last but that like *tout le monde* at that season he had gone on vacation and that he is now back, a fixture of the place and the stereotype of his kind.

Even if you should watch him from six o'clock, when he arrives, until eleven, when he leaves, you will seldom see this man catch a fish, what you will see him do steadily all that while is drink. And there you have the two components of the stereotype: patience to the point of downright imbecility and drunkenness. An idle man is contemptible in the eyes of all the world, one who believes himself amply rewarded for his morning with a four-inch-long fish, and it out of water that makes it inedible, is hopeless. The reputation of the Seine fishermen is not enhanced by their being seen to pull more often on their bottles than on their lines.

To a man, the French believe that fishing in the Seine is insane, for they can tell you that there are no fish in the river, and who should know better than they? All their lives they have watched the fishermen and none of them ever catches anything. Fifty million Frenchmen can be right about one thing and wrong about another. The fishermen seldom catch them, it is true, yet in the very heart of Paris the Seine teems with fish. There are fewer fishermen nowadays, for traditionally they were working-class men, small shopkeepers, *pensionnaires,* and Paris has become too expensive and housing too scarce for anybody on a pension to live there now, and chain stores and supermarkets and the decline in the number of householders, among their other ill effects, have reduced the numbers of that class from which the fishermen were drawn, while sending others to the suburbs to become commuters to their jobs, but there are more fish than ever.

Still, strollers along the Seine stop as did their *arrière-*
great-grandparents, Daumier's contemporaries, and
look down upon the fishermen on the *quai* and shake
their heads as they might at a madman fishing in his
bathtub, if not, indeed, in that other bathroom fixture,
the toilet. For as all the world knows, the Seine is a
running sewer. Another received notion impossible to
disabuse people of. Although it is not *eau potable,* to be
sure, the Seine has been greatly purified in recent years
by the installation of sewage-treatment plants upstream
of the city, and industrial pollution has virtually ceased.
(I saw a hatch of mayflies—*Ephemerella Dorothea* they were
—underneath the Pont Neuf one day: a sure sign of
purity, for they will not tolerate pollution. I saw a trout
caught just off the Île Saint-Louis—trout, that most fastidious of finned creatures.) It will come as a surprise to
many a Parisian to learn that the fish he is eating in his
restaurant this evening may have been caught this morning in the shadow of Notre Dame.

But not by the shirtless and suntanned, paunchy old
fellow in the freshly laundered blue overalls to be seen
every morning fishing from the Quai de Bourbon. This is
Pierrot le Plombier: Pete the Plumber. (The French add
an *ot*—the *t* is silent—to a man's name as we add a *y* to
make it diminutive.)

Pierrot le Plombier is not just familiar to, he is familiar
with, everyone with whom he shares his stretch of the
Seine: with the tramps who sleep under the nearby
bridge, the Pont Louis-Philippe; with the ladies who
come early in the morning to walk their dogs along the
riverbank; with the joggers; with the well-dressed old
gentlemen who for years have taken their morning con-

stitutional there. All have for Pierrot a handshake and a friendly word. Some of the ladies chide him good-humoredly for his drinking.

He drinks red wine, taking swigs that half empty the bottle. It is the cheapest possible wine, poisonous wine, with a sour and stagnant smell even from a distance, a smell as though it has been drunk once already. The floridity of his face and his bald dome and the distension of his liver indicate that he has been doing this for a long time and that it is taking its toll. When his bottle is empty, as it soon is, he goes up the steps to the street and to a blue *camionette*, a three-wheeled motorcycle truck with an enclosed cab, parked always in the same spot, and replenishes his bottle from the seemingly inexhaustible source that he keeps there.

Meanwhile, Pierrot le Plombier, almost as though he were posing for Daumier, fishes with the bland oblivi-ousness to the world and its amused condescension to-ward him which only the fisherman can bring to his pas-time and which to nonfishermen is at once so intriguing and so boring. He fishes without success with three rods at a time. One is an ordinary spinning rod baited with a scrap of fish from the one small one he caught yesterday, during the one short spell when nobody was there to see him do it, like the bit of "batch" saved daily for leavening tomorrow's loaf of bread. With this he hopes to catch a walleye pike. Another is a spinning rod as big as a surf caster's rod baited for carp with a kernel of canned corn or with a piece of boiled potato. The third is a Long Rod. I capitalize because the Long Rod has a special niche in Seine River fishing. It is the rod of tradition, associated with the place, and it is a highly specialized weapon.

They used to be of cane, now, like everything else, they are plastic. They come in different lengths, all long. Mine was 6.80 meters—that is a bit over 22 feet—in eight telescoping sections. Standing facing the water, you remove the cap of the tube, give a shake, and the diminishing sections come out as if propelled by a charge until the full length is extended. The butt section, which is the tube, is as big around as a rolling pin, the tip is as fine as a coarse needle. The fineness of the tip is dictated by the delicacy and slyness with which the fish you are after with this rod take the bait. No reel, no running line, just a length of monofilament tied to the tip, a lead sinker, a float, formerly a quill, now plastic, and a size 30 hook. That is smaller than the very smallest trout fly. The hook is baited with either a strand of *mousse,* the hairlike moss that grows on the stones of the riverbank, or with an *asticot*—a maggot—handily on sale at Martin Pêcheur, the tackle shop on the Quai du Louvre next to the bird sellers with their stacks of cages on the sidewalk of domestic and exotic songbirds, barnyard and waterfowl. *Asticots* are the bait for *chevaine*—chub—and they are sometimes taken by *gardon*—roach—even by carp, as well. Kept cool and without being fed, they last almost indefinitely without hatching into blueflies. Artificially reared, they are quite antiseptic; however, I saw no point in mentioning to our dinner guests that in the same refrigerator from which their meal had come I kept my maggots. They were kept in a plastic box, tightly sealed, animation suspended, chilled into mass immobility.

This is *la pêche aux poissons blancs:* literally "white-fish fishing," to distinguish it from trout and salmon, colorful fish. You might say, to distinguish democratic fishing from aristocratic fishing. It was what I had come to Paris to do. Reviewing my fishing experiences, I had found a pattern emerging. In fishing for trout in the Catskills and the Poconos and in the chalk streams of England, for salmon in Wales, Ireland, and Scotland, for bluefish off Nantucket, for bonefish in the Bahamas, I had been doing aristocratic fishing. What I had not done was democratic fishing.

In Anglo-English it is called "coarse fishing." American English has got no proper name for it. "Still fishing" is our closest equivalent. We do not go in for it as a separate sport in itself, or perhaps we do not go in for it as a "sport" at all; with us it is a pastime for kids and old folks. Some of the species comprehended in the name *poissons blancs* we do not even have. These species are the *ablette:* bleak; the *goujon:* gudgeon; the *tanche:* tench; the *chevaine:* chub; the *brême:* bream; the *gardon:* roach; the *rotengle:* red roach; the *sandre:* walleye, the *perche* and the *carpe.* The latter is despised as a trash fish by Americans and is not fished for but is sought after only by a few specially equipped archers. The roach does not exist in the United States. Yet the roach, despite the fact that its eating qualities have been described as cotton wool stuffed with needles, is the world's most popular fish. In Europe, where much of the water is privately owned and closely guarded and where trout and salmon are the prerogative of the well-to-do, not to say, in these days of inflation, the wealthy, the roach is the great democratic fish, the sport of the common man. It is prolific, unparticular about its habitat, like modern man himself, urban, and it is a challenge to the fisherman, for while it may not be aristocratic, it is very finicky and shy. It is fished for with tackle to which the fly-fisherman's is coarse in comparison. None of these species is easy to fool, hook, and land. For each of them there is a preferred bait. For the *ablette* it is the maggot. For the *gardon* it is a strand of moss. Carp will eat anything, which would seem to simplify matters but it does not, rather it complicates them, for these undiscriminating omnivores must be trained by the fisherman to crave what he has got his hook baited with. As I was to say to my friend Jean-Michel Dubos, after weeks of trying, "Jean-Mi', I have learned why the fishermen of the Seine are so seldom seen catching anything. These city fish are very sophisticated. I have learned that *la pêche aux poissons blancs* is harder than fly-fishing for trout." And he to me, "Now you know. It *is* harder."

That is not an easy admission for Jean-Mi' to make. He is in the business of holding *la pêche aux poissons blancs* in disrespect, not to say contempt. Jean-Mi' owns a fishing tackle shop on the Île Saint-Louis, a lovely old shop left just as it was when he inherited it from his father, where treasured rods are expertly repaired and where the articles on sale are made from genuine materials like bamboo and willow and leather and silk, one which caters exclusively to trout and salmon fishermen outfitting themselves for expeditions to Iceland, Canada, Scotland, Ireland—very elite fishing indeed. I could not outfit myself at Jean-Mi's for the fishing I was in Paris to do. Eighteen hundred patterns of artificial flies, but no maggots for sale there. But on days when he is not eager to get out of town and on a stream to fish the evening rise for trout, the *volets* are lowered over the shopwindows and the door locked and Jean-Mi' brings out a bottle of

The Famous Grouse and one of Perrier water and old pals are invited to settle down for talk of fishing. There I could meet men who knew the habitués of the Seine from whom I might learn how the fishing was done. It was there that I heard talk of that very unsuccessful fisherman, Pierrot le Plombier, of that very successful one, Albert Drashkovitch, and of that outlaw, Paulo le Trépané.

Albert Drashkovitch, Yugoslavian-born, long established in France, has, as far as I know, the unique distinction of having discovered for his (adopted) country a sport fish previously unknown. Albert is not an ichthyologist or an oceanographer, he is a landscape painter. He is also a passionate, worldwide fisherman. Several years ago he interested himself in the reports of occasional and unintentional catches of *sandre,* the fish we call the walleye pike, although it is not a pike, it is a perch. If there were some, Albert wondered, might there not be more?

In a country where for 130 francs one can buy a license entitling him or her to fish all the public water in every *département,* a country of fishermen, to add to the sport a species that reaches a weight of twenty pounds and more, that puts up a pretty good fight when hooked, and —a very French consideration, this—one good to eat is an achievement meriting the Légion d'Honneur. This recognition Albert has yet to win, but his fame is great. The day I went fishing with him a boy with a bicycle stood beneath a bridge watching us out in our boat for as long as we remained in view, then when we upped anchor and moved two miles downstream he biked down there and watched us. He followed us wherever we went, finally putting in four hours at it. When we went ashore to make a phone call from a bar, he came up, begged to introduce himself, and said, starry-eyed, that he had recognized Albert from his television appearances.

It is believed that *sandre* were not in France until the 1930s. Canals cut then between the Rhine, the Rhone, the Moselle and the Seine spread them. They were reported in the Seine by the 1950s. But these sightings were infrequent, happy accidental catches made by men fishing for other varieties of fish. For unless fished for with the proper bait and at the proper depth, *sandre* are not purposely caught and their presence goes unsuspected. They are bottom feeders, and so people were fishing over their heads, so to speak, for who knows how long? It was Albert Drashkovitch who, perfecting the tackle for it as he went along, discovered that they were present in large numbers. His invention is a wire harness, a *monture*, weighted with lead, for *vairons*—live minnows. The *monture Drashkovitch* is now sold in tackle shops throughout France. On each one sold Albert collects a royalty. As in all bottom fishing, one frequently hangs up and has to break off, thereby losing the lure or the bait and the hook. This and the spread of the sport he invented, and has helped to popularize through his appearances on national television, has made Albert quite comfortably off.

It was between the Pont de Puteaux and the Pont de Neuilly that we were fishing that day, off the Île de la Grande Jatte. Seurat's famous painting will come to the reader's mind. Dismiss it. Even in Seurat's time, life on the Grande Jatte was not the idyl he chose to depict. It was then a rough and rowdy place, bawdy, and the bourgeois who went there on a Sunday afternoon in summer were going slumming. Nowadays it is a place of abandoned and decaying warehouses and garages, disused factories and a dumping ground. Across from it on the northern bank of the river lies La Défense, named after a monument there commemorating the defense of Paris against the Germans in 1870, now a jungle of skyscrapers of frenzied and uninspired originality and incomparable ugliness.

But just a short way upstream, past the Pont de Puteaux, although you are actually that much nearer to central Paris, you are farther out in the country, for the river there loops back upon itself and flows through the Bois de Boulogne. Skyscrapers are screened from sight by the trees along both banks. The sound of horns and sirens is a distant sound. The only rooftop visible is that of Bagatelle, once the home of Sir Richard Wallace, art collector, philanthropist, who among his many benefactions gave Paris the green, ever-flowing water fountains that are one of the city's symbols.

That day, while sculls from the sculling club near the Pont de Puteaux, like large water spiders, skimmed past us, our boat anchored sometimes alongside houseboats where we could have shaken hands with the woman in her galley washing dishes at the sink, we caught seven fish, six *sandre* ranging from five to fifteen pounds and one pike of twelve pounds, and losing in the course of it half a dozen of Albert's *montures*. When I asked when was he going to design one that never hung up, his reply was that that would be bad for business.

A catch of around fifty pounds of fish in a river well-known to have none—not bad, eh? Well, good enough for your average Seine fisherman perhaps but certainly not anything for Albert Drashkovitch to boast about. He remembers a day when in this same stretch of the river he caught seven hundred kilos. I asked to have that repeated, not once but twice, to be sure my French had not deceived me. Seven hundred kilograms. It was so many, he could not sell them all to the restaurants of Paris. The rest he took down to Orléans and sold them there, where they are featured as a local *spécialité* from out of that city's river, the Loire.

When you eat gefilte fish in a Paris restaurant the odds are that the carp in it was caught in the Seine by the man known as Paulo le Trépané. In addition to the Jewish ones, he keeps many of the city's numerous oriental restaurants supplied with carp, too. And your *sandre de la Loire*, as it is called on all the menus, may not have come from the Loire, either; it may well have been snatch-hooked by Paulo le Trépané from one of the bridges in that stretch of the Seine between the Pont Sully and the Pont de la Concorde which for a certain portion of each day is this one man's personal preserve. I had heard about Paulo le Trépané at Jean-Mi's tackle shop and one morning in Pierrot le Plombier's spot beneath the Pont Louis-Philippe I met him. It was eight o'clock. Unlike Pierrot, who is stationary, Paulo fishes the length of the river daily, and eight is his hour for the Pont Louis-Philippe. At eight o'clock in the morning Paulo is nearing the end of his day.

What I saw was a man doing something quite mad—

that it was also illegal I did not know at the time. This fellow was on the bridge, on one of the pilings in the middle of the bridge, fishing over the rail; he was outside the rail, standing on the ledge, which is only about a foot wide, maybe less. As if that were not reckless enough, he was not even holding on; with both hands he was jerking his rod, obviously trying to snatch-hook fish, with motions of such violence, he seemed sure to lose his precarious footing and fall fifty feet to the water, maybe in the path of one of the many *bâteaux-mouches* or of one of the block-long *péniches,* the Seine river barges.

We call it snatch-hooking, or foul-hooking, and we consider it unsportsmanlike; the French call it to *alpaguer,* or to *grappiner,* or to *prendre par la veste,* and they make it illegal. Paulo le Trépané has been apprehended at it many times, fined, even jailed. His defense does not work with every *garde-pêche;* some of them know him too well by now to be fooled by it, and know too that the identity card he produces is not his but is one he found. His defense is to fall into a crazy fit. He rolls his eyeballs and lets his tongue loll and waves his arms akimbo and he points to the two craters, with their ugly scars, in his forehead just at the hairline. Out of jail now, he is in debt to the government for some twenty-thousand francs in unpaid fines. "They will wait a long time for it," he says.

Paulo was trepanned for his wounds incurred in battle as a soldier in the Algerian war. He was shot from his lookout post on the roof of a building and fell five stories to the ground. He was hit in the hip and the leg, in both arms, in the head, and his injuries from his fall were even more extensive and more severe than his gunshot wounds. His disability is one hundred percent and for this his pension is 2,200 francs a month. He feels his country owes him more than that, and he takes it. He has a wife and two children to feed, house, and clothe. He supplements his pension in two ways. He doesn't care who knows how he does it.

In his musette bag, along with his fishing gear, on the day I met him was the rearview mirror of a truck. He had "liberated" it, on commission, from a parked truck earlier that morning. The commission was from a butcher friend of his, whose delivery truck had lost its rearview mirror. Paulo was expecting a nice roast of beef for his.

It is very early in the morning that Paulo gets to his other job. Every morning for twenty-two years he has been on the river by 2:00 a.m. to fish. Every morning of the year, for open and closed seasons mean nothing to Paulo. Within the city's confines he works the entire length of the Seine. Gainful employment would be worlds easier, but Paulo likes to fish.

I met him, by arrangement, one morning at three. We met at the Pont du Louvre, on the left bank, just by the old disused Gare d'Orsay, soon to become a museum of nineteenth-century art. Ordinarily, Paulo would not be that far downriver by that hour, but he did not want me to be inconvenienced by having to walk too far for our rendezvous. Precisely on time he materialized like the nocturnal prowler he is out of that half-light of the short summer night in that latitude which one forgets is so far north. That day by the Pont du Louvre when we were almost the only persons in all of Paris awake and abroad Paulo took off his shoes and socks and rolled up his pantlegs and waded the Seine to do his snatch-hooking. The fishing was unproductive so we crossed the river and went downstream to the Pont de la Concorde, reputedly the best spot in town for carp. There earlier in the year a fisherman had made the papers with one weighing thirty pounds. The photograph of this old fellow stiffly holding up his fish with the Eiffel Tower in the background had transported me to that earlier Paris of the Douanier Rousseau. But Paulo had no better luck there and, unless he improved his lot by lifting something off somebody's parked car after leaving me, he went home that day empty-handed.

Paulo is the first fisherman of my acquaintance to do his fishing by bus. A lifetime pass, his owing to his service disability, entitles him to ride them free. Of course, they do not run as early as he gets to the river in the morning, so he must hike in from the suburb where he lives, but later on, in going from bridge to bridge, from the Pont Sully sometimes all the way to the Pont Mirabeau, he takes the bus. One day this spring he was denied entry to one by its driver, who said, "You can't come on this bus with a fish that big. It will make a mess. It stinks." The fish was a carp of twenty-seven kilos and to sell it to his regular customer, Goldenberg's, the kosher restaurant in the Jewish quarter of the Marais, he had to walk with it all the way from the Pont de la Concorde. Goldenberg's? Wasn't that place the target not long ago of a terrorist attack in which several customers were killed? It was. These guys with submachine guns sprayed the place inside and out at just the hour when Paulo is usually there with his fish to sell. That day he was lucky in his bad luck. He had caught nothing.

My last encounter with Paulo was again in Pierrot le Plombier's spot beneath the Pont Louis-Philippe. He said good-bye to me. Maybe he had found a way, despite my warning that their loss would have been reported and he would be identified by worldwide satellite before he could get out of the door of the bank, to pass himself off as the owner of the wad of traveler's checks he had found on the riverbank a few days earlier and forge the signature and cash them. He was off on vacation to Brittany for a month of fishing.

It was the summer of the falling franc. Eight to the dollar it got down to, and all the world, especially the student world, was in Paris. They flocked, as students have done for a millennium, to the Latin Quarter, my *arrondisement*. Some came porting backpacks and sleeping bags and made their homes in the streets and under the bridges. Early in the morning in the Place du Parvis, in front of Notre Dame, when I passed through it on my way to the river, you would have thought that a children's crusade was sleeping until the doors of their shrine were opened. On the morning of July 14, Bastille Day, the Seine was solid with soft-drink and beer cans, wine and whiskey bottles, and the streets were just as solid with litter from the celebrations of the night before. But that one morning stands out as the exception to the rule; usually for me the city put on her freshest face. I was never out as early as Paulo le Trépané, but the hours I kept, fisherman's hours, ensured that for a while each morning Paris was mine, and it was another Paris, one unseen by tourists, almost the one photographed by Eugène Atget during that epoch called *la Belle*, an earlier Paris, that of the blessed era before the internal-combustion engine, the jet plane. It was like a reward to me for my sacrifice of sleep.

In this, the first and most photographed of cities, photography kept coming to my mind. Seen at dawn, before any activity has commenced, the section near the two islands in the Seine will be found to have changed surprisingly little since Daguerre's day. At that hour of all shades of gray, the empty scene is reminiscent of those first-ever photographs of his taken when lenses and plates were too slow and insensitive to stop and record people in motion.

My old friend, young Pierre Affre—Parisian, veterinary surgeon, fabulous fisherman—had no alarm clock. I did not need one. On mornings when Pierre was going fishing with me I would phone him, getting a sleepy *"Allo?"* for an answer, apologize for the earliness of the hour, and say that I would be seeing him in fifteen minutes.

I got my maggots out of the refrigerator, slung my musette bag over my shoulder, hung my landing net on my belt, and shouldered my rod. Rather than risk a malfunction of the elevator at that hour, getting stuck in it, which would necessitate setting off the alarm and rousing and being rescued by the concierge, I walked the four flights down to the *rez-de-chausée.*

At the corner of the rue de Fleurus I crossed to the other side of the rue Guynemer and went northward alongside the tall iron palings of the Jardin du Luxembourg. At that hour the garden gates were locked and in the absence of the usual children noisily at play, the old men at their games of *pétanque,* the pony riders, the tennis players, there could be heard coming from the chestnut trees the plaintive sobs of the wood pigeons and the eerie wail of a screech owl. The street sweeper with his besom would be out, the water for washing the street flowing at the curbs, and along the walls of the buildings the bins would be lined up waiting for the trash collectors. The cool of night lingered in the air, which at that hour still smelled cleanly of nothing.

I crossed the rue de Vaugirard, went through the vine-covered Allée du Séminaire and down the rue Bonaparte. The street was the one taken by young Ernest Hemingway en route from lunch at the Brasserie Lipp to the Closerie des Lilas, there to work on his fishing story, which is only incidentally about fishing, "Big Two-Hearted River," or when going to the rue de Fleurus to visit the Misses Toklas and Stein. Routes rich in associations, literary, artistic, historical, whichever one I chose on any day, conducted me to my fishing, and with time at a standstill at that hour, ghosts from all periods of the city's long and rich past were abroad. The little rue Ferou, which I might take as my path down to Saint-Sulpice, was the one in which Madame de la Fayette, France's first great novelist, was born and died. There had stood Shakespeare & Company, meeting place for Joyce and Pound, Eliot and Valéry. On that site had stood the house in which Chardin was born, there Danton's, the one in which he was arrested, subsequently to be decapitated by the "humane" new machine the invention of Dr. Guillotin who lived just across the street from him in the Cour Saint-André.

At my hour, the water of the fountain in the Place Saint-Sulpice with its larger-than-life-size statues of France's four greatest preachers would not be turned on

yet. In the enclosed Marché Saint-Germain, where the
merchants' stalls were set up permanently, the doors
would still be shut, but in the rue de Buci, on the other
side of the Boulevard Saint-Germain, usually so
thronged with traffic but now deserted, where the stalls
had to be set up in the street each day, the vendors would
be at work stacking mounds of tomatoes and eggplants,
strawberries, peaches, artichokes. There I would be
greeted by one greengrocer with, "Bonjour, Monsieur
Texas! Bonne pêche!" It was my hat, he said, that had
told him I was a Texan. I forbore to tell him that it was a
boating hat from out of the catalogue of L.L. Bean of
Freeport, Maine. From him I would buy peaches or big
crisp black cherries and when Pierre met me at his door
in the rue Dauphine I would give him some of whichever
and we ate them as we went down his street to the Pont
Neuf. At the Wallace fountain there we would wash our
hands and, cupping them, have a drink.

On mornings when one of Pierre's all too many irons
in the fire kept him from going fishing with me, at the
corner of the rue Guynemer and the rue de Vaugirard I
would turn right and go up to the Palais du Luxembourg
where even at that hour a uniformed guard was on sentry
duty at the gate, for the palace is the French Senate, there
turn left and go down the rue de Condé to the Carrefour
de l'Odéon. I was then on my way to fish farther upriver,
off the Île Saint-Louis, and my path took me through the
rue Saint-André-des-Arts to the Place Saint-Michel.

Later on, the cars would stream along both banks of
the river in both directions. At first they were few and
occasional, then the gaps between them would begin to
fill with others and finally at the *heure d'affluence* they

would follow one another like machine-gun bullets. Forty-seven tourist buses I counted parked alongside Notre Dame one morning on my way back home. At that number I quit counting. By then the city would have awakened to another day with its disasters and sensations and the sirens would howl, but now all was relatively still and quiet.

All things are relative, and solitude is a state of mind. Said one of my fellow fishermen to me on one of those mornings, "I come here because I want to avoid all the people and I like my peace and quiet. It's so pleasant to get away from television and enjoy nature." The Seine was this one man's Walden Pond. And there is something to be said for being reminded wherever you look of all that you have gotten away from.

Fishing in the city one saw sights not usually seen by fishermen. One morning a team of two *pompiers,* whose job it is, in addition to fire fighting, to fish the corpses of suicides out of the Seine, were scuba-diving for one underneath the Pont Neuf, the man on the bank holding the man in the water with a leash in the form of a length of rope. On another day, very early in the morning, in one of the semicircular banquettes on the Pont Neuf, a young woman was giving her young man a haircut. A sight novel to me, though one common enough on the Seine, was that of the wives of the bargemen issuing up from their cabins to hang out a wash or to drop a pail to the water and haul it up and mop the deck, quite blasé about living their daily lives in the heart of, yet so detached from, the city.

My luck at fishing is never very good; in Paris I had more compensations for my bad luck than I have ever had fishing anywhere else. Done for the day by eight or at the latest nine o'clock in the morning, when the traffic of the barges and the *bateaux-mouches* grew heavy and the waves they made scared the fish, I would put up my rod and shoulder my bag and go up to the street for a café au lait and croissants at one of the outdoor cafés. After breakfast I might stroll down to the eastern tip of the Île Saint-Louis for a visit with Jean-Mi' Dubos. Coming home late one morning I stopped in the Place Saint-Sulpice for over an hour to watch another reminder of Daumier, a little traveling circus troupe consisting of a dancing girl in tights and spangles, a magician, a clown and a barker, their majordomo, who played the tuba, juggled, walked the tightrope, did feats of strength and acrobatics, and ate fire. Where else but in Paris could a fisherman coming home empty-handed be rewarded with such a show?

But if it was a day together with Pierre, between him and me as we drank at the Wallace fountain a look would pass. It was something of a mischievous look. We were playing a prank on the city by being awake and abroad at this hour while the world slept. We might have sneaked out of our beds and shinnied down the drainpipes. It was our river down there and all that lay along its banks, and with some little allowance for the difference in years, we felt like Huck Finn and Tom Sawyer in that era that now seems the age of innocence. Mark Twain says that when, as a youthful Mississippi riverboat pilot, he first saw the city of St. Louis he could have bought it for six million dollars, and that it was the mistake of his life that he did not. Saint Louis himself was crowned king of France in Notre Dame just over there, and I felt, at least for an hour or so each morning, which is as much of such heady joy as anybody should be permitted, as if I did own his city without having been out of pocket a centime.

At the Pont Neuf Pierre and I would go either left, down to the little park beneath the statue of Henri IV, the *Vert Galant,* on the prow of the Île de la Cité, or right, down another flight of stone steps that took us a little farther upriver. Either way we went we often saw wall-eyes in the water and always carp, some of them big carp, some three feet long, rubbing themselves against the stones of the bank like cows scratching their flanks against a tree trunk.

Carp: to fish for them properly one must first *amorcer.* To *amorcer* is to chum, and in the tackle shops like Martin Pêcheur you can buy ready-made chum. The French are great users of it. One manufacturer alone puts up in half-kilo packages sixteen varieties of *amorce.* Most of them are basically ground-up peanuts. You mix a bit with water, squeeze it into a ball, and chunk it into the river. It tastes pretty good to a hungry fisherman. And that's about all it's good for, according to Pierre. He had nothing but scorn for the fishermen we saw chumming with their little balls of commercial *amorce* or with pieces of two or three potatoes. That was why they never caught anything.

"Do potatoes grow in the river?" asked Pierre. "Do peanuts? Carp don't know what potatoes are. You must teach them. They must be fed enough to develop a taste for them."

To chum as it should be done, Pierre insisted, we must boil up a hundred kilograms of potatoes, even more would be better, and come early in the morning every day for a week and throw in a tubful or so, always in the same spot. We would have to come early enough not to be seen by Paulo le Trépané or else he would poach our fish. After a week of this we would have carp in our chosen spot like pigs at the trough. Even allowing for the decline in the value of the franc, a hundred kilograms of potatoes would cost money, not to mention the work in the apartment kitchen (Pierre was not keeping house, so it would have to be done in my place)—and Paris lay in the grip of a stifling heat wave—of boiling up thirty or forty pounds of them every night, then toting them in their washtub down to the river, there perhaps to be observed by the police on our furtive midnight mission. Nevertheless, that was our plan. We were waiting only for Albert Drashkovitch to get back from Alaska, where he had gone salmon fishing. We needed him, his boat we had to have. We would never be able to get back up the stairs to the street with all the fish we were going to catch. We would fill Albert's boat with carp as he had once filled it with walleyes and for the next several days carp would be featured on the menus of not just the Jewish restaurants but on those of all the Chinese, Cambodian, Laotian and Vietnamese restaurants in Paris and *les environs*. What spoiled our plan was that on returning home from Alaska, Albert found an agent from the income tax bureau waiting for him on his doorstep with a big bill. No time for fishing. He had to paint a picture and go off to the Côte d'Azur to sell it before the paint was barely dry.

Pierre had grown up on the banks of this river and knew its every centimeter. He was my guide. On my own, without him, I fared poorly. I was then about as productive a fisherman as Pierrot le Plombier. Like him, I drew watchers; like him, I provoked shakes of the head for my doggedness—maybe I should say my mindlessness. When one day a *bateau-mouche* drew in close to my spot on the bank of the Île Saint-Louis and cut its engine while the lady guide with the loudspeaker identified me in French, English, and German—in Japanese the message must have been the same—as a typical fisherman of the Seine, I felt with a mixture of pride and chagrin that I had arrived. To be sure, I had come too late to be an inspiration to Daumier, but the camera shutters clicked away at me with a noise like katydids and I am now in photo albums all the way from Tulsa to Tokyo.

But if the Parisians smile tolerantly at the fishermen of the Seine, they know how to laugh at themselves, too. They tell this story. Says the stroller to the fisherman, "Monsieur, you have got the patience of a dumb ox. Here I have been watching you for two hours by the clock, and in all that time you have caught not one thing."

# Ditches Are Quicker

By clearing a swamp in the service of humanity as his last earthly deed, Goethe's Faust saved his soul from the Devil, to whom he had sold it. "To many millions let me furnish soil" was Faust's dying wish, and this act of public land reclamation earned him the remission of all his many grave sins.

It says something about the commonly accepted attitude toward swamps that the clearing of one should win such favor in the eyes of God. Many Italians who otherwise detest the memory of Mussolini will allow that he did at least one good thing: He drained the Pontine Marshes and made the land tillable. Henry David Thoreau might say, "Hope and the future for me are not in lawns and cultivated fields, not in towns and cities, but in the impervious and quaking swamps. When, formerly, I have analyzed my partiality for some farm which I had contemplated purchasing I have frequently found that I was attracted solely by a few square rods of impermeable and unfathomable bog." But his was for long an eccentric point of view; indeed, until very recently, almost a lone one. Most people think of swamps as pestilential and profitless places, and regard anybody who drains one as a public benefactor.

"To many millions let me furnish soil" might well be the motto of the Soil Conservation Service of the U.S.

Department of Agriculture, which has long been engaged on a scheme of social betterment through earth and water engineering on a scale so vast it would stagger Faust's vaulting imagination. This it is empowered to do by Public Law 566: The Watershed Protection and Flood Prevention Act of 1954. In explaining its program the Soil Conservation Service presents a vision of nature, particularly water, tamed and harnessed in the service of man. Water brought to where needed and removed from where not wanted results in higher farm income, more industry and thus more jobs, more products, higher wages. Visitors come to enjoy the new recreational opportunities created by artificial lakes and new state and regional parks. Land values rise. Hospitals and social services are made possible.

In the attainment of this Faustian vision of the good life the Soil Conservation Service employs one practice which has aroused opposition from the growing number of people who share Thoreau's feeling for swampy places and his conviction that "in wildness is the preservation of the world." Who fear that we are daily destroying, in the name of Progress and the Gross National Product, what little wildness there is left in the world. What these people oppose is "channelization"—a practice which the Soil Conservation Service calls "stream channel improvement." By whichever name it is called, it means the deepening, clearing, and straightening of streams in the interest of flood prevention and soil conservation. This has been going on all over the country at a great rate and will continue to do so, according to plans already approved. Among sportsmen this raises fears of the virtual disappearance of our natural streams and the wildlife along their banks.

You do not have to go to Alabama, as I did, to see streams being channelized, or improved. Unless you live in Alaska, you can, or you will soon be able to, see them in your home state, whichever that may be. It is because there are so many of them there, and because there are plans to create two thousand miles more of them in the state, that I went to Alabama to see one. If that is what the countryside is going to look like in the near future, its streams deepened, cleared, and straightened, Alabama would be a good place to get a foretaste of it.

I went with a mind prejudiced in favor of both sides of the dispute. I was prejudiced by my memories of two men who lived close to nature, close to the land, whose attitudes toward them were diametrically opposed, though they were father and son: my grandfather and my father, both long dead now, yet they continue to shape—and to divide—my feelings about nature and the land.

My grandfather was a sharecropper all his life, in east Texas. He farmed, with hand tools, about thirty acres. Off these thirty acres he picked, in a good year, twelve to fifteen bales of cotton. Half of these went to the landlord; on what he got for the rest, my grandfather and his family of four lived for the year. Or rather, with it he paid his creditors for the living expenses of the year past. For like all of his class, my grandfather never got caught up on his debts but was always a year behind. Because sometimes, after bending from daylight to dark to the handles of a Georgia-stock turning plow drawn by a twenty-dollar

mule breaking furrows to plant cotton, then after bending over a hoe chopping it from daylight to dark beneath
a sun hot enough to broil meat, he might, even after the
boll weevils had taken their share, he might still have
enough standing cotton for that old never-to-be-discour-
aged hope to blossom yet another spring: the hope of
finally ginning enough bales to make a down payment on
"a little place of his own." And then the rains, the torren-
tial east Texas spring rains would come, the creeks would
rise and leave their banks and flood the bottomlands and
drown the crop my grandfather had plowed and planted
and hoed, and that year he would not make even the two
hundred dollars which he once told me was the most
cash money he ever made in a year in his life. I have seen
close up and at its hardest what it means to a man to get
his living working the land, and depending on nature's
help for the bread which he must eat in the sweat of his
face. Remembering my grandfather, I was for a federal
program which had, among its aims, that of sparing people the kind of hardship I had seen him endure. One case
of what my grandfather suffered chronically from—ma-
laria—might cure even a Thoreau of his partiality for the
impervious and quaking swamps, where it is bred.

My father hated, as only the son of a poor sharecropper could hate, cleared land, plowed land, row crops. He
also hated, as did another hunter, Fenimore Cooper's
Leatherstocking, "towns and cities, farms and highways,
churches and schools, in short, all the inventions and
deviltries of man." What he loved was swamps. Nor were
they for him impervious. He made his way in them with
the same accustomed ease as the game he hunted there.
Sulphur Bottom, our swamp was called; it belonged to

my father. Actually he owned not one of its countless and unsurveyable acres; but because he was the one man of his time who could go in one side of it and find his way out to the other, Sulphur Bottom was generally allowed to belong to him. He began sharing it with me when he judged I was ready; I was four. To be on Sulphur River at dawn when the woods came to life was like being present at the Creation, for just as I saw them, so those woods had looked since the dawn of time. If one bend, just one slight bend of Sulphur River were to be, at taxpayers', which is to say his own, expense, straightened so that some farmer—very likely one already being paid by the government not to grow anything on other parcels of his land—might grow a few more bushels of corn, my father would have gone to law to stop it. Had he known that in straightening a stream the trees, all of them—the hickories and the walnuts and the oaks, where the squirrels den and the coons and foxes prowl—are cut down, then the man whose son I am might have taken the law into his own hands.

The stream I had come to Alabama to see being channelized is called Granny Branch, in Lawrence County. On the day I was there the narrow wooden bridge I stood on divided the stream into Before and After, into Past and Future—divided it, for me, into the two attitudes toward nature and man's place in it symbolized by my grandfather and my father: Production and Preservation. Downstream from the bridge ran, straight as a railroad cutting, a drainage ditch. This was After; this was nature as the servant of man; this was the Future. Upstream from the bridge a narrow brook with grassy banks still wound across a peaceful low-lying meadow. Straight across the meadow marched parallel rows of wooden stakes with strips of white cloth tied to them marking the new course the water would take after the stream had been improved.

If you see a stream as an engineer sees it—a soil engineer or a social engineer, or the Soil Conservation Service's combination of the two—as a channel for the drainage of water, then you are bound to believe you can improve on nature's handiwork. Left to itself, a stream dawdles along, wanders about. Its bed is not level but is deep in some places and shallow in others. It is in these places that fish spawn and feed, but they impede the flow of the water. An unimproved stream will have boulders in it and fallen logs; around these, too, fish spawn and feed, but they also impede the flow of the water. Worst of all, from the engineer's point of view, the stream will be wayward and meandering. All these irregularities will cause the stream to overflow in times of heavy rain. The stream will carry away the overflow in time; but not in time, perhaps, to suit the farmer through whose land it flows.

To improve a stream by deepening, clearing, and straightening it as the Soil Conservation Service does, the trees as far back as two hundred yards from its banks are felled and cleared. This had been done upstream of the bridge on Granny Branch; now the dragline and the bulldozer were at work.

A dragline is a scoop hanging by a cable from a crane mounted on caterpillar treads. I watched as the scoop was hoisted to the tip of the crane, swung over the stream, and dropped. It struck with a splash that emptied the stream of water for a stretch of twenty feet, followed instantly by a thud that made the little bridge shudder. It made me shudder, too. The lip of the scoop had teeth, and when the winch was wound and the cable tightened, these teeth bit into the bed of the stream. When the scoop was full it was hoisted and swung aside and turned upside down, and a mound of what had been the living riverbed but was now what the engineers call "spoils" was dumped on the bank. Meanwhile on the opposite bank a series of these mounds was being flattened by the bulldozer. Thus the stream was deepened both by digging out its bed and by raising its banks. Being bare, the banks permit the return of the dragline at some future date for the rechannelization of the ditch; for with no roots to hold them back, these treeless banks soon crumble and erode. Had I come upon this scene without knowing what was being done, I should have said this looked like terrain being readied for trench warfare. The dragline lumbered up the bank and stopped and aimed its scoop again. As the scoop fell and struck I turned away. I turned about on the bridge and looked in the other direction. There being nothing in the prospect to detain my eye, I seemed to see for two thousand miles, at least. I tried to imagine the people who would inherit this landscape. To such unshaded sluices as this would tomorrow's people—those like me, who find public parks too public and artificial lakes artificial—come to picnic? Would tomorrow's lovers stroll hand in hand along such bare banks? I knew then that I had taken sides: my father's side—probably the losing one.

I left the bridge and went downstream, or rather

downditch, away from the clank and the roar of the bulldozer and the thud of the dragline's scoop, and sat myself on what had been the bank of what had been Granny
Branch to get the feel of the countryside of the future.
For of just such as this there will soon be two thousand
miles more in Alabama alone—time to begin getting
used to it. There was no shade to sit in, so I sat on the
bare ground. A breeze was blowing, a strange breeze,
hot, and though quite strong, totally silent, there being
nothing for it to rustle, not a leaf. The banks will in time
bear a growth of brambles, like a tangle of barbed wire,
but as yet the red subsoil was raw, scored by the bulldozer's tread. There being no trees, no birds called. Between its parallel, sheer, straight walls, over its flattened
bed, the water of the drainage ditch slid past without a
ripple, lifeless as one of the canals of Mars.

# The
# Trick-shot Artist

During my boyhood, hardly a month passed without a road show of some kind coming to my hometown of Clarksville, Texas. They invariably came to town on a Saturday, when school was out and when the farm folks from all over Red River County were in town for the day. Circuses, tent shows (as we called carnivals), medicine shows, minstrel shows: these were our diversions, and welcome ones they were in those times of the Depression and the Dust Bowl.

As I was growing up, the changes taking place in the outer world began to be reflected in these touring attractions. Now came barnstorming airplane pilots, teams of motorcycle stunt riders, daredevil auto racers. From out in the country, people came in creaking, horse-drawn wagons to marvel at these pioneers of the new age of speed.

In the fall of 1936, my twelfth year, and the last one that my father would see to its end in his short stay on earth, there came to town a performer from out of that older time that was being so speedily replaced: a touring trick-shot artist. Once—back in the days of Buffalo Bill and Annie Oakley—the trick-shot artist had been the stellar attraction of circuses and Wild West shows. Now, when mechanization and urbanization were transforming the country and relegating the mighty hunter to the nation's past, to find an audience the trick-shot artist came to places like Clarksville where that vanishing America lingered on, and where men of the mold admired by that world were admired still. The act was admission-free, sponsored by one of the sporting-arms manufacturers, and meant to stimulate interest in shooting and to promote the sale of the company's products. I bear upon my body, and will take with me to my grave, a memento of the trick-shot artist's visit to my hometown.

On the fairgrounds that day to watch the trick-shot artist perform was almost the entire male population of the county, among them men who, once the hog they butchered in the fall was eaten, went into the woods in bland disregard of the game laws (no effort was made to enforce them in our parts) and by their woodcraft and marksmanship furnished meat for their table until hog-killing time the next autumn. To these men ammunition was a medium of exchange, one more acceptable than the currency of the realm, which was not edible in any case and was subject to fluctuations in value beyond a common man's control, whereas a cartridge was still worth the same as always: one head of game. Their fathers had made hunters of these men just as they had put them to the plow, and at about the same early age, and trained them never to waste a bullet. Now they had put aside for the day their cotton picking and crop gathering to come watch a man do better than what they themselves did surpassingly well, and to judge whether he was a better shot than their local champion, whose son and only child I was.

When the trick-shot artist was satisfied that all had come who were going to come, he picked one rifle from his array of automatic .22s. It might have been a piece of chalk, except that his blackboard—actually a sheet of copper two feet wide and three feet tall, mounted on plywood—was fifty feet from it. With a noise like a woodpecker attacking a telephone pole, which was barely interrupted as his assistant passed him a fresh, loaded rifle, the trick-shot artist drew on his copper sheets, in bullet holes, a profile of George Washington, a bonneted Indian chief, Franklin D. Roosevelt with his cigarette holder in his mouth. He asked for requests from the audience and drew whatever comic-strip characters were called for: Mutt and Jeff, Maggie and Jiggs, Barney Google, Krazy Kat. He tossed handfuls of colored glass balls into the air and shattered them. They were like rockets bursting. He snuffed lighted candlesticks, drove nails in boards. He struck a match in his assistant's hand with a bullet, then when that cool customer had lighted a cigarette and put it between his lips, the trick-shot artist turned his back to him, laid his rifle over his shoulder, and, sighting with a pocket mirror, shot the ash from the cigarette.

A man in the audience called to my father, "You reckon you can beat that, 'Ump?"

The trick-shot artist, whose job it was to foster local shooting talent, was quick to pick up on this. Too quick for my father to steal away, which was what he would have liked to do. For it was one of the many contrarinesses of my contrary father that while he was a show-off in everything else and never refused a dare to fistfight, wrestle, race cars, drink, he could never be coaxed into displaying the skill for which he was famous, his shooting. Maybe that was a way of showing off, too: above having to prove to anybody that he was as good as he was said to be. Whether calculated to do so or not, this only magnified his legend. At our annual county fair he was the one man who could not be drawn near the shooting gallery, and of the men present that day, few had ever seen him fire a gun; they knew of his prowess because he hunted on their land and they were regular recipients of game from the full bags he brought in.

"Pretty good, is he?" said the trick-shot artist, sizing up my pint-sized father and concealing any doubts he may have had. "Well, 'Ump, show us what you can do. Maybe you can teach me some new tricks."

"Mister, it don't look to me like anybody can teach you anything. Certainly not me," said my father. "I don't know any tricks. I do a little bird-hunting, that's all."

"Don't bet your money against him, mister," said the local man who had addressed my father earlier. "Lose it if you do."

If looks could kill, my father's would have dropped him in his tracks. "Don't pay any attention to him, mister," my father told the trick-shot artist.

"Now don't be bashful," the visitor said, and he put his rifle in my father's hands. My father looked about as awkward and uncomfortable as he did when obliged to hold a baby. Fetching a sigh, he said, "Well, have you got a half-dollar on you? One that you won't mind if you lose, maybe?"

The trick-shot artist produced a half-dollar. My father regarded it, shook his head, and said, "Shame to waste a whole half-dollar in times like these." He handed it back to the man. "Give me just a quarter instead," he said.

My father laid the rifle on the ground. Beside it he laid

the coin. He straightened and looked up. Everybody looked up. There was nothing in the sky to see—what was my father shaking his head over? His face bore the pained expression of a man certain he was about to make a public fool of himself.

What happened next, following upon my father's reluctance and slowness, went so fast it was hard to follow. He knelt, picked up the coin and spun it high in the air, picked up the rifle and threw it to his shoulder as he rose to his feet, fired; there was an audible *ping* and the coin disappeared. His was the most dubious-looking face present.

"Can you do that every time?" the trick-shot artist asked.

"I doubt it," said my father, and did it twice more.

"There's a trick to it that makes it easier than it looks," he told me afterward. "Now, nobody could hit something that small with a rifle ball while it's moving. So you wait for it to stop moving. There is a second when it gets as high as it's going to go and before it starts to fall, when it just hangs there. That's your moment. Shoot then and you're shooting at a still target. That's the trick." Which has always seemed to me a little like Bach's saying that there was nothing to mastering the keyboard: all you had to do was strike the right note at the right time and the instrument played itself.

The trick-shot artist stayed overnight in Clarksville and the next morning came to our house.

"What do you do for a living?" he asked my father, and without waiting for an answer said, "Whatever it is, you're wasting your time. Quit. Resign. Sell out. Come with me. Here you're hiding your light under a bushel."

I could see it all already: us traveling across the whole U.S.A. and me earning the envy of every boy in it. Loading the rifles, setting up the copper plaques. And that was nothing to what came later. At first people would be scandalized—which was not to say any the less envious—at a boy my age lighting up a cigarette. Then . . . When the shot was fired that took off the ash I wouldn't even blink. The show over, my father and I would sign autographs. If only he would have the courage to stand up to my mother's objections!

My father's smile brought down these dreams of mine on the wing. "It's mighty nice of you," he said, shaking his head. "But in the first place, I'm not all that good a rifle shot. It's shotguns I'm better acquainted with. And in the second place, I wouldn't want to be on the road all the time. Thanks, but I'll stick with what I know: grease monkeying. If you're ever through this way again, it would be a pleasure to take you hunting. I'd like to see you on quail."

Now it was the trick-shot artist's turn to smile and shake his head. "Thanks," he said, "but I can't hit them things for love nor money. When I'm not working, what I like to do is play golf."

So, if my father wouldn't become a trick-shot artist, I would, in partnership with my pal, Pete Hinkle. We stocked up on BBs and practiced with our air rifles. As our skills sharpened, our targets got smaller and smaller. We became sharpshooters. We became daredevils. We took turns shooting first half-dollars, then quarters, then nickels and finally dimes from each other's fingers at twenty paces. We did it dozens of times. We couldn't miss. It was time to take our show on the road. First stop:

the alleyway behind my father's shop downtown, a performance for him alone.

We tossed the coin. Pete won. He would shoot, I would hold. Pete paced off the distance, took aim, fired, and shot off my right thumbnail. Last performance of Hinkle & Humphrey's trick-shot act.

"I blame you," my mother told my father when he brought me home from the doctor's office. "You ought to have had better sense than to let them do it."

"Mother, we'd done it a hundred times before," I said. It was not out of bravery but out of shame for myself and to protect my father against her scolding that I concealed the pain I was enduring. "Don't blame him. Blame me."

She glowered at my father. My defense of him made her all the angrier at him.

"I never knew a damned air gun shot that hard," he said.

"Well, I just hope you have both learned your lesson," she said.

"I'll grow another thumbnail, Mother," I said.

"Hear that?" said my father. "That's the spirit! Sure you will. You'll grow another thumbnail."

It was black for a long time afterward, a source of mutual embarrassment, thus a further bond, between my father and me. My new nail was just about fully grown in, only the tip of it still black, when, the following summer, my father died in the wreck of a speeding car.

In the more than forty years since then, I have grown many thumbnails, each of them with the identical dent where that pellet struck. I never rub it but what it brings back to me these memories.

# Guardian Dragon

In my time, Sulphur Bottom, in the east Texas woods, remained much as it had been from the beginning. Clearing was confined to its edges. Within it towered virgin oaks. Rattan vines connected the trees in webs that looked as though they had been spun by spiders from the age of the mastodons. Cane grew rooftop-tall in brakes as dense as fur, impenetrable. Its guardian monsters had kept the place inviolate.

But now in the mid-1930s signs of change were appearing, and my father, the man most responsible for them, was the one to whom they were least welcome. Game bags of the size he brought out of there emboldened others. Motor cars—kept running by him—got more men there more easily. To discourage these trespasses upon what he considered to be his private preserve, my father periodically shot and put on display at his shop a particularly big water moccasin, propping open the mouth to show its fangs and its deathly white interior. Or— But for this he needed help.

Whenever my father needed help, in anything, he got it from Wylie West, his carbon copy. Wylie had no more sense than he had. Wylie would have walked through fire if my father had gone first—as he would have done on a dare.

Wylie worked for my father. He worked at my father's

garage. However, he did not work for the garage, he worked for my father. To Mr. Barton, my father's partner, Wylie paid no mind.

Had he been asked what his feelings toward Wylie were, my father, if he had not said, "That's none of your business," would have said, "He's a good nigger." In fact, Wylie was the one man he liked, trusted, and respected. But the code governing relations between the races forbade that he show this, or even altogether admit it to himself—although my father was just enough of a maverick, and enough of an outsider without all that much social standing to lose, to test the code to the breaking point. Thus he saw to it that other white men, his customers at the shop, treated Wylie with a difference which must have galled them, and to Wylie said that if any of them gave him any trouble outside the shop, to let him know. With himself, of course, he expected Wylie to know his place. Wylie had gained my mother's approval by never turning his back on her, or on any other white woman. He bowed himself away from her back door. He mistered me. We took such deference as our due. We never questioned that Wylie did, too. Just one thing bothered me. I liked Wylie to an unacceptable degree, beyond what was tolerated. I had heard the term "niggerlover" and the contempt and hatred with which it was spoken. I had to be on guard against letting my fondness for Wylie show. In town, that is—another reason for my love of the woods. There, with no one to see us, we could be more free and easy with one another.

Whenever my father got to feeling that too many other hunters were poaching on his preserve, it was Wylie he took with him—and, once, me—there to find and bring out something to put a little caution into them.

The time they took me with them it was early fall. We boated in. We were going in deep. Because alligators, although there is the occasional odd man-eater, mostly shun people widely. We took with us a live duck in a cage. It was one of the flock of wild mallards that my father kept penned in our backyard for use as decoys.

A boat seemed hardly to be wanted on that water. It was so thick, so motionless with mud, it looked as though it could more easily be walked upon. The river led straight through the woods like an aisle, and down it we passed as silently as barefoot believers, our shoes left outside on the temple porch. When we had paddled a short distance, it was as though a door had closed behind us, shutting out the sounds of the world: a door as heavy as a temple's, a silence in which to have spoken would have been an irreverence. Yet it was not an empty but a populous silence, an attentive, even an inquisitive silence, one sensed. I felt myself to be an explorer, a discoverer. To have been met around a bend by a band of unknown Indians, holdouts in this, their last fastness, would not have astonished me.

The stillness, the sea-calm silence: that was the thing that struck me first about the deep woods, and which as it steadily deepened, steadily challenged and put in doubt my sense of myself, of everything. Timelessness hung like a vacuum over that vast, unvisited domain. For me, time was associated with sound, inseparable from it: the chatter and bustle of human affairs, the dependable chiming of my town clock, which I had heard within, at most, an hour after coming into the world, and with the comforting conviction that others were regulating their lives in synchrony with mine. Time was people, social life, the sharing with others of measured portions of the day, at school, at work, at play. Time was schedules to meet, anniversaries, celebrations, communions. This journey into silence was a journey into timelessness. And since time was commitments, responsibilities, I understood as never before the lure of these timeless woods for that half-wild father of mine.

We were wet from getting into the water to lift the boat over fallen logs that stretched from bank to bank. In places the river parted the cane that grew as thick as hair down to the water's edge. At our approach, herons white as linen napkins and folded together in pleats unfolded themselves and rose stiffly into flight. A flock of buzzards hung high overhead, moving with us as though we had them on strings, like kites. The trees grew in height as we penetrated deeper into the woods, giving the sense that we were descending an ever-deepening and darkening canyon. Wherever a limb overhung the water we stopped and inspected it carefully before passing under it. More than once we found what we feared: a moccasin stretched along it. The thing would gape at us, baring its fangs, the unearthly whiteness of its mouth, then slide leisurely from the limb and drop to the water like a large, ripe, poison fruit. As big around as a man's calf, some of them were.

We lunched in the boat on cheese, canned sardines, deviled ham, beans, chocolate bars—the provisions of boys playing hooky from school—then paddled on.

It was fun to frighten oneself with the thought that a volley of arrows might come any minute from out of the bushes along the banks. Much more real was the sense of being the first of one's kind ever seen here—such a curiosity as to stop the birds in their flight, the animals on their rounds. We had left behind all that made us familiar to ourselves. Although I was older and bigger now than ever before, the vastness and the changeless antiquity of the place made me feel very small and very, very young.

We pitched camp early enough to kill our supper. I was of an age now to be allowed to go off hunting on my own —of an age to know when I had reached the end of my tether, which was, within call of my father's hunting horn. This was an old steer's horn, gnawed by mice. When it was time to call me in, my father put it to the right-hand corner of his mouth, compressed his lips, puffed his cheeks, and out came a sound that carried in the stillness of the woods like a ship's horn in a fog. To me it was as welcome as its mother's call to a strayed calf. He sounded it at intervals until I found my way to him.

We divided the camp chores among us. Wylie set the trotline, my father skinned the squirrels, I gathered wood. Together we peeled the onions and potatoes, scraped the carrots. While the stew simmered over the fire, the men drank whiskey. Night brought the woods to life with sounds. It was after dark that time was measured here: in the regular hooting of the owl. In bed after supper I felt my father reach over me and touch Wylie. I too had heard what he had heard; now I understood what it was. The distant bellow of a bull alligator, like some dinosaurian yawn in the night.

The men woke in the morning gray-faced with whiskers. This made them look even more ghostly as we all went about our chores in the gray light that filtered down to us from the narrow opening between the trees high overhead. Breakfast was fried catfish taken from the trotline, sweet black coffee. We broke camp and were on the water by sunup.

Now every twist in the river carried us farther from all we knew and were. No likelihood of being met by Indians here, hostile or friendly. Even the cries of the birds and animals that occasionally broke the silence were strange —surely they came from creatures different from the ones in the alphabet book. And yet along with the sense of deepening strangeness came a sense of familiarity, as though one had been here before, but in another life. Then the cries of the animals seemed parts of speech, the language that had been spoken in that other existence, and we were led on by the feeling that soon, perhaps around one more turn, that long-forgotten, universal mother tongue would all come back to us. Here, untended since our expulsion from it, was surely the Garden that once was ours, where we had given the creatures their names. A little farther on, those names would recur to us, and they would all come meekly in answer to our call.

Late that second afternoon we found the sign we were looking for. Holes—big holes—dug into the riverbank. We made camp, but not near our find.

Come meekly in answer to his name—the beast I heard that night? Vast as the woods were, they were filled by the bellows that began when darkness was deep. It was as if the thing wished to be heard in the outside world—and as if it had a mouth adequate to the wish. Listening to it, lying close beside my father and feeling his intentness, I sensed in him regions as vast, as wild, as unknown to me as the wilderness we had come through to get to this spot. Other men, from time immemorial, had cautiously avoided this place; what drew him in here to disturb the thing that made that dreadful noise? It was a sound both hideous and oddly pitiful—like the groan of some monstrosity, some horrendous mistake of nature, a creature of the darkest night, afraid to catch sight of itself or even of its misshapen shadow by day, raging against its own unbearable brutishness and the intolerable isolation to which it had been consigned.

We returned to the spot on the riverbank early next morning. Now we carried with us two long poles, two saplings that the men had felled and trimmed and pointed at one end. They put me on the bank opposite from and a short distance upstream of the holes, then rowed themselves across. They took off their clothes and put them in the boat, keeping on their tennis shoes.

When they were stripped to the skin it was as though the two men had been picked to illustrate a lecture on the difference between the races, to show nature's vast variety. Wylie was as black as my father was white, and each extreme accentuated the other. Both were an absence of color, and seemed to have been cut out from the surroundings, leaving their outlines. Rather broad outlines they were. No longer the slender young man who married my mother, my father now weighed around one hundred sixty. Wylie was somewhere near the same. Two short, thickset, muscular little men—big men in miniature.

They loaded their .30-30 carbines, feeding the first cartridge into the chamber, seven more into the magazine. The loaded rifles were stood against trees at a distance from each other. The poles were planted in the bank.

The duck was taken from its cage and launched, and, as decoy ducks always did, tried to fly. Paddling rapidly to get up speed for the takeoff and beating the water with its clipped wings, it succeeded only in churning up a commotion. Suddenly it sank. It did not turn tail up and dive as ducks do; it sank. One moment it was there, then, quicker than it could quack, it was gone. At that same moment there was a loud splash, or rather, two, and gone from the bank were the men.

They were under for a long time. First to surface was Wylie. A moment passed. Then for a second the surface swelled, as I had seen it do when a creek is dynamited: that instant after the detonation and before the eruption. Then out of the water and high into the air burst my father, hanging on to something long and live and in a convulsion of rage.

He had hold of an alligator fully nine feet long by its short forelegs, as one might pin a man's arms behind him. Wylie threw himself in their direction, and in the split second that the furiously lashing tail was away from him, lunged and grabbed the hind legs. The animal writhed, twisted, heaved. Firemen trying to hold on to the biggest and most powerful water hose were never more flung about, for the animal's power exceeded that, and it had a will behind it and a brain, always brutish, always hostile, now enraged. There was no letting go; they were joined to the thing; both had to hold on—hold on truly for dear life. Having recovered breath, both were laughing, between their grunts, as though they were having the time of their lives.

They wrestled that bundle of fury to the bank and heaved it out of the water. Sure as a cat, it landed on its feet, and like a cat it arched itself for battle. No step either toward the water or the woods did it take. It stood its ground.

It looked antediluvian, the one creature too totally malevolent to be taken aboard the Ark, a monster from out of the primeval slime, gratefully thought long extinct. For a moment, until it moved, it looked clumsy. Not confounded—anything but: alert throughout its length; but out of its element, ponderous, ill-equipped for dry land. Not so; it was highly adaptable. It circled now, seeking its enemy, and its motions were as sure as though it moved on treads—truly amphibious: an all-purpose engine of destruction, designed to be invulnerable. Armor-plated with a scaly hide as hard as horn and triply armed it was, formidable from every approach, with its powerful long tail, the claws of its huge, half-webbed feet, the terrible teeth of its enormous chops bared in a zestfully malicious, a murderous grin. Its forelegs folded like elbows, its hind legs like knees; it stood like a man lying on his stomach about to do a push-up. Now it straightened and stiffened its legs, erecting itself to its full fighting height. It hissed as loud as a steam locomotive and the spray of muddy water from its nostrils made it appear to be snorting smoke. The grating together of the scales of its tail as it lashed from side to side made a swish in the air like a volley of bullets. It stood its ground, ready and a match for anything that lived, superb in its fearsomeness.

Its only moment of irresolution came when the two men clambered onto the bank and it had to choose which one to go for first. It went for Wylie. And its gaping jaws made it appear to be guffawing at the puniness of its opponent. Wylie had plucked his pole out of the ground and now he jabbed the creature with it as it stalked him. Undeterred, it attacked, bellowing, hissing, its tail lashing steadily to ward off the enemy at its back, all the while making that metallic, multiscaled sound like the rustle of a coat of mail. As it forced Wylie back and back I expected to see my father go for his rifle, but he was enjoying the sport and instead he gave the creature a whack on its tail with his pole and a bellow in imitation of its own. It answered with a bellow, swiveled around and advanced, hissing hideously, on him, its tail keeping that wide swath cleared behind it. Now my father jousted with it while Wylie harried it with whoops and hollers.

Like a pair of matadors they teased it by turns, working it into a fit of fury. It seemed to grow, to swell with the mounting pressure of its frustration and to become still more menacing and terrible. Quicker, too.

It made a dash at my father. He thrust at it with his pole. Flinching, it retreated, then before my father could ready another thrust, it had his pole, snapped it with a bite, and as it came on toward him seemed to be grinning for the kill. In dashed Wylie from behind. But it was intent now upon its disarmed enemy and not to be distracted by the blows, thick and heavy as they were, on its back. They sounded as though they were falling on something as solid and insensitive as a turtle's shell.

My father was running backward but the animal was fast closing the gap that divided them, its jaws gaping wide, when Wylie found a vulnerable spot. Where the hind leg joined the body his spear drew blood. Blood, and with it, the loudest bellow yet. The animal turned on him. My father turned and sprinted for his rifle.

Goaded to a frenzy of hate and frustration, the animal propelled itself at Wylie, who dropped his spear, turned and ran for his rifle. He had not reached it when my father, with his, leaped over that constantly lashing tail and came down astride the animal, firing even before he touched the ground. Though it stopped, the animal gaped hugely, reared so high on its talons that it looked as though my father was riding on its back and it was trying to throw him, then gave its tail a lash that seemed meant to demolish all the world behind it. Then its legs folded and it sank upon itself, its weight forcing its jaws shut.

As the two men, like naked savages, did their victory dance around it, whooping and yelling and pounding each other's backs, the alligator's tail died segment by segment, down to the tip. When that final bit stopped twitching and death distended the animal, it flattened and widened on the ground, its relaxation causing its teeth to grate for one last time.

Afterward, when I asked my father whether he had not been scared, he said, yes, very. I disbelieved that of my father, but I was grateful to him for saying it. It took some of the taint of childishness off the fear I had felt.

Placed on exhibit at the garage with its jaws propped open, that dragon was more effective than signs posted all around Sulphur Bottom saying DANGER. KEEP OUT. C. HUMPHREY, PROP.

# The Guns of Boyhood

Out of the east Texas woods came the first money the boy ever earned. In the barn on one of the places they stayed on he found a few rusty old steel traps. These he baited and set in the sloughs and the bayous. He trapped muskrats, coons, an occasional red or gray fox. He ran his line in the morning before beginning his day's work. Lacking a gun, he carried a club to kill the animals with.

He made stretchers for his skins, sawing them from a plank and rounding one end and smoothing the edges with a piece of bottle glass. The skins were removed whole, like a pullover sweater, stretched over the boards and the flesh and the fat scraped off. When they were fleshed they were salted; when dried stiff, removed from the boards. He sold his skins to the keeper of the cross-roads store at Lone Star.

To the store at that season of the year came a special class of men—or men whom the season lifted out of their class and into a special one. Not there now for the dull business of trading, these men were hunters. The contrast between them and his own plodding, pleasureless father shamed the boy. Some of these men were share-croppers themselves, but they had in them a spark that his father lacked—that spark of response to a world beyond grubbing and hoeing in the dirt, a quality that took them out of themselves and into something bigger, older, and longer-lasting than themselves. Each pursuing the most solitary of pastimes, there was yet a feeling of fraternity among them. Their dogs were hunting dogs, not dooryard mutts, with bloodlines like nobility, bred and trained, with that look of the pampered and idle, the sporting class. Some of them had reputations countywide. Leaning against the wall of the store would be the hunters' guns. The boy dared not look at them as long as he would have liked. If no hunter appeared while he and his father were there, he could gaze at the two or three old muzzle-loaders that the storekeeper had for sale, battered veterans with the stocks splintered at the grip, held together with wire—even these hopelessly beyond his dream of owning. He gave serious thought to stealing one, was deterred by his certainty that his longing for one, which he supposed must emanate from him like musk, would point the finger of suspicion directly at him.

The little money he got for the sale of his skins kept alive his dream of one day owning a gun. A gun would free him, make him independent, self-reliant, and would arm him to resist recapture. With a gun he could run away from home and never be brought back. Good-bye to chores, to chopping and picking cotton, cutting wood. He would live like an Indian—which in part he was—live in and off the woods. He would make himself clothes from the skins of animals, shoes from their hides. What he required that the woods could not provide, he would steal, like the Indians, like the animals themselves. He would come out of the woods at night as the coons and foxes did and raid his father's cornpatch, his mother's kitchen garden. When he got to wanting a chicken he would steal one from the chicken house. And for his one essential, ammunition for his gun, he would trade—trap and trade skins.

Sitting on the gallery of the store or inside around the stove, the hunters complained of the scarcity of game. They remembered when they were able in half a day, in a half-mile walk, to fill a buckboard.

No wonder the boy had to go in deep to find them. What did they expect? For the animals never to learn, to adapt, to keep on coming back generation after generation for the slaughter? To keep coming back to woods that were thinned further each year, where there was less for them to feed on, less cover to hide in, more hunters than ever out to kill them?

"Go in there deep enough," someone always said, "and you'll still find them."

And someone else: "Yeah, but who's going to find you?"

The boy listened, solemn-faced, wide-eyed, unnoticed, and kept his silence. It was not for one his age to claim to know more than grown men knew. Besides, he was not aware of what he knew. By then he knew things about the woods that he did not know he knew, and certainly not that he was the only one who knew.

And so he was as surprised as the men, and possibly as skeptical, when the storekeeper said, "That boy there. Him there" (for it was possible in a sweep of the eyes to miss him)—"he can take you anywhere you want to go in there. What's more, he can bring you out again."

He looked hardly big enough to know his way home. But maybe if you did not take him far enough to tire out his short legs, so that you wound up having to carry him out on your back, he could make himself useful, in the absence of a dog, as your turner. You required a turner, hunting squirrels: a boy or a noisy dog to go around to the other side of the tree and keep the squirrel from turning as you turned and keeping the trunk between you, as one would do by the hour if the tree was an isolated one and it could not leap to another.

So he began to go into the woods with them, and hunters coming back with game bags fuller than they had been in years said to the storekeeper, "That boy is a cutter!" Then men he never saw before, from Clarksville, Bogata, Detroit, Fulbright, would ask for him, that little button-eyed, cotton-headed tyke that could take you in there and put you on game stands like you never saw before, and who could outlast you, was sorry to come in when you were ready to quit. His father even excused him from some work, because he took from the boy the dime or the two-bits he was tipped for his services. He was still as far from a gun as ever while craving one all the more, having had a taste of it, when he was sometimes allowed by a hunter to shoot his.

The boy's father was one of those row-crop farmers with no feeling but hostility for land not cleared, productive, profitable. He longed for a piece of farmland of his own so much, and so hopelessly, that he resented that worthless woodland of which a wilderness surrounded him. From such a father, a boy longing for a gun could hope for no sympathy, not even if he had had the money to give him for one. Too poor to buy a gun, even to hope to buy one so long as he was only a boy and not earning wages, son of a man who himself held cash money in his hand just once a year—and then just long enough to take it from the cotton buyer to the owner of the general store who had provisioned him on credit since the same time a year ago—the boy realized that there was only one way for him to satisfy his longing.

A breechloader, using factory-made shells, was beyond him. Boughten shells using smokeless powder were too powerful, required a gun made of proof steel, a firing chamber capable of withstanding great gas pressure, a moving block, a firing pin too complex for his tools, his skill. But in those days there were still in use a great many old percussion cap and ball muzzle-loaders, and stores still stocked black powder, caps, and bulk shot for them.

His father had tools and a forge, as did every farmer, for home blacksmithing jobs, and the boy, already mechanical, was always using them to make himself something or other. No notice was taken, no questions asked about what he was up to now. Questions from his father, or mother for that matter, about what he was up to usually got no response anyway.

He found a length of small-gauge iron pipe threaded and capped at one end. Its thickness made it heavy and so he dressed it down with a file. Only a child or a life-term prisoner, a sailor or a lighthouse keeper would have had the patience. He filed a hammer and trigger out of a bar of scrap iron, shaped a lock and fitted it with a flat spring. Three stocks he had to carve, with grooves for the barrel and the ramrod, before he got one right. He forged two barrel bands from harness rings. From the hickory handle of a worn-out hoe he whittled a ramrod. He made himself a powderhorn. By then he had turned thirteen.

On his annual trip into Clarksville to the gin that fall he brought the metal parts with him, secreting them beneath the wagon bed. He took them to a machinist in town. He ordered the man to drill and tap a hole in the barrel and insert in it the threaded nipple for the caps, drill screw holes in the lock. Fingering in his pocket the dollar and a quarter that was his capital, he asked how much he owed. The man refused payment. He would repay that mechanic's favor to him many times over by making and repairing in his own shop anything he could that any boy in town asked him to.

It was the last of his many guns that he would really care for. He used a gun hard, taking care only of its mechanism, not its looks, and when one was used up, got another one. So long as one came to his shoulder right, functioned mechanically, he cared little or nothing about its appearance. His were strange-looking things, built like he himself was built: sawed-off. Not at the muzzle, but at the butt. Standing, a gun of his looked as though it was resting in a hole. The reach of his arms was short; to accommodate it, he sawed about three inches off his gunstock. This made the gun muzzle-heavy, but the muzzle could not be shortened without removing the choke. To compensate, he drilled holes in the stock beneath the butt plate and filled them with lead. Once that was done to a gun, he was deadly with it.

The boy hid his finished muzzle-loader in the rafters of the barn. Next time his father drove to the store he went along with a bundle of skins which he meant to trade, on the sly, for powder, caps, and shot. He clambered up the wheel spokes, onto the hub and over the sideboard, and he saw lying on the wagon bed, beneath the seat, his gun.

He took his place on the seat. As they were crossing the bridge over Scatter Creek, his father whoaed to the team. He reached under the seat, brought out the gun and flung it into the creek. Whereupon, from his side of the bridge, the boy flung his bundle of skins into the creek. His father flicked the reins and the team moved on.

My heart broke for the poor boy when my father told me this story. He laughed. "He" (meaning his father) "was right," he said. "I doubt" (trans: I do not doubt) "that thing would have blown up and killed me the first time I pulled the trigger."

My first shotgun cost a nickel. One chance on the punchboard in a diner on the Paris road where my father stopped one day just when it was getting time his boy, about to turn twelve—which was to say, going on thirteen—had a shotgun and learned how to use it. It was a four-shot bolt-action .410—the smallest of all the gauges. Being the lightest to carry, the cheapest to shoot, and the one with the least kick, it was the gauge boys were apprenticed on. From that beginning the grades up were 20, 16, and 12. It ought to have been just the other way round. Throwing the smallest charge and carrying the least far, the .410 ought to have been the gun for the most refined wing shot—the one in a thousand who is born, not made.

Now instead of stationary targets I began shooting at moving ones, or rather, I followed with the gun waiting for them to stop moving and become stationary. Finally, before the bird flew out of range or the rabbit hopped out of sight, I fired, and watched it fly on, hop faster.

"You're trying to aim. Don't. You've got to shoot at where it's going to be," my father told me. "If you shoot at it, then you've shot at where it just was." For my age I was a pretty good rifleman—and for a wing shot I was a pretty good rifleman. To my father it was being a wing shot that separated the men from the boys. He was the best of them all, and I, his only son, his sole hope for a successor, could not get the hang of it. My father was patient with me but I was impatient with myself.

During my twelfth summer I would meet my father at the garage at quitting time and we would drive out of town to the nearby farms where mourning doves flocked to feed on the sorghum and the durum and to the stock ponds to drink. That was the summer I shared with my chum Pete Hinkle a passion for casting, painting, and warring with lead soldiers, and after a day of this, Pete sometimes went with my father and me dove shooting. I was not embarrassed to have Pete see me miss time after time, for Pete was no better shot than I was, though with his gun, a 20-gauge double barrel, he ought to have been.

We crouched in the tall grass at the edge of the pond, the telltale white of our faces shaded by long cap-bills. A whistle from my father signaled the approach of a bird: one if from the left, two from the right. He gave first chance at every bird that winged in to us, and Pete and I took turns missing them, sometimes missing the same one in turn, before my father brought it down. It ran head-on into the charge of shot waiting for it in the air, crumpled and fell. It was left to lie where it fell. When the day was over, Pete and I gathered them up like nuts from a thrashed tree, wading for those fallen into the pond, searching for the others among the grass, my father directing us to them, he having marked them down, and kept tally of the bag.

In the course of the summer both Pete and I unavoidably got a little better at it. I began to think that the knack was not hopelessly beyond me after Pete lent me his gun a few times. My improvement with the 20-gauge raised my self-confidence and I shot better with my own gun. I had learned what deceptive birds doves are. They looked slow and as if they ought to be easy to hit but they were fast and their flight erratic and unpredictable, capable of sudden acceleration, full of dips and flares, tricky as a pilot dodging flak. You swung from behind, passed it firing and followed through, stringing out the charge in a path on the air ahead of the bird. And you still missed a great many more than you hit.

My performance on doves qualified me to be taken quail shooting in the fall. For, although quail are actually easier to hit than doves, they occupy a higher niche in the hierarchy of game birds, possibly because of their comparative scarcity, possibly because they are more prized on the plate. Whatever the reason, the rule is immemorial and inviolable: doves are boys's game, quail men's.

But I could not hit them. On this superior bird, this man's game, and being privileged for the first time to shoot over dogs, I did less well than I had done on doves. The joy of shooting over field dogs had been impressed upon me but it was something that until now I had had to take on faith from my father, just as I took on faith (although about this I had reservations) that the time would come when I would enjoy doing what he had recently told me men did with women.

His bird dogs at that time—"ours," he now began calling them—were Mack and Kate, brother and sister English setters, he white speckled with black, she black spotted with white. Though still young, they were, in my father's opinion, already the best dogs he had ever owned. They were completing their training as I was commencing mine. We could look forward to years of pleasure out of them.

He was right about the joy of watching good bird dogs at work—maybe about that other business too, then. To see Mack and Kate divide a field between them in quarters and cover its every yard, their tails like flags for us to follow, watch one of them suddenly brake, stiffen, straighten its tail, and the other one then come to honor its set, to watch them inch up on the covey just enough to hold it, not enough to flush it, was as thrilling as my father had told me it was.

That was my job: to flush the covey, and it was one reason I could not hit the birds. They could never be seen until they broke, for they were the color of autumn, of nature: of dead leaves, dry grass, twigs, mottled rocks, sunshine and shadow, and, up to the last moment, they could hug the earth as though made of it. When I kicked and they burst at my feet it was as though I had stepped on a land mine. Like shell fragments they went whirring off in all directions. Their flight was low to the ground and short. You had to be steady, cool and quick, and I could never recover from my shock in time to get off a sensible shot before they had all pitched to the ground. To think of ever being able to drop one, then swing on a second, even a third, on a single rise, as my father did consistently, seemed as unlikely for me as did that other business. The long fall season reached closing day without my having cleanly killed a single bird. Some at which we had both fired my father credited to me, but he was just being fond.

By then—closing day—no longer was the burst at my feet when I kicked quite so explosive. The big coveys, disbanded by gunning, thinned by predators, were broken up into singles, doubles, triples now. Still, I was sluggish in my reflexes, and instead of pointing my gun, I pottered.

We had had the morning to hunt. Now it was almost noon and we were working our way back to the car, my father's game pockets, as always, bulging, mine, as always, empty, when, emerging from a woods into a clearing, the two dogs simultaneously set. Tails stiff and straight out behind them, heads high, they seemed to be holding the birds transfixed by their steady stare.

When I kicked, three birds flushed, two one way, one another. So rapid were my father's two shots that they seemed one, and to each a bird, in a burst of feathers, fell. I in my pottering way was following the lone bird, when my father swiveled, found it, and fired. He scored a clean miss. I fired, and in a third burst of feathers on the air, that bird fell.

I acted as though I was used to doing it daily. So did my father, and he was offhand in his congratulations to me. But he was almost visibly puffed with pride. That he himself had missed the bird doubled his pleasure.

Forgotten were the uncountable number of quail he had brought down in his time whenever he told the story of that one of mine. Before long he was omitting to mention the two he had gotten on that rise before I killed the one he had shot at and missed.

Counting my one, we took home fifty-three quail that day. Game was not a treat for us, it was the staple of our diet; butcher's meat was the rarity in our house. My girl-mother, until late in the night, plucking birds into a washtub and sneezing as the feathers or the down tickled her nose, is one of my most vivid images of her, as is the one of my father stepping on the tail of a squirrel and peeling it out of its skin. Despite my mother's thoroughness as a housekeeper, pinfeathers and wisps of fur floated around doorjambs and lingered in corners of our house. The habit of watching for bird shot in my meat was so ingrained in me that I sometimes forgot and did it while eating fried chicken.

Yet it would have surprised my father to be called a gamehog. He was simply providing for his family. To the question, "What if everybody killed as many as you do?" he would have answered, "But not everybody does" (refraining out of modesty from saying, "*Nobody* does"), and would have expected that answer to quiet the fears of anybody concerned (in those days few were) over the future of wildlife. He had heard men complain about the scarcity of game, but he had been hearing that all his life, and always from the same ones: those who were not very good hunters. There were good years and bad years, as there had always been, as there were for any of nature's crops. The long recent drought had had an effect, but that was coming to an end now, and once the birds and the animals rebuilt their numbers, we would see good times again.

\* \* \*

That one closing-day quail of mine earned me the right to be taken a time or two that winter to shoot over the water, at the game bird supreme: wild ducks. Only a time or two, for duck shooting is where not merely the boys but the lesser men are separated from the men. Not just because ducks are the hardest to hit of all moving targets, but also because duck shooting is done under conditions demanding uncommon patience, stamina, and strength.

The use of live decoys in shooting ducks had been outlawed the previous year, or maybe the one before that; but my father was never a strict observer of any of the game laws. In this he was not alone among hunters in our parts—just the most flagrant violator. Game laws were unenforceable there in those times. No effort was even made to enforce them. The post of warden, if not vacant, was held by somebody I had never heard of. Somebody who wisely worked not very hard at the job. To have done so would have made a man highly unpopular there where men had always hunted for meat, and took it as their fundamental and inalienable right to go hunting whenever they felt like it and to be limited in their kill by nothing but their own prowess—and where judges and juries agreed with them wholeheartedly. Gentlemen sportsmen are not found on the frontier; and although the frontier was gone, and my father was one of those responsible, men like him had yet to learn this. Federal laws like those protecting migratory game birds they thought were something applicable to the other states of the Union, perhaps, but not to Texas.

My father kept his flock of live decoys in our backyard
—whenever we moved, they moved with us—and he still
drove through the square with them quacking loudly in
their cage affixed to the rear of the Model T touring car
he used for hunting, and which could get with equal ease
through the mud of Sulphur Bottom or the sand spread
thickly for miles by the Red River in its periodic risings.
Mallards, his were: three dozen of them, the imbalance
between the sexes favoring hens over drakes. Siren
songs they quacked to their former fellows.

The wildfowler loves foul weather. Then the birds are
on the wing. When days are short they must be active
during the few daylight feeding hours. Rain and fog
hamper their vision. Fearing freezing of their feeding
grounds, they are on the move. The gunner endures
these conditions in order to take advantage of the pressures they put on the birds. Always on my initiatory
expeditions to the Red River, it had been raining, was
raining, and was going to rain—cold, cutting rain, often
mixed with sleet, with a steady north wind driving it.

Even the Model T could get us only so near the water.
From our stopping place we proceeded on foot—all
thirty-eight of us.

My father had rigged a stout cord, like a trotline, to
which every few feet, instead of a fishhook, was attached
a snap swivel. Each duck was banded on one leg, and like
convicts in a chain gang marshaled out of their van and
manacled and marched to their work on the road, they
were snapped to this cord—we two their shotgunned
guards. Leading the column was always the same bird, an
old drake that had established himself as gang-boss.

When the decoys were on the water we took our places

in the blind, my father wiping out behind us with a bough the footprints we had left in the wet sand. The blind was a pit dug into a sandbar and slant-roofed with reeds. To see out, I stood on a crate.

Our watch of the gray skies would go long unrewarded. Then out of the mist they would suddenly appear like a squadron of fighter planes in formation streaking to intercept the enemy. Immune to the seductive quacking of our decoys, some, high out of range, swept on. But another flock would bank and turn, circle, circle again more narrowly, dip, dive, and then you could hear the whistle of their wings as they swooped low overhead. "Pintails," my father would whisper, or "Mallards." What he said that gave him the most satisfaction was, "Canvasbacks!"

He considered that the new law limiting duck shooters to three shots, one in the firing chamber and two in the magazine, was also for those who chose to obey it. As he always had, he carried five in his hammerless pump 12-gauge with the long, full-choked barrel, and I was to see him drop five birds on one pass, beginning with the hindmost and working forward so the flock could not count its losses.

When hit, ducks did not fold up and tumble down. Their speed seemed hardly to slow. They sailed on in a steadily falling trajectory and crashed into the water like a plane with its pilot dead at the controls.

The newly established daily limit on ducks was twenty-five. Since I was not able to fill mine myself, my father did it for me. That was only fair, as I was a beginner, and handicapped, undergunned. I tried my father's big gun and did no better with it than with the .410, getting nothing but a bruised shoulder in reward. I never minded. I was started now, in me my father was rediscovering the joys of just starting, and under his eager tutelage I was sure to show steady improvement.

On mornings when my father took me hunting with him we would get to the woods at about the hour my mother and I had gotten to the Paris hospital in the ambulance with him that morning. But in the woods it would seem like the hour just before Creation. It was as if God said again each day, "Let there be light." Looking just as they must have on the first day, the woods took shape out of the void. The change seemed chemical, like a photographic print in the developer in the dimness of the darkroom, the image appearing out of nothingness, then rapidly becoming distinct, recognizable, familiar. The transformation in my father seemed chemical, too. Perhaps even more in recent years, when illness and disappointment and worry had borne him down, that old boyish wonder of his whenever he went to the woods made a boy of him again. In me he saw the boy he once had been and then for a time he was one again himself. My oneness with him gave me some of his sense of oneness with that world.

He and I had long ago dispensed with talk while hunting. I knew what was expected of me. If, for instance, we were there now, as soon as the woods were light I would have crept around to the other side of that oak, and that first squirrel that came out to feed and chatter would now be lying on the ground, brought down by that keen right eye that would never look down a gun barrel again.

*Birds of a Feather*

It was in the foyer of the Metropolitan Opera House at Lincoln Center in New York, during an intermission between acts of Verdi's *Don Carlo,* that I first met Paul de Nemeskeri-Kiss. He was there as the guest of his daughter Ursula, I as the guest of Ursula's boss, the producer of the Met's satellite telecasts, my friend Klaus Hallig.

It was a Saturday matinee that we were attending, yet it was the premiere of this production, and thus many were there in evening clothes. The chandeliers turned day into night. Chagall's giant mural looked down upon us. A more unlikely setting could hardly have been found for a conversation about woodcock hunting. But in the taxi en route from our hotel to Lincoln Center, Ursula, who had come with our tickets to pick us up, had told me that her father was to be there—this was her parents' wedding anniversary—and that, like me, he was an enthusiastic outdoor sportsman. In fact, said she, he was a fanatic.

I had nothing, not a word, to say about woodcock hunting, because I had never in my life done it. Though I have spent much time outdoors since then, not since I was a small boy, in Texas, many, many years ago, had I ever seen a woodcock, and even then I had seen but few —the few that my father brought home from a day afield when quail were what he was really after. That was more than most people had ever seen; indeed, most people went through life unaware of the bird's very existence, this man said.

Hunting was in his blood, as it was in mine, I learned during the few minutes of that intermission. His father had been gamekeeper to Admiral von Horthy. Since Admiral Horthy had been the between-the-wars regent of Hungary, that made him the overseer of thousands upon thousands of acres of forests and fields. In these, on a diet of game, this man had grown up. With his father he had hunted and killed roebuck, chamois, boar, wolves, Hungarian partridge, the legendary *auerhahn* which men spend their whole lives hoping to get a shot at one specimen of. After the war he came to America, did postgraduate studies in engineering at Columbia University, and went to work for the then one and only telephone company. From this job he would retire next year. Then all his time would be his to fish and hunt. Of both sports he liked all kinds, but of the first he liked best to fly-fish for trout and of the second, well, it was hard to choose, but perhaps best of all he liked woodcock hunting.

The season for this year was just over, as of this very week. For him it had been a good one. Eighty-five birds. Whereabouts did he do his hunting? In several places as the season progressed, beginning upstate in the Helderberg Mountains, Albany County, then in the Catskills and down along the Hudson, then in Jersey, following the bird in its annual migration southward. Except for Jersey, those were places not far from where I lived and where I too fished and hunted; yet I had never seen a woodcock anywhere in them. Was I a wing shot? Well, I did a bit of duck shooting on the river, otherwise I got little chance to practice on anything in these game-poor times except clay pigeons.

Before the bell rang to summon us back to our seats for the next act of the opera, he invited me to go woodcock hunting with him next year. I accepted with an easy mind, knowing I need not worry about being put to shame shooting along with a man who could kill eighty-five birds in a season. You learn to take lightly such long-range and indefinite invitations made at such times and under such circumstances. You will never hear from that person again. You won't even mind that you don't. In the course of a year he will have forgotten all about it, and so will you.

"Paul what?" I asked.

"I don't know," said my wife. "I've asked him to repeat it twice and I still don't understand. I can't ask him to tell me a fourth time."

If she had asked twice then I could not ask once, so it was not until the word "woodcock" was mentioned, and not for another moment even then, that I was able to connect the man on the phone with the man I had met at the Met. It was ten months since that meeting. I felt somewhat ashamed of my initial doubtfulness.

Triggered by cold in Canada, the flights had begun, according to reports reaching him from his scouts in the field. Now the question was, what had our weather been lately? Had we had rain? That was essential. For if the ground was dry and hard, the earthworms burrowed deep and the birds quickly moved on south in search of them elsewhere. It was raining at that very moment, had been raining off and on for days. The ground was well soaked. I had seen earthworms on the paved roads. Then we would meet a week from today. He named the time, 9:00 a.m., and the place, a motel across the river—that is to say, on the western bank—and a few miles north of me.

"Why not come and stay overnight with us?" I asked.

"I'll have the dogs with me. The people at the motel don't mind if they sleep with me, as they do here at home. Your wife might not like that—at least, until she gets to know them."

Our call concluded, I called my friend Klaus to learn the man's name.


Never expecting to go woodcock hunting, I knew nothing whatever about the bird, its habits, its habitat. Now in just a week I was to go in armed pursuit of it, in the company of a man of great experience. I must not impose upon him a thoroughgoing ignoramus.

From books and articles in the local public library I learned in that week all that I could, cramming as I used to do for school exams. The first thing I learned was why I knew so little about the bird.

It is not because its numbers are sparse that the woodcock is so seldom seen. It is by no means a rare or a narrowly distributed bird; on the contrary, its range is wide, extending throughout all the states east of the Mississippi and into southeastern Canada, it is quite prolific, and, despite its many predators—crows, owls, shrikes, hawks, foxes, bobcats, house cats, dogs, skunks, raccoons, weasels, squirrels, snakes, human hunters, and those threats common to all wildlife, diseases, pesticides, parasites, land developers—it is in no immediate danger of becoming endangered; the cock is a regular lech and the hen, a conscientious, even a formidably protective, mother, succeeds in bringing to maturity most of her annual brood of four. The chicks are adept at foraging for themselves from a precocious age. The reasons that woodcock are so seldom seen are two. The bird is inactive during the daylight hours, and it is so perfectly camouflaged that you might step on one never knowing it was there. Even in a photograph of one you must stare for a long time before it emerges, materializes out of its natural setting, for it is woven warp and woof of the same overall russet yet parti-colored, finely figured, motley pattern. The regularity of its feathering matches the irregularity of a leaf-littered forest floor in the fall.

The woodcock is nocturnal—even more of a creature of concealment by night than are the owls, for, unlike an owl, it does not give away its presence by a call—except during its mating ritual, and that is not during hunting season but in the spring. No wonder most people go through life never knowing of its existence! A silent creature of the night. In most parts of our country it is a transient, appearing briefly—or rather, slipping in unobserved—in the spring to mate and nest, then moving on farther north, not to reappear—and then only to pass through—until the fall, on its southward migration, all this under cover of darkness, in silence, nothing resembling the honking of wild geese announcing their arrivals and departures like passenger trains, and not in flocks, like other migratory birds, but singly or in small groups at most. A shy, elusive little feathered phantom, inactive, invisible, and unsuspected by day, foraging by dawn and by dusk for the earthworms that are the staple of its diet and of which it must eat its own weight every twenty-four hours, migrating, mating in the dark, always shrouded in crepuscular obscurity. The for-centuries-extinct dodo bird is sighted about as often and by as many watchers.

When seen, the woodcock is almost as peculiar-look-ing, in his own way, as the dodo, with his long bill, his big bug-eyes, his stubby tail. His peculiarities do not stop, they only start, there. From my reading I learned that of all birds that fly (and of those that do not—some of them very strange birds) the woodcock is surely the oddest. He is, in fact, an anomaly. He is a shorebird, cousin to the snipe, who, however, long ago quit the shore and moved inland. Though sometimes in some localities called the bogsucker, he is not particularly partial to bogs, he pre-fers the lowlands of the high uplands. He does suck, however, using his long soda-straw of a bill, instead of pecking and throwing back his head to swallow, as other birds do. He gets curiouser and curiouser. His brain is upside down. His ears are in front of his nose. He flies, as I said, by night. *He* is smaller than *she* is. Biologists are skeptical, but hunters maintain that the hen bird carries her chicks in flight. Like the salmon returning from sea to spawn in the same spot where he himself was spawned, the woodcock returns north to the same mating ground every spring for as long as he lives. Showing off to attract a mate, the cock bird spirals into the air a dizzying three hundred feet.

I have said it of fishermen, I believe it to be true of hunters as well: They are attracted to a game species by a similarity of its disposition to their own. Like the woodcock, I too am an odd bird; I know I am, and I would change if I could, because being odd is uncomfortable, but, no more than the woodcock can, I can't, not anymore—it's too late even to try. My brain, I often think, must surely be upside down, so out of step with the world am I. Like the woodcock, I'm a loner. I don't sleep well of nights, either. It's true, I am bigger than my little mate, but not by much. I don't migrate from south to north annually, but I did it once, performed my courtship rites, and settled in the nest. The kind of terrain said to be favored by the woodcock is terrain of a kind I favor, too. I felt drawn to this queer little fellow creature by everything I had read about him. Birds of a feather . . . For me, there was no contradiction between that and my wanting to kill some of them. *L'uomo è cacciatore.* Though most people go through life without ever seeing one, they are quite numerous, and I would not greatly deplete their numbers. Long ago and faraway as it was, I could still recall the flavor of those my father brought home, cooked by my mother—and my wife is every bit as good a cook as my mother. But now I was eating my kill before I had killed it. I felt sure I was going to enjoy my hunt with an experienced companion, if only I did not shame myself by my shooting.

To help prevent that, I spent some time each day of that week banging away at clay pigeons thrown by the trap in the hayfield out behind my house. My wife pulled for me. She cocked the arm of the trap, placed a bird on it, I steadied myself, gun butt below my waist, running through in my mind all the things I must remember: my stance, feet the proper distance apart, left foot forward, knees slightly bent, hips loose, easily swiveled, neck craned, head forward, the gun to be brought to the cheek, not the cheek to the gun; quickly find and track the target, both eyes open; don't rush yourself, you've got more time than you think; don't aim: point; lead, pass, fire, follow through; and above all, keep your mind *off* what you're doing! don't think: shoot—then I called, "Pull!" the arm of the trap sprang, and the little flying saucer, going sixty miles an hour, sailed off into space, either to disappear with my shot in a black puff of powder or, all too often, fall to the ground intact and there shatter. For a change, I stuck to one gun, a side-by-side double-barreled 16-gauge, instead of switching from one round to another among the all too many guns, of all gauges and both side-by-side and over-and-under, that I have accumulated. Beware of the man with only one gun, goes an old saying.

It was not that I was readying myself to be competitive. I am not competitive, not in anything I do—at games the world's best loser; the attraction of field sports for me is that your rivals are yourself and your quarry, not your companion. Compete with a man who had killed eighty-five birds his previous season? One who had been doing this all his life long? I who had never once done it? My hope was just not to disgrace myself in his eyes.

With each day of that week of practice on clay pigeons my shooting steadily improved.


Perfection in anything is quickly sketched—hardly needs sketching. It would be downright dull did it not happen so rarely. Perfection is performance without fault, form without blemish. In the case of the woodcock hunter, perfection is filling his daily limit of five birds, and on our second day afield together Pauli and I both did that, each of us with just six shots. Three out of five on the average is considered good shooting.

In addition to his five woodcock, the upland hunter is allowed a daily bag of four grouse. That is to laugh. It is said that for every one flushed he will walk five miles, for every one he gets a shot at ten miles, and for every one he bags twenty miles. We reckoned that in our two days we walked—"climbed" would be the better word for what we did—our full forty miles. Their generous limit of four grouse per day is made tongue-in-cheek on the part of those jokers in the conservation department who fix it. In getting our one apiece along with our limits of woodcock Pauli and I had done ourselves proud, and we were befittingly humble.

Our second day having proved to be like that second million dollars which one is advised to make first in order to become a millionaire, let us go back now to our first day.

We were where the southernmost range of the Helderbergs meets the northernmost range of the Catskills. Land never much good for anything, hilly and rocky, it was once, long ago, for a pioneer people willing to work harder for a living than the generations that have succeeded them, hardscrabble farm country (humbling, even heartbreaking, the sight of the endless high walls of huge stones heaved up by the frosts each and every spring, lifted onto horse- and ox-drawn stoneboats, carted to the site, lifted and fitted into place, year after year after year), then for a while after that a never very fashionable summer vacationland; today it is all but abandoned, gone rank, reclaimed by its original, its primal growth, a place of long, harsh winters, late and sluggish springs, short summers, and glorious falls tinted with a spectrum of colors as replete as a painter's full-spread palette. Now the year's first gentle frosts had alchemized the landscape, transmuting into gold and old gold and golden-orange the tremulous and scintillant poplars and paper birches, to ruby red the sumacs and the swamp and sugar maples, to topaz and opal the oaks. Only the hemlocks and the pines high on the slopes surrounding us remained untouched. The medley of colors was that of a macédoine, the salad of fresh fruits of all kinds upon their bed of green.

"Bill?"

"Here!"

"Good!"

These frequent exchanges between Pauli and me, much like birdcalls, kept us posted at all times of each other's exact whereabouts. Should a bird flush wild anywhere within the fifty-odd yards we kept between us we knew where and where not to fire. When we had beaten through a covert and emerged within sight of each other, Pauli silently signaled with his hand where to turn next. He was familiar with every foot of this terrain, having hunted over it for years—the only person permitted by its owner to do so. His brain was upside down, too—a woodcock's brain, for sure. He thought like one. He knew just where to look for them with a good chance of finding them there, and where not to bother. He knew which way out of any spot one would fly when flushed. He knew every bush and berry, weed and flower, fungus and fern, and could tell you its name. White-haired and a lover of good living, he was nonetheless in condition to have run a marathon. I was in safe hands, and I was hunting with a very savvy old hand.

Some of those coverts were almost impenetrable. Nothing daunted, Pauli tore his way through the worst of them, hoping to drive birds to me out on the edge. He had hunted a couple of days earlier this season, before my joining him, and already his hands and his wrists were scratched raw and scabbed by brambles.

Meanwhile, the dogs' bells tinkled incessantly as they ranged. The two bells were identical and produced the same pitch, yet you could distinguish one dog's from the other's by their different tempos. The slightly slower, more deliberate, though by no means plodding, bell was Ipsy's; the slightly quicker one was Ipsy's daughter's, the younger, more enthusiastic, but less woodcock-wise, less energy-conserving Aïda. *Celeste Aïda! Forma divina!* We were far from the Metropolitan, but not all that far. German shorthaired pointers they were, the mother all-over unbroken brown, the daughter brown speckled with gray. It was music to our ears, that syncopated twosome of a tinkle, but in so closely attuning our ears to it what we were really listening for was that magical moment when it should cease. As with Grecian urns, so with woodcock hunting: heard melodies are sweet, but those unheard are sweeter. The sudden silence of the dogs' bells signified that they had located a bird and were on point, the one honoring the other who had scented it first, both rigid: two weathervanes indicating a wind from the same quarter. The wary and wily woodcock might sink itself into its surroundings as closely concealed as the chameleon, but those two saw with their noses.

Whenever the dogs went on point, Pauli would call me to the spot. There mother and daughter would be living statues, transfixed, motionless so long as the bird—invisible to you—remained mesmerized by their hypnotic glares. Should it move, the dogs moved with it, just so much and no more. In flushing the bird, Pauli and I took turns. The unspoken understanding between us was that old code of the field, that should the shooter miss, then the second shot belonged to whichever could make it. Yet not so did I kill my first, my virgin, woodcock.

I knew it for what it was precisely because it was my first. In its total novelty to me, it could be nothing else. The wild twitter it made as it flushed, I had read, was not a cry that it utters but is caused by the rapid rush of air through the feathers of its frenziedly beating wings. This bird was not pointed. I was hunting at a distance of some fifty yards from Pauli and the dogs when it flushed wild out of a poplar. I shot and missed. It was a good thing that I did.

Let nobody ever tell you otherwise: wing shooting is hard—all wing shooting. In woodcock hunting there is an added factor that can unsteady the hunter and throw him off his mark. Unlike grouse, woodcock generally hold close, either to the point or the set of the dog, or to the approaching hunter, and they are so perfectly camouflaged that you will never see one before it has taken wing. Thus the bird usually flushes quite close to you. You must curb your natural impulse, must slow yourself down, hold back for a moment and let it gain some distance from you before shooting. The charge of shot must have time to open and spread, otherwise it is the equivalent of a rifle slug of large caliber and, being so compact, will do one of two things, either miss the bird or demolish it. Though I was hunting them for the first time, I was not long in realizing that. You must not wait overlong, of course, else the bird will get away by putting too much foliage between itself and you, especially during the early season when the leaves are still on the trees. Some intervening foliage you will often have, for the bird is on the wing seeking protective cover, yet you must not let this deter you. Shoot into it, through it, at the departing and disappearing bird, or rather, at where it will be momentarily, when your charge arrives at its same spot in space. Some pellets, even tiny number 8 or 9 pellets, will get through, and not many are needed to bring down a woodcock; he does not take a lot of killing. It is a matter of very nice judgment, this waiting but not waiting too long, and his being tense and overconscious of it can throw the shooter's timing off, causing him to potter and thus to miss the bird by shooting behind it, or to let it get away with nothing fired after it but a curse, intended for himself. As in wing shooting at anything, from clay pigeons to wild geese, it must be instinctive. To think about it is to falter and to fail.

There is yet another difficulty peculiar to woodcock hunting, another difference between this one and other game birds. He is the helicopter among them. As all the others take off and travel horizontally, more or less, that is the flight pattern the wing shot is used to; when afield after woodcock he must readjust his reactions to shoot at a vertically rising target. This is hard to do not just because it is unexpected but because it is awkward; tracking no other airborne mark so contorts the body. It is as if a right-handed person had to do something left-handed. So, although the woodcock is far from the fastest of game birds, he does things with his usual difference. A lot of those shot at time and again arrive for their winter in Louisiana whole and hale, with no trace of lead poisoning.

Once clear of the treetops, the woodcock is erratic in flight. The shooter may, in his mind, have this rather slow, rather easy-looking mark already in his game pocket, and then it will sidestep as the knight progresses on the chessboard, or from the altitude it has attained it may drop as though it has been shot on the wing and killed. Its fluttering forward flight much resembles that of the butterfly, darting, dipping. And if you miss one with your first barrel, it has, this little feathered missile, auxiliary rockets that can send it into orbit.

Considering all these things, I was not at all disappointed that it was only with my second barrel that I brought down my first woodcock.

By lunchtime, shooting over the dogs on point, I had killed two more, each with a single shot. Pauli had missed two.

Lunch. Not back at the car but high on a mountainside, on the bank of a bone-dry, boulder-strewn stream. A pick-me-up of strong tea, scalding hot from the thermos, laced with cognac but only a little, for alcohol and gunpowder make an explosive mixture. Chunks wrenched from a loaf of heavy, coarse black bread. Butter. Cheese. Sliced ham. A wurst made by Pauli's neighborhood Hungarian butcher from venison supplied by him mixed equally with pork. Apples. Raisins. Chocolate. All this from out of the knapsack containing, in addition to these things and others too many to list, extra collars for both dogs, a can of Sterno, rope, space blanket, several knives, a sweater, a small hatchet: survival items in case while hunting alone he should sprain an ankle or break a leg. And with this on his back Pauli not only hunts all day, walking as much as twenty miles over terrain as rocky as a stream bed, up hillsides steep enough to turn back a tank, he actually gets his doublebarreled 12-gauge shotgun to his shoulder in time to pluck from the sky a rapidly disappearing woodcock, often a pair, grouse that go off underfoot like a land mine.

But not that day. That day was my day, not Pauli's day, and when it was over, back at the car, with my five birds and his one lying on the ground, Pauli said, as the dogs were being rewarded with a feed, "Well, Ipsy, Aïda, it's a good thing we had our Uncle Bill along with us, eh?"

I didn't like this. Didn't like it at all and was worried over what might come next. You don't make a friend by badly outshooting a man over his dogs and on his grounds, and you don't inspire trust in your honesty or the uprightness of your character by doing it on what you claim is your first time. I was glad, at least, that no bets had been made on the day. I would have looked like a sharper.

Back at the bar of the motel where we had met that

morning, and where I was buying the drinks, Pauli said, "Now come clean. You lied to me, didn't you? You've done this before. Many times before. You can't tell me that you can kill five birds with six shots the first time you ever try it."

I said, "I was shooting way over my head today, Pauli. You had a rare bad day, I had a rare good one."

"If I promise to do better tomorrow, want to go again?" he asked.

"Same time, same place," I said.

And we drank up.

How perfectly everything had turned out! What an enjoyable time I had had, following upon all my fears for my performance! How lovely the setting and the season, how fine the dogs, what a good companion, how well and with what scant communication needed between us he and I had understood each other, gotten along together! How pleased I was with myself, how pleased must be the spirit of my father, who never lived to train me in that pursuit that was his passion! And it all began with their invitation to *Don Carlo* at the Met! This was what I told our friends Klaus and Bobbie Hallig days later when they came to have dinner with us. I had just finished when we were summoned to the table, the cover was removed from the main dish, and, to their surprise, they were served the very stuff of the story they had just been told.

By law wild game may not be sold. You must either get your own or else you must be given it. As a gift from a sportsman friend, it tastes good. But nothing else tastes as good as game you yourself have gotten. It savors of so much more than mere meat. It is food for the soul. In it are the sights, the sounds, and the smells of a landscape, the weather of a day, the companionship of a friend, your rapport with the dogs and theirs with each other, the moment when their ranging bells suddenly fall silent as they freeze on point, the memory of the rush of your blood as you walk in to make the flush and the heart-stopping instant when the bird bursts from cover and towers, the shot, the puff of feathers on the air, and, yes, that ineffable moment, compounded in equal parts of self-satisfaction and self-reproach, when the dog brings it to you and you hold in your hand the creature you both love and love to kill.

*Royal Game*

We would go after them on the first fine Sunday—if we ever saw another one—following the rain. Essential conditions: a fair Sunday, following immediately upon a spell of bad weather. The bad weather we were having this winter—*parbleu!* Days indoors while the window-panes streamed. Day after day as dark and dank as a cave. Days when you could part the fog with your hands. When you groped your way to the *boulangerie* for your daily bread, encountering in the Cimmerian gloom some bent old woman swathed in her widow's weeds. When, in a short-lived lifting of the fog, the low, little half-timbered farmhouses appeared again in the nearby fields like a fleet of fishing boats anchored in port, afraid to venture beyond sound of the church's muffled bells. Our first condition was being met. *Bon!* For our purposes, the ground must be soft, muddy. We must be able to track our quarry to their lair. They travel in droves, and they range widely—here one day, miles away the next. Unless their signs have been freshly sighted and they are known to be in a certain covert, then you are wasting your time hunting them.

Droves? Wild boar in droves? Could this be? When I, in a novel set in east Texas, had required one for a character to kill, I had had to import the boar from over the line in Louisiana. But here in the Sologne, a district of France less than a hundred miles due south of Paris, they have them in droves. They have got entirely too many of them, more than they want, more than they know what to do with. Here they are a nuisance, a pest, a varmint. For this is a region of grain farming (especially corn), truck gardening, and plant nurseries, and the wild boars, the *sangliers*, are voracious, omniverous, and prolific. It is impossible to deplete their numbers; impossible, except around small plots, to fence strongly enough to keep the brutes out.

The Sologne has long been the hunting center of France. Game of all kinds abounds there. You lose count of the pheasants in the roadside fields after driving for a quarter of an hour. Game may legally be sold in this country, and outside the shops at this, the open, season hang mallards, partridges, rabbits and hares, deer and roebuck. It is not cheap, but it is plentiful.

The area, always sparsely populated, went strongly Protestant in the religious wars, lost, of course, and was desolated. A marshy place, low-lying and flat, periodically flooded by its many rivers, it was then practically abandoned, shunned as savage and pestilential. Wild animals took it over. The nobility used it as their hunting grounds; it was good for little else. Not until Napoleon III was draining and reforestation undertaken. Odd, that penchant of dictators for glorifying themselves and currying favor by reclaiming swamps.

Now, though much of the district is still wild woodlands, still held as hunting preserves, much of it is cultivated—despite the poorness of the soil. This proximity of crops to coverts has increased the amount of game—

especially those impudent, wily, and gluttonous creatures, wild boars.

The long tradition of hunting, here in the valley between the rivers Loire and Cher, has produced attendant
crafts, fine arts, history, legend and lore, much of it preserved in the Museum of the Hunt in nearby Gien.
Gunmakers in towns along the Loire still turn out fine
shotguns by hand—lock, stock, and barrel—with side-by-
side double barrels (that lost art in America) and with, if
you prefer, the hammers on the outside in the old fash-
ion; these will cost you not less but rather more. Hunting
horns are still made, the making of the great ones for the
stag hunt being a skill passed down from father to son.
The tubes for these are hand-drawn, hand-curved, the
bells hand-hammered, the whole thing gold-plated,
chased in silver with scenes of the hunt; the finished
product is a piece of jewelry, and costs accordingly. The
chipping of flints for flintlock fowling pieces was a local
cottage industry lasting well into the age of photography.
The museum in Gien has a photograph—circa 1875, I
would guess—of a man and wife seated outside their
door engaged in this work, along with a flintmaker's
bench and hammers, and flints in various stages of com-
pletion. They would not have had to look far for flint.
The solid part of this part of the world is made of it.

Hunters come here, in season—mid-September to
early January—from all parts of the country, for the
French are a nation of hunters. Indeed, the patron saint
of hunting was French: Saint Hubert. His devotees tend
to overlook the fact that it was not because of his hunting
that he was sainted but rather because he forswore it. He
gave up his sport when a stag he was after one day turned

on him and said, "Hubert, how long are you going to keep this up? How long are you going to allow this mania of hunting to distract you from the care of your soul?"

On weekends for the preceding month the banging of shotguns had been daylong right up to the village edge. The streets at noon were filled with men in hunting clothes and boots. They crowded the bars. They brought their dogs with them into the dining rooms, tied them to the table legs, ordered food to be served to them. In large parties, they got loud and boisterous and started dousing one another from the water and wine bottles. One glimpsed young blades in full formal hunt regalia: calf-length black frock coats with broad lapels, scarlet redingotes, frilled white shirts, riding breeches and tall gleaming boots that always look as though they are being worn for the first time, or as though the wearer has a manservant whose only duty is to tend them. These glorious gallants will be off to take part in Count Something-or-other's mounted hunt for the stag. The horses will be purebred coursers with lineages centuries long. There will be a head huntsman with one of those golden horns, resplendent in his uniform, a *valet de chiens* in charge of a pack of eighty or ninety staghounds. Stirrup cups in foot-less goblets of chased, precious metals inset with gem-stones will be handed by uniformed servants to the hunt-ers and huntresses on their restless mounts.

Boar hunting, though done on foot, is party-hunting, too, unlike the upland game-shooting going on in the fields around the edges of the village, which involves a solitary man or a group of two or three friends out with a brace of dogs. Indeed, much organization must go into a boar hunt—too much work to take chances, too many people to be disappointed. So, conditions must be right. Until the day comes when they are, you must wait. In the meantime, you might remember what you know and have read about it, and, being a stranger, study up on how it is done here.

The combination of disgust, respect, and fear that he inspires in man makes the wild boar the ideal game animal. "Of all quadrupeds," says Buffon, France's premier naturalist, "the boar would seem to be the ugliest. His imperfections of form seem to affect his nature. All his habits are gross, all his tastes foul, all his feelings reduced to a furious lewdness and a brutish gluttony, which makes him devour indiscriminately anything put before him, even his own offspring at the moment of their birth. The coarseness of his pelt, the thickness of his hide, the density of his layer of fat, all make the animal insensitive to blows; one has seen mice living on their backs, gnawing their hides and their fat without their feeling it. But if they are obtuse in their sense of touch, and even more so in taste, their other senses are very sharp. Hunters are mindful that wild boars see, hear and smell at long range, thus obliging them to stand and wait in silence through the night, and to place themselves downwind in order to keep their scent from reaching the animals, for it will carry a great distance to them, and always strongly enough to turn them aside."

In those places where the people have left written, oral, and pictorial records of themselves, the wild boar was the only game animal that would attack a man if

provoked. Thus he became the test of prowess and bravery, the stuff of heroism, legend. One of the assignments
given Hercules was the capture of a destructive wild
boar, a feat to rank with eleven others describable only as
Herculean. Meleager, son of a king, at whose birth the
Fates themselves attended, killed the mighty Calydonian
boar that had been ravaging the countryside. He presented the boar's head to Atalanta, the great huntress,
who had wounded but failed to kill the animal. Meleager's uncles tried to rob Atalanta of her prize. Meleager
came to her defense and, in the ensuing fight, slew his
uncles. Whereupon their sister, his mother, in a fit of
anger, extinguished the torch upon whose continued
burning, the Fates had prophesied, the life of her son
depended.

An enviable trophy, then—for all its ugliness, the
coarseness of its habits. Ferocious and prepotent, and
thus conferring upon its killer the same attributes. A
beast with a bad disposition, so churlish and unamiable
that its very name in Latin, *singularem,* means "the one
who lives by himself," or, as we might say, "the loner,"
and who must be sought in the deepest and most thickset
part of the forest. A dangerous animal, one

> Whose tushes never sheath'd he whetteth still,
> Like to a mortal butcher, bent to kill.
> On his bow-back he hath a battle set
> Of bristly pikes, that ever threat his foes;
> His eyes like glow-worms shine when he doth fret;
> His snout digs sepulchres wher'er he goes;
> Being mov'd, he strikes what'er is in his way,
> And whom he strikes his crooked tushes slay.

So Venus warns Adonis, who, indifferent and cold to the advances of the very goddess of love (a deficiency, or a superiority, fairly common among fictional hunters—Cooper's Leatherstocking, Faulkner's Ike McCaslin), goes off on his hunt for the wild boar, with direful consequences. Hunting has been known to do that: make celibates of its most ardent devotees, of either sex—witness Diana, chaste goddess of the chase; look how hard Atalanta made it for her suitors to win her in wedlock.

In the course of time, when heroes came to be born, not made, and a whole, self-declared, hereditary class of them sprang up, they reserved the wild boar hunt unto themselves as a proof of their innate superiority. One explanation for there being so many of the animals in present-day France may be that for as long as the country was a monarchy—and that was a weary long while—they were a protected species, protected, that is, against the common people: they were royal game. In the *sanglier,* that fabled creature, mythologized, versified, painted, sculpted, the French nobility found a quarry worthy of them and decreed that they alone were worthy of it. Not for the commonalty, because to challenge one was a test of bravery and manliness, which, of course, you did not have unless you had it in the blood. The peasants might complain that the animals were devouring their crops, but to the nobility, who were devouring the peasants, those complaints were immaterial so long as they themselves had their sport.

As late as 1818, the wild boar was still *gibier royal.* That year, the young Alexandre Dumas was taken on his first boar hunt. Not a drop of blue blood in Dumas, of course, but by that time notice had been served by the people of France that they would not always remain fodder for pigs, biped or quadruped. So, when the Duke of Orléans's neighbors complained of the depredation of their crops by those pernicious and protected beasts, the *sangliers* that his grace's forests harbored, and petitioned him to have his gamekeepers exterminate them to the last one, he acceded. The duke's head gamekeeper was Dumas's friend; thus it was that he was privileged to hunt the royal game. In the Fifth Republic, there are still some privately owned hunting preserves of royal dimensions where boars make their lairs, and around these are small farms where crops are grown for a living. Between these two divisions of landowners the clash of interests over the wild boar continues to this day. For farmers, there is never a closed season on them now, and in France any man, properly licensed, may carry a gun; but along the edges of the woods where the boars have repaired to digest the corn which they glutted on in the night, the angry farmer may find signs on every other tree saying, PROPRIÉTÉ PRIVÉE. ACCÈS INTERDIT.

In the interest of détente, some of the owners of large preserves now permit boar hunts on their land. That very word, "détente," is used in a pamphlet put out by an association of parish priests here some years ago in an effort to air, and to settle, some of the local tensions growing out of hunting, such as resentment by the game-keepers over their wages and working conditions, hikers' fears for their safety, protests by anti-blood-sports groups—and the frustrations of the farmers. Some of the owners of the preserves welcome the hunts. For, in these difficult, late years, a number of them have cleared more

land—though there remain forests that are truly vast—
and planted it to moneymaking crops. As regards the
wild boar, now legally classed an *animal nuisible* (a nox-
ious animal), the owners, too, have begun to feel that
there can be too much of a good thing. They are ready to
provide the services of their own gamekeepers in the
democratic control of these destructive creatures. We
have come a long way from the days of the *gibier royal*.

One Saturday morning in mid-December the church
bells that woke us every day had a different ring, a higher
pitch, a quicker tempo. They did not sound, as they had
for weeks, like the slow, muffled tolling of a buoy bell in a
fog, but like bells pealing for a holiday. I threw open the
shutters to find that the world had reappeared. It was like
sighting land after crossing the ocean in a ship. The
skies, long so low overhead and so heavy they made you
stoop, had lifted high over this broad, flat land. The thin,
slightly crooked spire of the church had reasserted, if not
righted, itself in its place. The garden plots behind the
houses steamed. From the village, where for weeks all
had been so silent, came stirrings of life. There was the
noise of traffic on the roads. The first shots from the
rabbit hunters went off somewhere close by. The phone
rang. It was the call I had been waiting for. The weather
looked fair to hold through tomorrow, the *gardes-chasse*
on two estates had reported finding fresh signs: tracks,
rootings, wallows. The call was going out over the wires
like the starting blast from the huntsman's horn—*à la
chasse!*

\* \* \*

It was Monsieur Hatte (pronounced Ott) whom the gamekeepers called to report their findings, for in and around Souvigny-en-Sologne he is the master of the boar hunt. As will presently be seen, this kind of hunting requires someone firmly in command, and M. Hatte is something of a disciplinarian, for he knows well, having been gored and having twice been shot, once in the head, what can happen when things are allowed to get out of hand. M. Hatte is also a farmer, and farmers are natural enemies of wild boars. Just the week before, M. Hatte had gone out one morning to harvest a field of corn, and found that overnight it had been razed by a drove of the beasts. Instead of going hunting he ought, in fact, to be spending this fine day on his tractor, and indeed, he would have to pay for taking the day off by spending the night on it. Never mind. It was worth it, and not just because he was out to destroy some number of his old enemy—whom he loves—but for the passion of the chase.

Our hunt was a far cry from the days when the wild boar was game for the aristocracy only. On ours there was *égalité* and *fraternité*—*liberté* being the understood prerequisite of the two. Along with a Parisian-looking gentleman addressed as "Docteur" were the village grocer, farmers, farmhands, a road mender, me—not only not to the *manoir* born, but a foreigner. Old companions of the hunt who had not seen one another for a long time, and people who had never seen you before—certainly not me —stuck out their hands for a shake, that rather limp French handshake. Nothing exclusive about it; by the time all were assembled there were seventy-five of us. M. Hatte had been right about wasting the time of a great many people unless you had an idea where the game was.

There would be two hunts today, on two separate domains, and they would be conducted differently. On this first one, we would each be assigned a stand, and the gamekeepers, along with some volunteers from our numbers, would be the beaters. The four gamekeepers were in uniform: green corduroy breeches tucked into knee-high rubber boots; corduroy jackets with a huntsman's horn embroidered on their lapels in gold; on their caps, the same emblem repeated. Each hunter was to keep closely to the stand assigned to him.

In Buffon I had read, "Since the boar flees but slowly, deposits a strong scent, and since he defends himself against the dogs and often wounds them dangerously, it is not necessary to hunt him with fine hounds meant for the stag or the roebuck." Indeed, says Buffon, running a dog on boars spoils him for anything else. The scent he follows is so rank it ruins his nose, and he gets accustomed to hunting slowly. A few curs are all that are needed to hunt boars. Pretty lowly labor is his implication.

Even so, I was not prepared for my first sight of our ragtag-and-bobtail pack of eight. Underbred in every line, they appeared to be unadoptables from the SPCA. One mutt looked as if he had picked his separate features from as many ashcans: pug nose, short ears, long tail, nondescript, castoff-looking coat. Another looked like the last representative of a once presentable family of hounds after generations of misalliances and some matings of too close consanguinity. All were undersized. But they had a certain air. A certain shabby insouciance. Rather raffish. They seemed to say, "We know we're a sorry sight to see. That our work is that which everybody else is too good for. Our noses are not fine and we're not fast on our feet. But you've got a dirty job to do; here we are to do it." For me, it was precisely their runtiness that was impressive. They might lack breeding and polish, but to be no bigger than that and yet to bring to bay and fight a wild boar, and then go back and do it again another day, they had to have something in them that many of their soi-disant betters of my acquaintance had been lacking.

Although M. Hatte called for volunteers—and there was no lack of them—to assist the gamekeepers as beaters, he chose deliberately the men he wanted, telling others who were importunate, to their faces, that they were amateurs. The danger to which the beaters are exposed comes not so much from the boars, though an old one, one with tusks, when wounded and cornered, can be ferocious, charging through the dogs to attack the man. The greater danger is from themselves, from the guns of inexperienced hands in the melee and excitement of the *battu,* the confrontation when the boar turns, stands, and fights the dogs. The closeness of the battle, with men firing buckshot from 12-gauge shotguns—there is where the danger lies.

We were ready.

Looking rather like a mob of vigilantes, gun barrels bristling in each of twenty-odd cars, we sped to our hunting area. So huge was this holding—the property of one of the richest men in France—that, without once leaving it or ever seeing any of its boundaries, we were fifteen minutes getting there. The roads we traveled, crossed, turned onto, all sliced straight through the woods without a crook. They parceled the domain into innumerable perfect squares. Seen from above, it must have looked like a tiled floor. Incongruous—the wild woods, precisely squared by the neat, level roads.

Along three sides of one of these large squares our numbers were deployed, stationed some fifty yards apart. At that range, buckshot could wound but not very likely kill a man, I reckoned. This kind of hunting, with all its regulations, regimentation, its sheer number of men, was more military than any known to me. We stood facing the woods, awaiting the bugle call and the onrush of the enemy like a line of militiamen prepared to resist an attack.

Everyone else was alone, on his own, but I, being new, was assigned a partner, the village grocer. Not a word of English could he speak, and he had been told—we all had—not to speak at all. He first broke the rule to observe how futile it was for us in our position to keep silent; we would see no action here, for we had the wind at our backs. Now he asked, "Is it like this in your country?" Unlettered in English though he was, he might have been reading my mind, for I was thinking how very different from mine this country was. The ground, where bare, was blond as a beach—finely ground flint and coarse pale sand, the deposit of the ages from the Loire and its many tributaries, inexhaustible rivers of sand, in their periodic floods. Heather, bracken fern, and gorse, plants indifferent to their soil, which can thrive on nothing, were rife. Stunted, gnarled little starveling trees, leafless now and unidentifiable, so covered with lichen they looked moldy. Ground-growing juniper. Paper birches. Then the woods. To one side, a pine plantation, the trees uniform in shape, height, and girth, spaced to the centimeter, in ranks as straight as squadrons standing at inspection. Off to one side, a hardwood forest: huge, ancient, acorn-bearing oaks, burdened with mistletoe in bunches that looked like evergreen nests of some large species of bird; lofty chestnuts—gone from my country, victims of the blight, before I was born. Their burrs littered the ground at this season, and on these and the acorns the wild boars grow fat and nutty-tasting.

From deep in the woods, far to our left, came the sound of the horn blowing the *lancer,* the call that signals the unleashing of the dogs, the start of the hunt. It silenced us. It put an end to thought. It stiffened and strained to attention every man along the line.

Our section was about midway in our side of the square, quite distant from the hunt's starting point, and so for a long time—it must have been almost an hour— we listened to the progress, the slow approach of the chase through the woods. Repeatedly the keepers blew their horns to urge the dogs on. The beaters shouted constantly at them, *"Chasse! Chasse! Chasse!"* Whenever they found a scent, the hounds bayed, the dogs barked frenziedly. Next we heard blown on the horn another, different call, louder and more urgent. It was rather like the call of a bugle in battle, sounding the advance, the charge. Then down the line ran a sequence of shots as the boar ran the gantlet, seeking an out from the trap in which it was caught. For that particular call upon the hunting horn there is a word in French. The word is *hallali* (the *h* is silent), and it denotes both the call itself and the event that the call announces. It means "to be in on the kill."

Now the hunt was in our sector. The keepers and the corps of beaters came into view. *"Chasse! Chasse!"* they cried, and the horns sounded a tattoo. The dogs were on a trail, barking, baying. Our men tensed. We heard crashings in the dry, dead bracken, which made the hunters visible along our line lean forward, each taking his cue from the one on his left, and raise and ready their guns. The dogs came our way, veered, and the chase swept past us. Again and again we heard the shots and the trumpeting of the *hallali*, and each time the faces of the men near me showed that in imagination, in memory, they were there, "in on the kill." But along our section of the line, no shot had been fired when, an hour later, the horn sounded the call signaling the end of the hunt.

"A great economy of cartridges," commented the village grocer, making a moue.

Eight dead boars lay thrown together on the ground in the courtyard of the farm, our assembly point. Wine bottles appeared—delicious, dry, white Sancerre. The boars ranged in color from ginger to chestnut to near-black, as they ranged upward in size. The males had been castrated. This is done because the odor from the testicles is so strong that, unless they are removed, a few hours is enough to spoil the meat of the whole carcass.

Not only in temperament, but also in almost all aspects of its appearance, the wild boar bears only a distant resemblance to the domestic pig. It has tall, powerful shoulders. It is short and compact in body. Its hams are long and lean. Its forelegs are short, its hooves delicate. Its snout is long, the muzzle dark and callused from its constant rooting. But the most striking difference is its pelt. Next to its hide grows a thick, fuzzy fur; from out of this fur grow bristles as long as seven or eight inches. They grow abundantly, from snout to tail. It is a shaggy beast. Buffon was right—not a pretty creature. But, even in death, one to respect.

We drove fifteen miles to the site of our second hunt. This was on higher ground, with roads less well tended. Ours shortly became impassable. The cars were left alongside it and we took to our feet. We had lost some few of our number—people anxious to beat the traffic jams on the road back to Paris—but we were still a good sixty strong. It was getting late, the light failing fast. *"Dépêchez-vous, messieurs! Dépêchez-vous!"* M. Hatte urged as we hiked to our starting place.

No dogs, no gamekeepers on this hunt. No beaters. Or rather, more beaters than before. On this one, we—one half our number—were to be our own beaters, driving the game toward the other half, in wait for them, as all of us had been on our first hunt. And in order that I might experience both aspects of the *chasse à sanglier,* I would be one of the beaters.

Now I began to wonder if I really wanted to take part in this, for I was unarmed, and had been from the start. I was there strictly as a spectator. A pity that I was not allowed to carry a gun; but, because application must be made months in advance for all the many permits required, the liability insurance, etc., etc., it is far too complicated for an alien to hunt in France. Now, standing in my spot on the road at the woods' edge, one of a long line of men awaiting their marching orders, the only one of them without a gun, I began to have visions of the hunter on one side or the other of me wounding but not killing—just enraging—one of those big old fellows with the curved and whetted tusks.

*"En avant!"* Down the line came the word, and bursting into a din of shouts, calls, and grunts, the column of men entered the woods.

From M. Hatte, on my left, to me came this command: *Allo? Monsieur Enfré! Faites de bruit! Faites de bruit! Ce que vous voudrez. Parlez à ces cochons! Faites de bruit en anglais!"* I did as ordered. I made as much noise as anybody in the line—more, being unarmed. I was such an enthusiastic beater that I earned myself a rebuke from the hunter on my right. *"Vous, à gauche, ralentissez!"* he yelled at me. I was getting ahead of the line, and maybe thereby flushing the game before guns had come up within range of it. Meanwhile, I talked to those pigs in three tongues— theirs, my own, and that of my companions. *"Allez-là! Allez-là!"* I yelled in French as good as the best of them. "Pig! Pig! Pig! Uh, pig! Uh! Uh! Uh! Show your dirty snouts, you *sales cochons,* you!"

I came upon a wallow so fresh, the tracks were filling with water as M. Hatte and I bent over them. Big ones and little ones—a drove of half a dozen at least—there just moments before us.

Down the line went the command to close ranks and to pass the order on: *"Serrez à droite! Relayez la commande!"*

We heard the fusillade to our right and the bugling of

OPEN SEASON

the horn. Between M. Hatte and me a roebuck flushed
and bounded over the bracken.

Twice more before we emerged from the woods to
rejoin our stationary companions we heard the fusillade
and the sound of the *hallali.* Then as the last men came
out into the dusk, there came from the woods the other
traditional, long-drawn call on the horn that signals the
conclusion of the hunt. "The hunter's adieu," de Vigny
has called it in a famous stanza of verse. It is impossible
to hear that sound at that hour and not be reminded of
his lines:

> *J'aime le son du Cor, le soir, au fond des bois,*
> *Soit qu'il chante les pleurs de la biche aux abois,*
> *Ou l'adieu de chasseur que l'écho faible accueille*
> *Et que le vent du nord porte de feuille en feuille.*

(I love the sound of the hunting horn, at
  day's end, deep
in the woods, whichever its melody—that
  of the quarry
brought to bay, or the hunter's farewell,
  gathered in a faint
echo, and carried by the north wind from
  leaf to leaf.)

The following evening, at cocktail time, there came a
knock on our door. M. Hatte was there. He carried, in a
transparent plastic bag, a shaggy slab of *sanglier*—my
share. For that is how it is done in these democratic days:
to each man who assists in the hunt, a share of the meat.
Mine was from one of the young ones, M. Hatte assured

me, saying that the big old boars get so tough that only their heads are edible. He laid his package on the drawing room table and accepted, *volontiers,* my offer of a drink.

It was M. Hatte's first meeting with my wife. The presentations concluded, we recounted the hunt, heard from him stories of others he had been in on in his time. I gathered much of the information I have here relayed. Meanwhile, the room—the whole house—was filling with an odor. It was not a stench, exactly; in fact, it was rather sweetish. But it was powerful. It was almost stifling.

M. Hatte declined a second drink—his tractor awaited him. The moment he was gone I fell to dressing the chunk of meat, resisting my wife's demand that it be thrown out—far out. I had my opportunity then to verify Buffon's statements about the coarseness of the *sanglier*'s pelt and the thickness of its hide. You could have soled boots with it.

The pelt gone, the meat smelled clean. For seven days we aged it; for two days more we marinated it in red wine. We invited friends to share it, on the understanding that we had in readiness the makings of a quick substitute dinner. It was the best meat that any of us had ever tasted. It was, truly, *gibier royal.*